RELIGION AND POLITICS

A Reference Handbook

Other Titles in ABC-CLIO's
CONTEMPORARY
WORLD ISSUES
Series

Books in the Contemporary World Issues series address vital issues in today's society such as terrorism, sexual harassment, homelessness, AIDS, gambling, animal rights, and air pollution. Written by professional writers, scholars, and nonacademic experts, these books are authoritative, clearly written, up-to-date, and objective. They provide a good starting point for research by high school and college students, scholars, and general readers, as well as by legislators, businesspeople, activists, and others.

Each book, carefully organized and easy to use, contains an overview of the subject; a detailed chronology; biographical sketches; facts and data and/or documents and other primary-source material; a directory of organizations and agencies; annotated lists of print and nonprint resources; a glossary; and an index.

Readers of books in the Contemporary World Issues series will find the information they need in order to better understand the social, political, environmental, and economic issues facing the world today.

RELIGION AND POLITICS

A Reference Handbook

John W. Storey and Glenn H. Utter

A B C ● C L I O

Santa Barbara, California   Denver, Colorado   Oxford, England

Library of Congress Cataloging-in-Publication Data is available.

ISBN 1-57607-218-5

08 07 06 05 04 03 02   10 9 8 7 6 5 4 3 2 1

ABC-CLIO, Inc.
130 Cremona Drive, P.O. Box 1911
Santa Barbara, California 93116-1911

This book is printed on acid-free paper ∞
Manufactured in the United States of America

For our students

Contents

Preface

Given the enormity and complexity of the relationship between religion and politics, we concluded that the introductory essay would be more illuminating if it focused in some depth on three basic patterns in different parts of the world rather than skimming the surface of every possibility. Accordingly, this book deals primarily with separation of church and state in the United States; domination of the state by religion in Iran; and control of religion by the state in China. But the print and nonprint resources point students toward the numerous other relationships between religion and politics, which are many and varied.

In western Europe alone, for instance, there exists a remarkable mosaic, the result in part of the sixteenth-century Reformation, which shattered the unity of Christendom and divided the region broadly into the Protestant north (excluding Belgium and Ireland) and Catholic south. And today church-state patterns vary widely, ranging from the Nordic countries (Denmark, Iceland, Norway, Sweden, and Finland) in which Lutheranism is the established faith to Italy, Spain, and Portugal where Roman Catholicism enjoys a privileged, though not established, status. And in between fall England and France. Although the Church of England has never been a state church as such, it has always enjoyed certain privileges. For instance, the twenty-six most senior Anglican bishops have seats in the House of Lords and Anglican priests preside at most state ceremonies. Yet, the Church of England is subordinate to the state in that the British sovereign serves not only as head of state but also as supreme governor of the church. With a population that is predominantly Catholic, France belongs to southern Europe. But since 1905, when the Catholic Church was disestablished, the French state has become rigidly secular, showing no preference for any religious group and prohibiting clerics from teaching in the public schools.

There is a parallel between France and Mexico, in that both are predominantly Catholic countries that have become increasingly secular in politics. But the contrast is sharper in Mexico. Despite a population that is still overwhelmingly Catholic, almost 92 percent in 2000, Mexico has implemented perhaps the most anticlerical legislation in the Western Hemisphere. Church property belongs to the state; worship services outside churches were forbidden until very recently; the government has the authority to open any place of worship and to determine the maximum number of clerics; the clergy cannot vote, participate in politics, wear vestments in public, or criticize public officials; and the church cannot own radio and television stations. There have been efforts in recent years to ease some of these restrictions, but polls show that 70 percent of Mexicans still want the church to stay out of politics.

Debts are always incurred in the preparation of a manuscript, and this one is no exception. Special expressions of gratitude go to two members of the Lamar University history department. Patty Renfro, the department's administrative assistant, typed most of the chapters, and in so doing kept the project on schedule and saved us from many typos. Carol Stokesbury-Atmar, a graduate student and adjunct instructor in the department, offered helpful suggestions regarding content and style. Mark Asteris, media services coordinator, Gray Library, Lamar University, furnished information on video materials, while Jeff Lacy, also in the Gray Library, made reference materials readily available to the authors. And, finally, we extend our thanks to Alicia Merritt of ABC-Clio for her assistance. Of course we accept full responsibility for any errors of fact or judgment.

John W. Storey and Glenn H. Utter

1

Introduction

The Lord said to Moses, "Come up to me on the mountain,
stay there and let me give you the tablets of stone, the law
and the commandment, which I have written down that you
may teach them." (Exodus 24:12–13)
   Moses came and told the people all the words of the Lord,
and his laws. The whole people answered with one voice and
said, "We will do all that the Lord has told us." (Exodus 24:3)

Stories such as those of Moses descending Mount Sinai with
God's laws are a staple of ancient mythology. King Menes of
Egypt, for instance, obtained a code from Thoth, the god of wisdom, as did Hammurabi of Babylonia from Shamash, the sun-god.
The gods had sent him, proclaimed Hammurabi, "the obedient,
god-fearing prince, to cause righteousness to appear in the land, to
destroy the evil and the wicked, that the strong harm not the
weak."[1] Additional similarities to Moses are seen in the accounts of
King Minos returning from Mount Dicta with a legal code for Crete
and of Dionysus's stone tablets inscribed with laws for the Greeks.
From the Far East come comparable tales of the heavenly origins
and earthly responsibilities of ancient Japanese and Chinese emperors.[2] Such mythology does more than confirm an intimate link-
age since the dawn of civilization between religion and politics. It
also bestows a certain legitimacy upon government that endured
in much of the world until as recently as the eighteenth-century
Enlightenment, a legitimacy that some religious fundamentalists in
the late twentieth and early twenty-first centuries apparently
would like to reestablish. Just as politics and religion once rou-
tinely bolstered one another, with religion infusing politics with a
touch of divinity in return for the state's enforcement of religious
dogma, many of today's religious and political leaders around the
world would seem to welcome the return of such an arrangement.

To generalize even broadly about relationships between religion and politics in modern times is definitely risky, maybe foolhardy, given the enormous diversity of religious expression, from established institutionalized faiths to less formal folk varieties, and the almost equally diverse forms of politics. The task is simplified somewhat by taking a rather narrow view of both religion and politics, but even then the distinction is more theoretical than real. Whereas religion deals with the supernatural and centers around institutions such as synagogues, mosques, and churches, politics concerns the manner in which society organizes and governs itself and maintains order. Whereas religion is often a private, personal experience involving spiritual matters, politics is a public expression of society's collective wishes. Whereas religion sees temporal existence as preparation for higher spiritual purposes, politics regards earthly existence as an end in itself. Whereas religion looks to prayer and ritual, politics turns more to the rational, scientific, and material.[3]

This division of religion and politics, of course, is entirely too neat, for it suggests clearly defined and mutually understood boundaries between spiritual and secular authorities. Nothing is farther from the truth. Religion and politics, appealing to the deepest human passions, have always interacted, and that interaction has often been confrontational if not violent. Problems inevitably arise when religion, presuming itself to be the sole custodian of society's moral values, employs the state to impose its will on the larger community, or when the state charts a new course at sharp odds with prevailing religious sentiment. From the twentieth century alone testimony abounds. Unable to persuade Americans to stop drinking, for instance, churches in the United States in the early twentieth century readily turned to state coercion, supporting enthusiastically the Nineteenth Amendment to the Constitution. The Islamic fundamentalists who took power in Iran in 1979 had no qualms about using political means for religious ends. On the other side, people of a more secular bent have just as frequently relied on political power to curb religious influence. Such was the case of Mustafa Kemal Atatürk, the founder of modern Turkey, whose programs came at a high price for Muslim clerics. Similarly, Communist China's incorporation of Tibet in 1950 brought about the flight of the Dalai Lama to India in 1959 and the eventual destruction of thousands of the Himalayan country's Buddhist monasteries and nunneries and the deaths of numerous monks. As for the United States, Supreme Court decisions of the early 1960s on prayer in the public schools that attempted to clarify the boundary between religious practice and public institutions still rankle religious conservatives.

Further complicating the interaction of religion and politics have been attacks by one religious group upon another, usually a dominant body against minority ones. That such conflicts have political repercussions is apparent, as seen in modern India. With over 80 percent of its population classified as Hindu, it would seem that the small Muslim (12 percent), Christian (2.5 percent), and Sikh (2 percent) elements posed no threat. Yet, Indian nationalists who consider Hinduism a unifying aspect of their culture see it differently. As a result, in December 1992 a sixteenth-century Muslim mosque in northern India was razed, apparently with the blessing of members of the Indian Peoples Party (BJP) and World Hindu Assembly (VHP), two of the more aggressive Hindu parties. Before running its course the resulting Hindu-Muslim violence claimed the lives of thousands of Muslims in western India, caused comparable numbers of Hindus to flee Muslim-dominated Bangladesh, and prompted Muslim terrorists to bomb Bombay.[4] Christians, too, have aroused the ire of Hindu nationalists, who loudly objected to the pope's visit to India in November 1999. At issue was an allegedly vigorous campaign by Christian missionaries to convert India's Hindus. One angry Hindu nationalist considered this "world Christian conversion campaign" a "grave threat," while another claimed that it jeopardized "the unity, integrity of the country" by fueling Christian separatist movements. Christians meanwhile blamed the unrest on the BJP, which had come to power in March 1998 at the head of a coalition government.[5] Such developments seriously test the traditional tolerance of Hinduism and cast doubt on the ability of India's more secular rulers to achieve a pluralistic society.

Complexities notwithstanding, at least three fundamental relationships between temporal and religious institutions exist today, two rooted in the distant past, one of more recent vintage. In two patterns exist a close, though not necessarily cordial, tie between civil and spiritual authorities, but religion is subordinate to the state in one, the state to religion in the other. The third model, that of separation and independence between religion and politics, springs from the eighteenth-century Enlightenment and finds classic expression in the First Amendment to the U.S. Constitution.

Contemporary China offers an example of the first relationship. Until 1911, when revolution ended the imperial rule of the

Manchu dynasty, the Chinese state wielded both civil and spiritual authority; the emperor was both a secular and religious ruler. Instead of autonomous religious institutions, there was an official state religion derived primarily from the ethical teachings of Confucius, the Chinese philosopher who lived 500 years or so before Christ. If Confucianism was a religion, authorities agree not only that it differed fundamentally from the more traditional faiths of Buddhism or Christianity, but also that its appeal was more to an educated elite than the unlettered masses.[6] This, along with the vastness of China itself, made it impossible to establish religious uniformity throughout the realm. Buddhism, Islam, Christianity, and Daoism attracted sizeable numbers, as did various expressions of folk religion. Imperial China responded to these alternative religions with tight controls, exemplified by restrictions on the number of Buddhist and Daoist priests allowed in any given geographical area. As long as these other faiths operated within the approved boundaries and posed no challenge, they were relatively free of government meddling. However, if a threat was perceived, real or not, it invited the state's wrath. In the early 1700s, for instance, Jesuit missionary activity in China was banned when the papacy instructed Chinese Catholics to stop the practice of worshiping their ancestors, a custom central to Confucianism. Those popular movements of the nineteenth century that emerged and flourished outside acceptable channels brought harsh government action. The Taiping enthusiasm of the 1850s and early 1860s, for example, inspired by a certain amount of Christian idealism and fueled by the anger of oppressed, land-hungry peasants, left huge numbers dead and caused enormous property damage in its confrontation with the state.[7] As this episode shows, the state would bend only so far with regard to departures from religious orthodoxy.

Dramatic religious change accompanied the Chinese revolution of 1911. New political leaders, seeking to create a modern secular society, severed the ancient connection between religion and politics. A period of hostility ensued during which the state seized Buddhist and Christian property, along with local village temples. This policy of subordination moderated with the emergence of Generalissimo Chiang Kai-shek, the Nationalist leader who wielded considerable power from 1928–1948. Though a secularist, Chiang recognized the value of religion in promoting certain national and political goals. World War II intervened, and in the postwar struggle between Communists and Nationalists, Chiang was defeated and fled to Taiwan.

Despite its official atheism, as well as the conviction that religion would disappear with the advancement of scientific information, the new Communist regime, the People's Republic of China (PRC), nevertheless permitted freedom of "religious belief." As Mao Tse-tung, China's new leader, declared in 1957, religion could not be abolished by "administrative decree" any more than could Marxism. The desired end, he elaborated, would come about through "discussion, . . . criticism, . . . persuasion and education."[8] Overseeing this dialogue would be the PRC's Bureau of Religious Affairs. Actually, the religious policy of the PRC was similar to that of the imperial rulers. It allowed room for China's five institutionalized religions—Buddhism, Islam, Daoism, Protestantism, and Roman Catholicism—but accorded no official standing to popular sectarian movements. Guided by the Bureau of Religious Affairs, the PRC expected religion to serve national interests.

Although presumably permitting religious belief, the PRC sharply limited religious practice. Spiritual activity was to take place only on religious premises, and foreign support of any kind to internal religious groups was outlawed. A longstanding suspicion of outsiders was evident in this last restriction. "The imperialist powers have never slackened their efforts to poison the minds of the Chinese people," wrote Mao in 1939. "This is their policy of cultural aggression. And it is carried out through missionary work."[9] Accordingly, Protestant and Catholic missionaries came under intense pressure, and by January 1953 all but a handful had been expelled, achieving an objective sought at various times by many Chinese since the midnineteenth century. Although it eventually failed, the Catholic Church attempted to hold its position in China. Priests and Chinese Catholics who remained loyal to Rome paid a high price. In 1951 China and the Vatican broke diplomatic ties, and by 1957 the state had essentially nationalized the Catholic Church.[10] The hostility persists into the twenty-first century. An announcement of plans by the Vatican to canonize on October 1, 2000, 120 Catholics killed in China from 1648 to 1930 brought an angry response from the PRC. To the Vatican, these were martyrs to the faith; to Chinese authorities, they were agents of Western imperialism and colonialism who had "committed monstrous crimes against the Chinese people."[11] That October 1 also marked the anniversary of the founding of the PRC added to China's resentment, the Vatican's claim that the date was coincidental notwithstanding. Predictably, the cessation of diplomatic ties between the PRC and the

Vatican led to cordial relations between the papacy and Chiang's government on Taiwan.

A similar concern of the Chinese government, in that it involved loyalty to an authority other than the Communist state, was Tibet's Dalai Lama. When China took control of the Himalayan nation in 1950, sending in troops on the pretext of ending feudalism, the Dalai Lama, who was both a spiritual and political leader to Tibetan Buddhists, was a problem for China's Communist leaders. They could no more tolerate his authority over Tibetan Buddhists than that of the papacy over Chinese Catholics. To the PRC, the Dalai Lama was a potential source of nationalistic and separatist activity. To Tibetan Buddhists, the official atheism of Mao's regime, to say nothing of political and cultural differences, was anathema. China's heavy-handedness in Tibet sparked an unsuccessful uprising in 1959, whereupon the Dalai Lama escaped to India, touching off something of an international incident. In a move that angered the Chinese, Prime Minister Jawaharlal Nehru of India not only granted the Dalai Lama political asylum but also allowed him to establish a government in exile in the northern town of Dharamsala. To this day the Dalai Lama remains an embarrassment to China and a source of tension in Sino-Indian relations. For instance, a fourteen-year-old monk recognized as the Karmapa Lama, the head of another Tibetan Buddhist sect whom many Tibetan exiles regard as the eventual successor to the Dalai Lama, eluded the Chinese in late December 1999, slipping out of Tibet and arriving at Dharamsala on January 5, 2000. China promptly warned India not to offer asylum to the Karmapa, a warning India ignored.[12]

Mao's Cultural Revolution from 1966 to 1976 was a particularly repressive period not only for Tibetan Buddhism but for all expressions of religion, whether Christianity, Islam, Daoism, or Confucianism. Young zealots known as Red Guards killed thousands of clerics and believers, imprisoned many others, and razed religious property. A 1966 wall poster in Beijing captured the mood. "There is no God; there is no spirit; there is no Jesus; there is no Mary; there is no Joseph," it proclaimed, adding: "Like Islam and Catholicism, Protestantism is a reactionary feudal ideology, the opium of the people, with foreign origins and contacts." It ended with a call to "all people to burn Bibles, destroy images, and disperse religious associations."[13] This brutal policy did not abate until 1976, after Mao's death and the emergence of a more liberal faction within the Communist Party. In 1982 China's new political leaders, seeing once again a certain practical use for religion, returned to a somewhat more tolerant stance on spiritual matters.[14]

Whether imperial rulers or recent Communist Party officials, state authorities in China have always been suspicious of popular movements that arise from the masses without any government sanction. This common stream linking past and present meanders like the Yangtze River through Chinese history. Consider the current case of Falun Gong. It was founded in 1992 by Li Hongzhi, a former government bureau clerk who left China for New York City in 1998 and who maintains contact with his followers via the Internet. Falun Gong, known also as Falun DaFa, meaning "law of the wheel," was an obscure religious movement until quite recently. It combines elements of Buddhism and Daoism with meditation and slow-motion exercises to produce spiritual enlightenment and physical well-being. It appeals to people of all ages and backgrounds, including among its members government researchers, factory managers, radio reporters, police officers, and even some Communist Party members. Estimates of the movement's size vary enormously. The state puts the figure at 2 million; Falun Gong claims at least 100 million.[15]

One thing is certain, Falun Gong startled Communist officials by quickly mobilizing large numbers for a rally in Beijing on April 25, 1999. Attempting to pressure the state into according their group official recognition, about 10,000 of Li's followers suddenly surrounded Communist Party headquarters. An angry and embarrassed President Jiang Zemin ordered a crackdown. Falun Gong's leaders were subsequently detained, its members harassed, and its Web sites blocked. Undaunted, Li's movement mounted protests in cities across China, prompting even more repressive measures by the government. On July 22, 1999, the state banned Falun Gong, labeling it an "evil sect," a "devil cult" that "brainwashes" members with "heretical ideas."[16] Resilient, resourceful, and defiant, Falun Gong stood its ground, and the state, despite increasingly tougher steps, seemed incapable of crushing "this evil force." The clash between Falun Gong and the state took a grisly turn in January 2001, at the beginning of China's Lunar New Year, the nation's biggest holiday. Witnessed by a CNN camera crew, five alleged members of the religious group, one man, three women, and a twelve-year-old girl, attempted collective suicide by setting fire to themselves in Tiananmen Square. One of the women died from her burns. Although other Falun Gong members disavowed the five, asserting such suicide protests were not condoned, the state used the event to prove the point it has made all along—Falun Gong is a cruel, irrational, and evil cult.[17]

Political issues definitely were at the center of this battle of wills over religion. Denying any political intentions for Falun Gong, the attitude of a thirty-eight-year-old Beijing woman was typical. "We are good people, and we are not interested in politics," she explained. "We have to persuade the authorities not to brand good people as evil."[18] Party leaders, of course, saw matters differently. To them, any movement or organization that competed with the party for the people's loyalty was political. So, regardless of statements to the contrary by its members, Falun Gong, from the party's perspective, was a political force as potentially menacing as the student demonstrations in Tiananmen Square in 1989. As one party official put it, the state's handling of Falun Gong was justified because of "the danger it posed to our country and our people. Any responsible government would do the same."[19] A meeting of about 1,200 Falun Gong members from around the world in January 2001 only strengthened government suspicion. From their safe haven in Hong Kong, where the group is legal, Falun Gong disciples rebuked the PRC for its religious oppression. "There's no human rights in China," said one, "because you cannot even say a word about Falun Gong in Tiananmen Square."[20] Such talk in Beijing's backyard was sufficient evidence of the sect's political motives and ties to subversive elements. "Li Hongzhi's claim that he doesn't take part in politics and doesn't oppose the government is a cheap lie," editorialized the *Beijing Daily*. "The result will only be to make people even more aware of the sinister political machinations of Li Hongzhi and his Falun Gong cult organization."[21]

This continuing internal religious tug-of-war could have significant external repercussions. In February 2000 the U.S. Immigration and Naturalization Service announced it was considering granting asylum to Falun Gong members, something unlikely to please the PRC.[22] And in January 2001 former assistant secretary of state for President Ronald Reagan and current chair of the U.S. Commission on International Religious Freedom, Elliott Abrams, after cataloguing a lengthy list of Chinese religious and human rights violations, urged the U.S. to initiate a resolution of censure at the annual spring gathering of the U.N. Commission on Human Rights and to use its diplomatic influence to thwart China's effort to host the 2008 Summer Olympic Games. China,

Abrams added, could avoid such punitive actions by releasing all its religious prisoners, responding to inquiries about people detained for religious belief, allowing international human rights groups access to China's religious leaders, engaging the U.S. in a high-level dialogue on issues of religious freedom, and ratifying the International Convention on Civil and Political Rights.[23]

Standing in sharp contrast to China is modern Iran, where the state has been subordinate to religion since 1979. The overwhelming majority of Iranians, about 93 percent, are Shi'ite Muslims, making Iran the only nation in which Shi'ism prevails. Elsewhere Sunni Muslims, representing the mainstream of the faith, generally predominate, but in Iran they comprise only about 6 percent of the populace. Ayatollah Ruhollah Khomeini was a Shi'ite, and so were the Pahlavi monarchs, but with a fundamental difference. Whereas the ayatollah looked to Islam's distant past for political direction, the shahs found in the West an example for separating religion and politics. The Pahlavi monarchy, not the ayatollah, was the aberration. To understand this requires some grasp of the origins and political significance of the divisions within Islam.

Beginning with the Arab conquest in the seventh century, Islam gradually but steadily replaced Zoroastrianism as the religion of most Iranians. By the ninth century Islam's triumph was more or less complete, but Islam itself by then had divided into rival factions. From Abu Bakr, the first caliph and Muhammad's father-in-law, emerged the Sunni tradition. This dominant body of Islam recognizes the first three caliphs as rightful heirs to the Prophet Muhammad and subscribes to a more moderate view of political succession. This position is more conducive to political stability, allowing for an easier transmission of power. From Imam Ali, a cousin of Muhammad who was married to the Prophet's daughter Fatimah, sprang the Shi'ite tradition. Muslims of this persuasion looked to Allah to provide an infallible leader, an imam who would guide the community with fortitude, justice, and compassion for the poor, and Ali was seen as the first such caliph; they insisted that only direct descendants of Muhammad could succeed to political leadership; and they believed that the twelfth imam, who had gone into concealment toward the end of the ninth century, would reappear at the end of time to create a perfect world. This was Twelver Shi'ism, and its so-called Hidden Imam, or the *Mahdi*, was the only legitimate authority on earth. All temporal political leaders were illegitimate unless they governed as his trustee.[24]

But even Shi'ism, derived from an Arabic term meaning *partisan* or *faction*, also became fragmented. Whereas the Shi'ism of Ali was to become the religion of the masses, a popular expression of the faith that saw in Imam Ali the classic virtues and expectations of Islam, the Shi'ism of the Safavid dynasty, which appeared in the late thirteenth century, became the religion of the monarchy, the elite, the establishment. It was not until 1501, under Shah Isma'il, that Twelver Shi'ism became Iran's official state religion, and since the early 1700s the vast majority of Iranians have been Shi'ites. Significantly, Ayatollah Khomeini harkened back to Imam Ali, whose collected speeches, *Nahj Al-Balagheh*, soon became the most popular book in Iran, next to the Qur'an.[25] Seen from the perspective of Khomeini's followers, the 1979 revolution was "an act of restoration—a halt to the rapid pace of development, and a revival of traditional cultural symbols" that "emerged from the very depth of Iranian society."[26] And by drawing support from the masses, the revolution of 1979 arose in classic Shi'ite tradition to oppose an allegedly illegal state. Just as Imam Ali had earlier challenged and defeated his rivals, so the Shi'ite mullahs challenged and defeated a despised and illegitimate shah.

In February 1921 Reza Khan, an imposing military officer in command of the Persian Cossack Brigade, seized power in Iran in a bloodless coup, supported apparently by British officers. Skillfully consolidating his political grip, he had himself crowned Reza Shah Pahlavi by a constituent assembly in 1925. What followed was a sixteen-year reign, from 1925 to 1941, remarkably similar in method and objective to that of Atatürk in neighboring Turkey. Modernization of Iran was his goal, and he tolerated no opposition to his plans. Though a Muslim whose first name recalled a revered Shi'ite saint, Reza Shah was actually indifferent to religion. Indeed, he was a secularist determined to curb clerical influence. Accordingly, in defiance of the mullahs, he banned traditional Persian garb in favor of Western dress for men and women, required licenses of anyone donning religious attire, raised the marriage age for women from nine to fifteen, introduced coeducation, permitted foreigners to visit certain sacred mosques, abandoned the Muslim calendar, and encouraged Western music, architecture, and cinema. Other actions struck at the institutional power of the clergy, particularly in the area of education. This customarily religious responsibility was transferred to a newly fashioned secular ministry of education. A French curriculum was taught at all levels, and foreign professors held positions at the University of Teheran, founded by Reza Shah.[27]

Suspected of being pro-German in World War II, Reza Shah was forced from power by Soviet and British forces in August 1941. Before fleeing to South Africa, where he died in 1944, he abdicated in favor of his young son, the twenty-two-year-old Mohammad Reza. Although deeply resented by Iranians, this foreign invasion was made somewhat more bearable by the collapse of an autocratic regime that Persians from all walks of life had come to hate.[28] After some reluctance by the Russians, the occupying forces, including Americans, withdrew by early 1946, but not until 1953 did the shah gain firm control of the reins of power. Thereafter he brooked no opposition, relying increasingly on the secret police, SAVAK, to silence both secular and religious opponents. To the shah these opponents were "black reactionaries"; even so, the mullahs had found by the early 1960s a forceful opposition leader who proved to have broad popular appeal. Until 1963 Ayatollah Ruhollah Khomeini, then in his early sixties and a respected but rather obscure teacher of ethics and philosophy in Qom, stayed aloof from politics. His reticence ended, however, as with ever-increasing stridency Khomeini lashed out at the shah. A particularly biting rebuke came in June 1963, when Khomeini urged the shah to avoid the pitfalls of his father. "Listen to my advice, listen to the Ulama of Islam. They desire the welfare of the nation, the welfare of the country," asserted the cleric, adding: "Don't listen to Israel; Israel can't do anything for you." With obvious contempt, Khomeini then declared: "You miserable wretch, forty-five years of your life have passed; isn't it time for you to think and reflect a little, to ponder about where all this is leading you, to learn a lesson from the experience of your father?"[29]

Although accusing the shah of hostility toward Islam, thereby capturing the mood of most religionists, Khomeini couched his arguments broadly enough to catch the attention of many secularists as well. Paralleling the shah's religious apostasy, according to the ayatollah, were financial and moral corruption, fraudulent elections, and a foreign policy slanted toward Israel and the United States. Such claims not only resonated with all manner of Iranians, but, given the fearless nature of their proclamation, also inspired confidence. Because the secret police were always lurking, Khomeini's verbal attack showed remarkable courage. It also won the admiration of some liberal, secular-minded Iranians who saw in this audacious cleric

an ally against the shah. Not until later, after the fall of Mohammad Reza, would the secularists discover the depth of Khomeini's religious conservatism. In the meantime, the ayatollah
paid for his outspokenness. Imprisoned for a time in 1963 and
1964, he was exiled in late 1964, first to Turkey, then to Iraq,
where he remained until the events of 1978–1979 unfolded.

Even though opposition steadily mounted, the swiftness of
the shah's demise nonetheless caught observers by surprise.
Without the support of middle-class professionals, civil servants,
students, and teachers, the revolution probably would not have
succeeded, but it was the religious leaders who identified with
the Shi'ite masses that gained control of the movement. Aside
from agreeing on the corruption of the Pahlavi monarchy, however, the mullahs were divided on Iran's political future. Some,
leery of direct religious involvement in the political process,
sought merely to reform the monarchy, to remake it in accordance with Islamic laws; others wanted to establish an Islamic republic based upon democratic values; others, those of a more
moderate temperament, favored a constitutional government of
some sort that would preserve much of the social progress of the
Pahlavi era, particularly regarding women; and yet others, the
most authoritarian and anti-Western element, would settle for
nothing less than a rigidly Islamic state. Khomeini belonged to
this last group, and he was easily the most towering figure of the
revolution. Here was a proven, charismatic leader who not only
spoke the religious language of the masses, but also had trained
a host of lesser clerics who now held positions in towns and vil-
lages across the nation.[30]

Once Khomeini and the forces loyal to him gained the upper
hand in early 1979, a movement begun primarily to oust a hated
shah became a crusade to restructure society. The result was the
world's only theocratic republic. If those secularists who at first
rallied to Khomeini had been listening, they would have known
the ayatollah's vision for the future differed from theirs completely. A 1971 series of lectures by Khomeini on Islamic government made clear his desire for a system in which political
authority was subordinate to Islam, a system drawn from Eastern rather than Western ideas and practices. As though nothing
had happened in the last 1,300 years, the ayatollah turned the
clock back to the seventh century, to the Prophet Muhammad
himself and Imam Ali. To prepare the way, Khomeini called upon
fellow religious scholars, beseeching them to "explain what the
form of government is in Islam and how rule was conducted in

the earliest days of Islamic history," to tell the faithful "how the center of command and the seat of the judiciary under it were both located in . . . the mosque."[31] For most Iranians of a secular bent, the elimination of the shah's regime was sufficient; for Iranians of Khomeini's persuasion, nothing less than a social upheaval would do. For this latter group, the existing social structure had to be totally dismantled and rebuilt with Islamic materials.

The constitution drafted by the Council of Experts in the summer and fall of 1979 disclosed the full triumph of Islamic fundamentalism. It established a theocratic republic composed of a supreme leader, a popularly elected president, a prime minister and cabinet (the Council of Ministers), a 270-member unicameral parliament (the Islamic Consultative Council), and a twelve-member Council of Guardians. Behind this republican facade the clergy exercised almost absolute authority. Based upon the principle of *velayat-e-faqih*, the guardianship of the jurist-theologian, the supreme leader was recognized as the trustee of the Hidden Imam, from whom all legitimate temporal authority flowed. Khomeini held this position until his death, and it gave him the power to appoint half of the Council of Guardians, declare war and make peace, and select supreme commanders of the military and revolutionary guards. The president's primary responsibility was to implement the constitution and act as a liaison of sorts among the various branches of government. He had to be a Shi'ite and supporter of the revolution. The appointment of the prime minister, who normally presided over the Council of Ministers, had to be approved by both parliament and the president. The parliament, whose members served four-year terms, considered legislation presented by at least fifteen of its own members or by the Council of Ministers. The Council of Guardians had the enormously powerful assignment of ensuring that everything harmonized with Islamic principles. Composed of six "Islamic jurists" and six "just and religious persons," this body not only had veto power over parliamentary acts, but also screened candidates for presidential and parliamentary elections. Thus, this council had the right to set aside what it saw as undesirable laws and to prevent undesirable candidates, those who had criticized the revolution or whose fidelity was in some way suspect, from running for office. The constitution also accorded legal standing to the revolutionary guards, those youthful zealots who sprang into action behind Khomeini during the first days of revolution. Thus from the wreckage of the Pahlavi monarchy quickly evolved an

increasingly authoritarian and intolerant theocracy. Revolutionary courts handed out swift justice for allegedly making war
against God; an August 1979 law silenced the opposition press;
classical Iranian music was banned from radio and television;
women daring to wear Western attire faced growing harassment;
Islamic uniforms became mandatory at girls' schools; the University of Teheran was closed; and street gangs of *hezbollahis*, or par-
tisans of God, saw to the enforcement of the new orthodoxy.[32] If
this was Khomeini's dream for the future, it was a nightmare for
Iranians of a different, more secular, more Western outlook.

The Islamic Republic remains intact despite major setbacks,
such as the failure to ignite Islamic revolution throughout the
Middle East, a costly eight-year war with Iraq, diplomatic isolation from much of the world community, and an economy unable
to provide jobs for more than 50 percent of its university graduates and plagued by a 15 percent rate of unemployment and a 25
percent rate of inflation. Yet there are some signs of change. In
May 1997 Mohammad Khatami, a relatively unknown mullah
and former culture minister, was permitted to run for president,
a decision Islamic conservatives later regretted. Though in his
mid-fifties, Khatami caught the imagination of youthful Iranians
with hints of a more open, tolerant society. Today 65 percent of
Iran's population is under twenty-five years of age, too young to
remember "the tyranny of the Shah or the euphoria of the revolution,"[33] but old enough to know and resent the constraints of
clerical rule. Of the 29 million ballots cast, Khatami received 20
million, or about 69 percent.[34]

Once in office President Khatami moved cautiously to loosen
restrictions. The special police force charged with enforcing public morals was disbanded, allowing young men and women to
mingle somewhat more freely; satellite dishes, once outlawed,
began to reappear on rooftops; some women began dressing in
more fashionable Western garb; newspapers became more outspoken; and subtle diplomatic overtures calculated to end the nation's isolation were made toward the West. Modest but
significant, these shifts marked Khatami as a genuine reformer.
His objective was to liberalize rather than replace the existing Islamic system. He offered a more moderate interpretation of Islam,
suggesting that the revolution begun in 1979 was not a finished
product but a "point of departure." When asked of Khatami's fidelity to the revolution, one grand ayatollah who supports the
new openness remarked that the president's "goals remain those
of the Imam [Khomeini], but the means of reaching them can

change."[35] So although he was taking a new course, Khatami posed no threat to the fundamental structure of the Islamic Republic itself. He was an insider seeking change from within rather than an outsider determined to topple the system. Even so, in a speech to students in Teheran in September 1999 he made clear his disagreement with those who "suppose that the more retarded a society is, the better protected its religion will be."[36]

Timid though they were, these steps toward a more open society nevertheless provoked a strong reaction. Khatami's overwhelming election notwithstanding, conservative religious leaders still controlled the key sources of institutional power. The supreme leader, Ayatollah Ali Khamenei, who has held that position since Khomeini's death in 1989, was resistant, as was the powerful Council of Guardians. Thus, the hard-liners struck back, closing several reformist presses, impeaching members of Khatami's cabinet, jailing dissident clerics, sentencing to death four students for their part in recent protests, and allegedly ordering the murder of some opposition writers. Such strong-arm tactics failed to intimidate Khatami's supporters, who handed the conservatives a stinging setback in the parliamentary elections of February 2000. Of the 270 seats, the reformers won 170, the conservatives 45, and the independents 10, giving the advocates of change control of parliament for the first time since the 1979 revolution. In runoff elections in April for the remaining seats, the reformers substantially increased their majority.[37]

Khatami's victory in 1997 and the parliamentary elections of 2000 buoyed reformers but did not foreshadow the demise of the Islamic Republic. As one observer noted, the youthful champions of reform were "not radical Westernizers or anti-Islamic zealots." Rather, they were Muslims who simply wanted "a less oppressive, less dogmatic system of government." Their goals, he concluded, were "jobs, an end to intrusive Islamic restrictions of individual rights and greater freedom of expression."[38] And this was precisely what the largest party in the reform coalition, the Iran Islamic Participation Front, promised shortly after the 2000 elections. The theocracy would become more tolerant and humane but otherwise endure. Politics would remain subordinate to religion. Change, of course, can be unpredictable, as that astute French observer Alexis de Tocqueville knew so well. "The most dangerous moment for bad government," he remarked in the early 1800s, "is usually when it begins to reform itself."[39]

Events in Iran may well bear out de Tocqueville's observation. Despite the recent elections, Islamic conservatives have resisted the popular will, and in March 2000 they lashed out violently. A gunman attempted to assassinate Saeed Hajjarian, a forty-seven-year-old newspaper editor and key supporter of President Khatami. Hajjarian had been the principal architect of the reformers' landslide victory in February.[40] Since then reformers and conservatives have clashed repeatedly. Fighting actually erupted in parliament in August 2000 as the two sides debated a law allowing greater press freedom. The measure pitted the elected president squarely against the unelected supreme leader. With twenty-three newspapers having been closed since April 2000, Khatami favored the proposal, seeing a free press as an essential means of making his case for change to the people; Khamenei opposed, viewing an open press as a threat to society. Said the supreme leader: "If the enemies of Islam and the Islamic system take control of the press or infiltrate it, a big danger will threaten the security and faith of the people."[41] Khamenei prevailed, whereupon hard-liners promptly closed another reformist paper, arrested a liberal journalist, and called for the execution of a particular member of parliament who had vigorously supported the press bill.[42]

As 2000 closed and 2001 began, Khatami and his followers were showing signs of despair. "After three and one half years as president," acknowledged Khatami in a remarkably candid statement, "I don't have sufficient powers to implement the constitution, which is my biggest responsibility." He added somewhat plaintively: "In practice, the president is unable to stop the trend of violations or force implementation of the constitution."[43] Many of the president's youthful supporters have also become more downcast. Typical was the attitude of one twenty-one-year-old student. "People voted for him because they expected more freedom," he observed. Khatami "delivers speeches for freedom and peace, but we don't think he's done anything." With reference to the upcoming presidential race in June 2001, the young man concluded: "This time many university students are not going to participate in elections at all."[44] Perhaps the time had come, one analyst speculated, for someone "more aggressive than Khatami."[45]

Change may yet demand someone more daring, but on June 8, 2001, an overwhelming majority of 76.9 percent of Iranian voters, most of them young, elected Khatami to a second term. Predictably, reformers saw the election as an unequivocal mandate for the beleaguered president's policies. "Friday's polls should have convinced hard-liners that the nation endorses Khatami's program," declared one lawmaker.[46] Perhaps so, but many conservatives remained defiantly intransigent, vowing to block "structural changes" that would restrict the powers of the supreme leader, increase those of the president, or permit dissidents "to write in newspapers." The hard-liners were unfazed by electoral results, for the "legitimacy of our Islamic establishment," as one proclaimed, "is derived from God," and "this legitimacy will not wash away even if people stop supporting it."[47] Thus, the present situation in Iran is definitely dangerous, volatile, and complex. On both sides of the country's religious-political divide one now finds moderates and radicals. In each camp the former show a willingness to compromise for the sake of domestic calm, the latter appear ready for violence.

It is a gigantic leap in temperament and practice from Iran's theocratic republic to America's policy of religious independence, or separation of church and state. The classic biblical justification emerged from an exchange between Jesus and a group of Pharisees. When asked if they should pay taxes to Rome, "Jesus answering said unto them, render to Caesar the things that are Caesar's and to God the things that are God's."[48] Not until the Revolution and shortly thereafter did separation of church and state become a reality in the United States, brought about by a coalescence of religious and secular interests. Chafing under the establishment policies then prevailing in most of the colonies, Baptists from Massachusetts to Virginia, along with other dissenting groups, wanted the state out of religion; George Mason, James Madison, Patrick Henry, Thomas Jefferson, and others who shared their outlook, aware of the potential for religious strife, wanted religion out of the state. In those southern states where Anglicanism had been established, religious independence was accomplished rather easily and quickly a few years after the Revolution; but in those New England states— New Hampshire, Connecticut, and Massachusetts—Congregationalism continued to receive state support until 1817, 1818, and 1833, respectively.[49] At the federal level, meanwhile, religious liberty became the governing principle with the adoption of the First Amendment, which went into effect in 1791. It reads: "Congress shall make no law respecting an establishment of religion, or prohibiting the free exercise thereof." Americans have never been in complete agreement over the meaning of those sixteen words. Do they call for a total separation between church and state, or neutrality by the state toward religion, or mutual support by the two?

The debate over these questions has grown more rancorous as the religious terrain has become more diverse. For a prolonged period after the Revolution, until about 1860 or so, Protestants easily dominated the landscape. Admittedly, Roman Catholicism had become the largest religious body in the nation well before the Civil War, but Catholics as yet wielded little national influence. By contrast, Protestants of diverse denominations, whose members held positions of economic and political prominence, labored zealously to ensure for the United States a Christian future. Through a multitude of interdenominational societies, Protestants shared Sunday school literature, promoted Sunday closing laws, and worked steadfastly to curb if not eliminate alcoholic consumption. It must have struck certain Americans of the revolutionary era as ironic that Protestants in this immediate postestablishment era seemed determined to make Protestantism the new establishment faith. Although persuasion was the preferred means, Protestants were ready to use state coercion if necessary to advance their goals for the United States.

Though not numerous, issues of church and state did arise in this age of Protestant ascendancy. In the midst of a cholera epidemic in 1832, for instance, a group of ministers implored President Andrew Jackson to proclaim a day of prayer and fasting. Citing separation of church and state, the president declined, prompting the scornful rebuke that all this talk about church and state was so much cant, "the watch word of infidels and drunkards and the very dregs of human society" (*Connecticut Observer*, July 16, 1832). A subsequent chief executive, Zachary Taylor, faced with a similar request during the cholera outbreak of 1849, readily complied, eliciting concern that religionists were attempting to reunite church and state.[50] The public criticism of these contrasting presidential responses discloses the ambivalence of Americans in the early 1800s. Jackson's critics took for granted that religion and politics should be mutually supportive, while Taylor's preferred strict separation.

A more vexing matter during this period involved the Mormons and plural marriage. Disclosed by the Prophet Joseph Smith in 1841, this new marriage doctrine was regarded as an important aspect of the Mormon faith. As such, Mormons insisted it was protected under the free exercise provision of the First Amendment. Not so, retorted evangelical Protestants, who condemned the practice as a dangerous threat to normal family institutions and demanded restrictive legislation from political leaders. Mormons fled the United States for the Mexican southwest in 1847 only to find themselves back in the Union at the close of the Mexican War in 1848. The difficult task of sorting out the dimensions of church and state fell to the Supreme Court, and with regard to the Mormons the justices made a distinction between belief and practice. In *Reynolds v. United States* (1878) the Court held that the state had no quarrel with theology; religious people could believe whatever they wanted. However, if religious practices were at odds with the law, the state certainly had the right to involve itself. Polygamy was such a practice, for it transgressed federal laws. The significance of the *Reynolds* decision was that it established that religious beliefs were no protection against punishment for the commission of secular offenses. Only when Mormons finally agreed to abandon plural marriage was Utah admitted to statehood in 1896.[51] As the Mormons discovered, the free exercise clause was not an entitlement to disregard polygamy laws or flout popular convention.

The century beginning about 1860 witnessed fundamental religious change in U.S. society. Specifically, it was apparent the nation was not going to become a Protestant republic. Increasingly assertive Roman Catholics and Jews were making room for themselves and forcing Americans to reexamine church-state relationships. Much of the tension centered on public schools, whose historically Protestant character offended Catholics. Public schools in Cincinnati, Ohio, for instance, had since their inception in 1829 opened the class day with scripture reading. Objections by Catholics brought a change in 1842, allowing pupils whose parents so desired to be excused from reading the "Protestant Testament and Bible." A decade later students could read from the Bible of their choice; then in 1869 a majority of the school board ended altogether the practice of starting the day with Bible reading. A minority of members sued the majority, and the state supreme court eventually ruled in favor of the majority.

The argument generated by the Cincinnati case has a remarkably contemporary ring. A lower court judge who supported the minority contended "that the mere reading of the Scriptures without note or comment" was not "an act of worship." He elaborated that "the lessons selected are, in all probability, those which elevate the mind and soften the heart—an exercise not only proper, but desirable to calm the temper of children, while it impresses the truth of personal responsibility for good or evil conduct." An Episcopal cleric made the case for the other side, asserting that in a nation of religious diversity "a school system in which a specific form of religion shall be taught or practiced at the public expense, is among such a people unjust to all who dissent from that religion, but are, nevertheless, compelled to contribute to its support."[52] This makes clear that the battle over religion in U.S. classrooms has a long history, and ongoing efforts today to post the Ten Commandments and permit student-initiated prayer at football games or around the flag pole, efforts that have gained momentum with each outbreak of school violence, only represent the latest phase of that struggle.

Just as the Mormons in the late nineteenth century had forced the Court to distinguish between belief and practice, the Jehovah's Witnesses in the midtwentieth century compelled it to examine again the implications of religious liberty. Founded in the 1870s, this small sect was fiercely antiestablishmentarian, rebuking with equal fervor the alleged corruption of mainstream religion, state tyranny, and oppressive business behavior. The Witnesses won support among the poor and disinherited, but angered the more affluent by ignoring Sabbath quiet laws, distributing literature in public places, and engaging in aggressive door-to-door proselytizing campaigns. Were such unconventional methods, methods irritating to many middle-class Americans, allowed under the free exercise clause? Relying on the belief-practice precept, the Court ruled against the Witnesses in the 1930s, but shifted positions in the 1940s. In *Cantwell v. Connecticut* (1940) and *Murdoch v. Pennsylvania* (1943) the justices accorded the practices of the Witnesses "the same claim to protection [under the First Amendment] as the more orthodox and conventional exercises of religion."[53]

Another and more controversial series of cases involving the Witnesses had to do with flag salutes, pledges, and oaths. Such ceremonial practices, the Witnesses believed, violated commandments against having other gods and making graven images. Yet in rejecting these symbols of allegiance, particularly in the early stages of World War II, the Witnesses struck many Americans as unpatriotic. Accordingly, Witness children, faced with an unusual degree of public animosity, were expelled from school for refusing to recite the pledge of allegiance. Upholding such expulsions in *Minerville School District v. Gobitis* (1940), the Supreme Court reasoned: "The flag is a symbol of our national unity, transcending all internal differences, however large, within the framework of the Constitution."[54] That the refusal of children should bring such reproach, even in wartime, is difficult to comprehend in retrospect. In any event, the composition of the Court changed somewhat, and so the justices reversed themselves in 1943. "If there is any fixed star in our constitutional constellation," the Court said in *West Virginia State Board of Education v. Barnette,* "it is that no official, high or petty, can prescribe what shall be orthodox in politics, nationalism, religion, or other matters of opinion or force citizens to confess by word or act their faith therein."[55] The Witness cases pushed the Court beyond the simple belief-practice rule to the conclusion that certain actions that would otherwise be illegal are sometimes permissible under the free exercise clause. In terms of personal freedom, therefore, all Americans were the beneficiaries of the Witnesses' perseverance.

Although most issues coming before the Supreme Court dealt with free exercise, an important case involving the establishment clause confronted the justices in 1947. The precise meaning of the establishment clause was always debatable. Although virtually everyone agreed that the state could not establish a church, considerable uncertainty about other questions remained. Was it all right for the state to aid religious institutions, so long as it showed no preference for any particular group? Or should the state adopt a strict hands-off policy, separating itself from any religious entanglements? These were the issues facing the justices in *Everson v. Board of Education* (1947), which arose from a New Jersey school board's practice of reimbursing parents for the cost of transporting their children by bus to parochial schools. Split 5–4, the Court arrived at a muddled conclusion. In unmistakable separationist language, Justice Hugo Black spoke for the majority: "In the words of Jefferson, the clause against establishment of religion by law was intended to erect 'a wall of separation between church and state.'" Yet, paradoxically, the Court upheld the school board. However, in 1952, reflecting the fluid nature of the debate, the justices backed away even from the hard separationist tone of the *Everson* decision. The issue in *Zorach v. Clauson* was released time for New York public school children for religious instruction. Since the program was voluntary and took place off school property, Justice William O. Douglas saw no violation of the establishment clause. Indeed, Douglas believed the kind of church-state cooperation involved in this case followed "the best of our tradition."[56] The division on the High Court was no doubt indicative of the divided mind of the U.S. public.

Twice during this period of emerging pluralism, religion and politics intersected at the highest level of public life—the presidential campaigns of 1928 and 1960. It is doubtful that Alfred E. Smith, a New York Democrat and the first Catholic nominated for the presidency, would have been elected even if he had been a

Protestant. Still, his religion was a liability, arousing among many Protestants concerns about federal money for parochial schools and papal control of Catholic politicians. Playing upon those fears, a nationally prominent Baptist fundamentalist from Texas, J. Frank Norris, reduced the race to a contest between God and Herbert Hoover on one side and Satan and Al Smith on the other. The flamboyant minister barnstormed the state, conjuring up images of Dark Age persecutions and papal abuses and imploring voters to oppose that "wet Catholic" Smith and support "that Christian gentleman" Hoover. More than once Norris asked: "Are we ready to permit a man to occupy the highest office, the chief magistracy over this Government, who owes his first allegiance to a foreign power which claims" to be supreme in all things, infallible, and unalterable?[57] The answer was self-evident to Norris, and multitudes of Protestants obviously agreed.

John Kennedy, a Massachusetts Democrat, confronted similar opposition, but with a different result. Kennedy's success was in part due to adroit handling of the church-state question. In a televised speech in Texas to the Greater Houston Ministerial Alliance, Kennedy astutely recalled the role of Baptists in securing religious liberty in the eighteenth century. He proclaimed his own belief in religious liberty and his opposition to federal aid for parochial schools and diplomatic recognition of the Vatican. "I believe in an America that is officially neither Catholic, Protestant nor Jewish," explained the candidate, "when no public official either requests or accepts instructions on public policy from the Pope, the National Council of Churches or any other ecclesiastical source."[58] If Kennedy's victory in 1960 eliminated Catholicism as a barrier to the White House, it in no way settled the debate over church and state.

It is significant that Kennedy used the phrase "neither Catholic, Protestant nor Jewish," for it signified what many Americans by 1960 had come to accept as the boundaries of religious pluralism. One scholar called this "mainstream pluralism," a view given classic expression by Will Herberg, *Protestant-Catholic-Jew* (1955). As Herberg observed: "Protestantism today no longer regards itself either as a religious movement sweeping the continent or as a national church representing the religious life of the people"; instead, it "understands itself today primarily as one of the three religious communities in which twentieth century America has come to be divided."[59] Acceptance of this reality had come only slowly and grudgingly to Protestants, and Jews, as vigorous in defending separation of church and state in the twentieth century as Baptists had been in the eighteenth, "nicely mediated between the far larger Protestant and Catholic communities."[60] Ironically, by the time Christians of varied persuasions and Jews were becoming more accommodating toward one another, the dimensions of America's religious pluralism were becoming ever more expansive. Protestants, Catholics, and Jews would have to make room for additional expressions of religion.

With changes in U.S. immigration laws in the 1960s came a sizeable influx from the East, producing a religious kaleidoscope unimaginable only a half century ago. Since the 1960s Islam has become the largest non-Christian body in the nation, and mosques have appeared in cities from coast to coast. It is too soon to gauge the political effect of this development, but it could eventually have some bearing on U.S.-Israeli policies. Though not as numerous, Buddhists and Hindus have been increasingly evident since the 1970s. The first Buddhist chaplain to the armed services was named in 1987, the same year in which the American Buddhist Congress was organized to advance greater understanding of Buddhism. Both Buddhists and Hindus today claim 3 to 5 million adherents, making them as numerous as any number of Christian denominations.[61] Add to this mix smaller groups of spiritualists, pagans, humanists, atheists, and New Age disciples and it becomes apparent that for the first time this nation is truly plural in religious configuration.

To be sure, these changes have not pleased all Americans, and since the 1980s many religious conservatives, particularly Christian evangelicals, have entered politics to accomplish cherished religious goals. Under the banner of the Moral Majority, then the Christian Coalition, these Christian conservatives joined the political fray determined to "save" the United States by restoring its alleged godly foundation. This entailed rejecting the new pattern of religious pluralism and challenging secular institutions. Again the Supreme Court found itself the principal arbiter of bitter constitutional clashes over church and state. Much of the fury stemmed from the controversial school prayer decisions of 1962 and 1963, *Engel v. Vitale* and *Abington Township School District v. Schempp*, respectively. *Engel* dealt with the daily recitation of a prayer composed by the New York Board of Regents, while *Abington* concerned mandatory prayer and Bible reading. In striking down both practices as violations of the establishment clause, the Court returned to the strict separation course charted in *Everson*.[62] A furor erupted. "With the possible exception of its ruling on racial integration [in 1954]," wrote E.S. James, editor of the widely-read Baptist weekly in Texas, the *Baptist Standard*, "nothing has so stirred the citizens of this country."[63]

The Baptist journalist was absolutely right. Since 1962 there have been repeated calls, including one from President Ronald Reagan, for a constitutional amendment to allow school prayer. This country must strike many outsiders as something of a paradox. It is a secular nation in which over 90 percent of all Americans believe in God and in which religion commands considerable public influence and absorbs an unusual amount of its elected officials' time. In 1999 Congress spent countless hours debating the posting of the Ten Commandments in schools and other public buildings, allowing student-initiated prayer, and calling for days of prayer and fasting. Not to be left out, President Bill Clinton joined the chorus in December 1999, announcing support for stronger ties between religious institutions and public schools. "Finding the proper place for faith in our schools is a complex and emotional matter for many Americans," the president declared, adding: "I have never believed the Constitution required our schools to be religion-free zones, or that our children must check their faith at the schoolhouse door."[64] These recent eruptions suggest that Americans are as divided as ever with regard to church and state. Do they want strict separation, neutrality, or mutual support? The issue remains unresolved.

An important question that definitely has a bearing on attitudes about the proper relationship between religious and political institutions is whether specific religions predispose one to think in a certain way about politics. It is true that numerous faiths make little or no distinction between the secular and spiritual, the profane and sacred realms. Such is the case with Islam, Hinduism, and Buddhism. As one scholar observed, Islam is a religion "that embraces all aspects of life and controls all the attitudes and actions of its believers. Religion is government. Religious law is the law."[65] This belief, rooted in the Prophet Muhammad himself, can be seen in practice throughout the Muslim world. It guided the Muslim Brotherhood and continues to inspire the more recent militant Muslim groups; it was evident in the Iranian constitution of 1906, which was drafted "in the name of God, the Compassionate, the Most Merciful";[66] it informed the writings and lives of such prominent twentieth century Islamic thinkers and activists as Sayyid Qutb, Hasan al-Banna, and Maulana Sayyid Abul Ala Mawdudi; it sustained the exiled Ayatollah Khomeini; and it presently drives Osama bin Laden.

But the belief that religion and politics are inseparable has not forced the Muslim world into a political straitjacket. Atatürk, for instance, as well as the Pahlavi dynasty in Iran, was a Muslim who pursued a modern course for Turkey. Despite the objections of religious conservatives, who have become more vocal and violent in recent years,[67] Turkey remains a secular state. A better example of a modern Muslim country that is attempting to harmonize Islam with political democracy, religious pluralism, ethnic diversity, and women's rights is Indonesia. Brought to western Indonesia by Arab traders in the thirteenth and fourteenth centuries, Islam gradually extended throughout the islands, where it fused with traditional animist practices to produce a moderate form of Asian Islam in which women were free to work and leave their heads uncovered. Today, with Muslims representing almost 90 percent of its 216 million people, Indonesia is the most Muslim-dominated nation in the world. Yet, since the 1960s its political leaders have endeavored to ensure religious equality for all inhabitants. Although the state encourages religious development, there is no formal connection between religion and the state. Indonesia is not officially an Islamic state, but rather accords equal rights to Islam, Roman Catholicism, Protestantism, Buddhism, and Hinduism. The Indonesian experience suggests that Islam does not require an Islamic state.

Of course, Indonesia, which has known both ethnic and religious violence in the past, is presently experiencing turmoil. Conflicts between Muslims and Christians have recently flared, fueled by staggering economic problems and the political instability accompanying the collapse in 1998 of longtime dictator Suharto, who had held Islamic fundamentalists in check for over three decades. Nevertheless, the victor in the presidential election of October 1999, Abdurrahman Wahid, promised to hold Indonesia on a moderate course. A respected Muslim religious leader, Wahid assured the nation of his commitment to a policy of tolerance and inclusion. Criticized by some Muslims for his openness, the new president asserted: "Those who say that I am not Islamic enough should reread their Koran. Islam is about inclusion, tolerance, and community." Wahid's words carry weight because of his actions. Unlike Muslim leaders elsewhere, he has refused to condemn Salman Rushdie, the British author whose *Satanic Verses* (1988) outraged much of the Islamic world; he journeyed to Jerusalem to pay respect to the assassinated Israeli Prime Minister Yitzhak Rabin;[68] he has rebuffed calls by Indonesian fundamentalists to impose Islamic law; and he has thus far managed to keep religion out of politics. Whether Wahid will succeed or not remains uncertain. Although considered a wily politician, financial scandals have plagued his administration, and parliament has twice censured the nearly blind and frail president. By May 2001 Wahid faced a serious threat of impeachment. Compounding his troubles was a series of church bombings across Indonesia on Christmas Eve 2000 that killed fifteen and injured about 100 worshippers. It was feared that outraged Christians, comprising no more than 10 percent of the population, would retaliate, initiating a round of Muslim-Christian violence.

Wahid's ability to hold Islamic fundamentalists in check remains unsure at this point. Even so, the Indonesian experience, though troubled at times by religious strife, shows that the Muslim world is hardly monolithic in politics, theology notwithstanding. Hinduism and Buddhism disclose similar parallels. Assumptions about the unity of the sacred and the profane have not precluded either from accepting political arrangements that accord equal treatment to all citizens regardless of religious persuasion.

By contrast, Christianity in the West has long acknowledged a distinction between the things of Caesar and the things of God, and in the United States that principle has undergirded political practice since adoption of the First Amendment. Religious liberty accomplished through separation of church and state has not only enabled this country to escape for the most part violent religious conflicts but also has contributed to an expanding pattern of religious pluralism. If anything, the U.S. experience shows that Christianity, or Protestantism, or Catholicism, or Islam does not require a religious state to flourish. On the contrary, by showing no preference to any one body, the policy of church-state separation affords all religious groups an equal opportunity to prosper—or to perish. As already shown, however, Americans remain perplexed over the exact meaning of church and state. Among these are many religious conservatives who, if they could have their way in the political area, would no doubt shorten if not eliminate the distance between the sacred and profane. To these Americans the story of Moses as a divine lawgiver has the ring of truth.

Endnotes

1. Quoted in Herbert J. Muller, *The Loom of History* (New York: Harper and Brothers, 1958), p. 101.

2. Will Durant, *Our Oriental Heritage* (New York: Simon and Schuster, 1954), pp. 331, 351; Will and Ariel Durant, *The Lessons of History* (New

York: Simon and Schuster, 1968), pp. 43–45; and Martin E. Marty and R. Scott Appleby, eds., *Fundamentalisms Observed* (Chicago: University of Chicago Press, 1991), p. 786.

3. John F. Wilson and Donald L. Drakeman, eds., *Church and State in American History*, 2nd ed., enl. (Boston: Beacon Press, 1987), p. ix.

4. Robert Wuthnow, ed., *The Encyclopedia of Politics and Religion*, 2 vols. (Washington, DC: Congressional Quarterly Inc., 1998), 1:324–328.

5. *Houston Chronicle*, Oct. 30, 1999, p. 26A and Nov. 8, 1999, p. 13A.

6. John K. Shryock, *The Origin and Development of the State Cult of Confucius* (New York: Paragon Book Reprint Corp, 1966), pp. 223–233; D. Howard Smith, *Chinese Religions* (New York: Holt, Rinehart and Winston, 1968), pp. 32–33, 145–147; Marcel Granet, *The Religion of the Chinese People*, trans. Maurice Freedman (New York: Harper and Row, 1975), pp. 97–119.

7. Smith, *Chinese Religions*, p. 159.

8. Donald E. MacInnis, *Religious Policy and Practice in Communist China, A Documentary History* (New York: MacMillan Co., 1967), pp. 13, 14; and Richard C. Bush Jr., *Religion in Communist China* (New York: Abingdon Press, 1970), pp. 15, 17–18.

9. MacInnis, *Religious Policy*, p. 12.

10. Bush, *Religion in Communist China*, pp. 38–169.

11. *Houston Chronicle*, Sept. 27, 2000, p. 15A.

12. Ibid., Jan. 13, 2000, p. 22A, Jan. 18, 2000, p. 9A, Feb. 6, 2000, p. 23A, and Feb. 8, 2000, p. 12A.

13. Bush, *Religion in Communist China*, p. 257.

14. MacInnis, *Religious Policy*, pp. 283–306.

15. *Houston Chronicle*, July 23, 1999, p. 22A, and Oct. 28, 1999, p. 16A.

16. Ibid., Oct. 28, 1999, p. 16A and Nov. 6, 1999, p. 24A.

17. Ibid., Jan. 25, 2001, p. 13A and Jan. 31, 2001, p. 10A.

18. Ibid. See also, Feb. 5, 2000, p. 28A.

19. Ibid., July 23, 1999, p. 22A.

20. Ibid., Jan. 15, 2001, p. 11A.

21. Ibid.

22. Ibid., Feb. 17, 2000, p. 29A. See also *Houston Chronicle*, Nov. 6, 1999, p. 24A; *Beaumont Enterprise*, Oct. 29, 1999, p. 11A; and *Newsweek*, Aug. 9, 1999, p. 43.

23. *Houston Chronicle*, Jan. 5, 2001, p. 23A.

24. Shaul Bakhash, *The Reign of the Ayatollahs, Iran and the Islamic Revolution* (New York: Basic Books, Inc., 1979), p. 5; John W. Limbert, *Iran, At War with History* (Boulder, CO: Westview Press, 1987), pp. 31–32; and John B. Noss, *Man's Religions*, 4th ed. (New York: MacMillan Co, 1971), pp. 542–552.

25. Manochehr Dorraj, *From Zarathustra to Khomeini, Populism and Dissent in Iran* (Boulder, CO: Lynne Rienner Publishers, 1990), pp. 42–47; and Limbert, *Iran*, pp. 11, 63–70.

26. Dorraj, *From Zarathustra*, pp. vii–viii.

27. William H. Forbis, *Fall of the Peacock Throne, The Story of Iran* (New York: Harper and Row, 1980), pp. 43–46; and Limbert, *Iran*, pp. 84–87.

28. Limbert, *Iran*, p. 88; and Forbis, *Peacock Throne*, pp. 48–50.

29. Limbert, *Iran*, p. 99.

30. Ibid., pp. 107–109.

31. Ibid., p. 119.

32. Ibid., pp. 120–127.

33. *Newsweek*, July 26, 1999, p. 63.

34. See Christopher de Bellaigue, *"The Struggle for Iran,"* The New *York Review of Books*, Dec. 16, 1999, p. 58; and *Houston Chronicle*, Feb. 21, 2000, p. 22A.

35. de Bellaigue, *"Struggle for Iran,"* p. 54.

36. Ibid., p. 51. See also *Houston Chronicle*, Feb. 19, 2000, p. 26A and Feb. 21, 2000, p 22A.

37. *The Washington Post National Weekly Edition*, Nov. 29, 1999, p. 18; de Bellaigue, *"Struggle for Iran,"* p. 57; *Houston Chronicle*, Feb. 19, 2000, p. 26A and Feb. 28, 2000, p. 14A; and *Beaumont Enterprise*, May 19, 2000, p. 20A.

38. *Newsweek*, July 26, 1999, p. 63.

39. Quoted in ibid.

40. *Houston Chronicle*, Feb. 28, 2000, p. 14A and March 13, 2000, p. 12A.

41. Ibid., Aug. 7, 2000, p. 14.

42. Ibid., Aug. 8, 2000, p. 15A and Aug. 9, 2000, p. 20A.

43. *The Washington Post National Weekly Edition*, Dec. 4, 2000, p. 12.

44. Ibid.

45. Ibid.

46. *Houston Chronicle*, June 13, 2001, p. 29A.

47. Ibid.

48. *Mark 12:13–17.*

49. William Warren Sweet, *The Story of Religion in America* (New York: Harper and Brothers, 1950), pp. 189–192.

50. Charles E. Rosenberg, *The Cholera Years, The United States in 1832, 1849 and 1866* (Chicago: University of Chicago Press, 1962), pp. 48–49, 123–124.

51. R. Laurence Moore, *Religious Outsiders and the Making of Americans* (New York: Oxford University Press, 1986), pp. 27–29; and Paul K. Conkin, *American Originals, Homemade Varieties of Christianity* (Chapel Hill: The University of North Carolina Press, 1997), pp. 195–196; and Robert T. Miller and Ronald B. Flowers, *Toward Benevolent Neutrality: Church, State, and the Supreme Court*, 4th ed. (Waco, TX: Baylor University Press, 1992), pp. 47–55.

52. Wilson and Drakeman, *Church and State*, pp. 122–125.

53. Miller and Flowers, *Toward Benevolent Neutrality*, pp. 45–55.

54. Ibid., pp. 55–63, 74–82.

55. Ibid., pp. 82–96. See also Conkin, *American Originals*, pp. 151–154.

56. Miller and Flowers, *Toward Benevolent Neutrality,* pp. 283–286.

57. See John W. Storey, *Texas Baptist Leadership and Social Christianity, 1900–1980* (College Station: Texas A&M University Press, 1986), p. 204; and Barry Hankins, *God's Rascal, J. Frank Norris and the Beginnings of Southern Fundamentalism* (Lexington: The University Press of Kentucky, 1996), p. 54.

58. Wilson and Drakeman, *Church and State,* p. 190.

59. Quoted in Storey, *Texas Baptist Leadership,* p. 201.

60. Wilson and Drakeman, *Church and State,* p. 161.

61. J. Gordon Melton, *Encyclopedia of American Religions,* 6th ed. (Detroit: Gale Research, 1999), pp. 14–18.

62. Miller and Flowers, *Toward Benevolent Neutrality,* pp. 286–287.

63. *Baptist Standard* (Dallas, TX), July 4, 1962, p. 5.

64. *Houston Chronicle,* Dec. 19, 1999, p. 13A. See also *Houston Chronicle,* June 23, 1999, p. 27A, July 11, 1999, p. 3C, and July 16, 1999, p. 10A.

65. Forbis, *Peacock Throne,* p. 145.

66. Ibid.

67. See *Houston Chronicle,* Jan. 26, 2000, p. 14A.

68. Ibid., Oct. 21, 1999, pp. 1, 18, 33A.

2

Chronology

c. 1750 B.C.   Babylonian King Hammurabi codifies the law. The Code of Hammurabi, as it is to be known, is a body of *conditional* law, stating that if *this* happens, then *that* will be the legal consequence.

c. 1200 B.C.   According to legend, Moses receives "the Ten Words," or Ten Commandments, from God on Mount Sinai. This is a body of *absolute* laws, as in "thou shalt not commit murder," etc., and it is of major importance to Judaism, Christianity, and Islam.

563 B.C.   Gautama Buddha, the founder of Buddhism, is born in northern India. His will be a religion of self-denial, one that promises peace and joy through the renunciation of things that bring pain to mind and soul, such as lust, pride, doubt, self-righteousness, and ignorance. Hence, Buddhist literature often consists of lengthy lists of things and desires to be avoided or given up. Significantly, since it is up to humans to control their appetites and thus their fate, there is no need in Buddhism for a supernatural, external deity to guide human behavior.

551 B.C.   The Chinese scholar Confucius is born in what is today the Shandong province. An itinerant scholar for most his early years, Confucius returns to his native province rather late in life and establishes a school for the education of future statesmen. In time, by the third century B.C., his moral and ethical teachings, rooted in familial ties, will become the official creed of China, embraced particularly by the educated elite. Confucianism will be

551 B.C., a humanistic moral philosophy in that, starting with
cont.   the individual as the measure of proper conduct, it
moves outward to the broader family and community.
One of its governing precepts will be, "Do not impose
on others what you yourself do not desire."

c. 30   When questioned about the payment of tribute to Caesar, Jesus answers: "Render to Caesar the things that are
Caesar's, and to God the things that are God's." (MK.
12:17)

313   Emperor Constantine of Rome issues the Edict of
Milan, ending years of persecution of Christians.

426   Augustine of Hippo completes *City of God*, a major influence on the Christian view of politics, which defends
the church against the charge that Christianity is responsible for the fall of Rome.

c. 570   The prophet Muhammad is born in Mecca, a city on the
Arabian coast that will become the holiest place of
Islam.

c. 1270   Thomas Aquinas, in *Summa Theologica*, clarifies the relationship between church and state. He posits the existence of divine and natural law distinct from the laws
of individual states.

1517   Martin Luther posts ninety-five theses to the castle
church door in Wittenberg. This revolt against Roman
authority contributes to the formation of nation states.

1787   Believing that religion should not prevent service to the
nation, the framers of the U.S. Constitution prohibit, in
Article VI, Section 3, religious tests for persons holding
federal offices. Unlike the Declaration of Independence,
which makes reference to a "creator," the Constitution,
making no such appeal, is a thoroughly secular document.

1790   Reflecting the increasingly anticlerical nature of the
French Revolution, the clergy is required to take oaths
to civil authority.

1791   Ratification of the First Amendment to the U.S. Constitution, which in part reads, "Congress shall pass no law regarding the establishment of religion, or prohibiting the free exercise thereof . . .," provides the legal framework for separation of church and state.

1802   Addressing the Danbury Baptists of Virginia, President Thomas Jefferson refers to a "wall of separation between Church and State," which in time becomes shorthand for the First Amendment.

1849   American transcendentalist Henry David Thoreau writes "On Civil Disobedience," an essay that informs the nonviolent protests of Mohandas Gandhi in India and Martin Luther King Jr. in the United States.

1891   Pope Leo XIII issues *Rerum Novarum* ("The Condition of Labor"), which is the modern Roman Catholic Church's first official declaration of social concern. It assesses the strengths and weaknesses of capitalism and socialism, examines the need of labor unions, and highlights the dire conditions of industrial workers.

1894   Mohandas Gandhi organizes the Natal Indian Congress to battle British mistreatment of Indians in the crown colony of Natal.

1906   A South African law requiring Indians to carry identification cards pushes Mohandas Gandhi toward nonviolent protests. This struggle lasts seven years, ending in 1913.

1917   After the Communists gain power in Russia, they initiate a vigorous attack on religion. They abolish private property, including that of the churches. Although the new constitution theoretically grants religious liberty, believers are nonetheless persecuted.

1919   Supported enthusiastically by the churches, the United States ratifies the Eighteenth Amendment to the Constitution. The churches thus achieve through political means the long-sought goal of national prohibition.

Mohandas Gandhi encourages a nationwide boycott in

1919,
cont.
India of British goods. The British respond harshly, arresting Gandhi and many of his followers.

1920
Mohandas Gandhi becomes the leader of the Indian National Congress and promotes nonviolent resistance to British authority.

1923
The state of Oklahoma enacts the first antievolution law in the United States, which proscribes the teaching of Charles Darwin's theories of biological evolution in the public schools.

The Republic of Turkey is established, and Kemal Atatürk is elected president. Although a Muslim, Atatürk sets about making Turkey a modern, Western-style secular state.

1924
Mohandas Gandhi conducts his first fast, this one in behalf of Hindu-Muslim unity in India.

1925
The state of Tennessee enacts a measure making it illegal to teach evolution in the public schools. This leads to the sensational trial of John Thomas Scopes, a young teacher from Dayton, Tennessee, who is prosecuted by the prominent William Jennings Bryan and defended by the famed attorney Clarence Darrow.

1928
Egyptian teacher and Islamic reformer Hasan al-Banna founds the Muslim Brotherhood, which promotes Islam as a way of life to be applied not only in religion but also in politics and economics. He also denounces British occupation of his country.

The Democratic Party nominates Governor Alfred E. Smith of New York for the presidency of the United States. Smith hopes to focus the campaign on economic issues, specifically the Republican Party's favoritism of big business, but the public, especially in the heavily Protestant South, seems more interested in the nominee's religion. Smith is the first Roman Catholic nominated by a major party for the presidency, and he falls victim to vicious rumor-mongering. It is hinted that if Smith is elected, the pope will run the country.

1930   Mohandas Gandhi initiates a concerted campaign of civil disobedience against British authority in India. Central to this effort is a 165-mile march to the Gujarat Coast on the Arabian Sea to protest Great Britain's salt monopoly.

1934   The National Assembly of Turkey bestows on Mustafa Kemal the honorary title of "Atatürk," meaning "Father of the Turks."

Elijah Muhammad, formerly Elijah Poole, assumes leadership of the Black Muslims, a group that adheres to a puritanical lifestyle and advocates black nationalism.

1939   Rumors and charges persist that Pope Pius XII, because of alleged anti-Semitism, does not offer much help to Europe's persecuted Jews during World War II.

1940   Muslim leader Mohammad Ali Jinnah proposes separate nationhood for those parts of the Indian subcontinent composed of Muslims.

The Muslim League adopts the Lahore Resolution, which calls for an autonomous Muslim state independent of India.

1941   Maulana Sayyid Abul Ala Mawdudi founds the Islamic Party in India.

Mullah Ruhollah Khomeini condemns Iran's Pahlavi monarchy for embracing the secular ways of the West.

1945   Although overwhelmingly Muslim, the newly independent Indonesia drafts a constitution granting religious freedom.

Dietrich Bonhoeffer, a Lutheran pastor, is executed for his active opposition to the German Nazi regime.

Following its defeat in World War II, Japan disestablishes Shintoism, the nation's ancestral faith, which had become the official state religion by the constitution of 1889, and grants religious freedom to all.

1946   Violence erupts between Hindus and Muslims in India, hastening the creation of Pakistan, a Muslim state, in what had been northeastern India.

Joseph Martin Dawson becomes the first full-time director of the newly fashioned Baptist Joint Committee on Public Affairs, a lobbying agency concerned with transgressions of the First Amendment to the U.S. Constitution.

1947   Prompted by violence between Hindus and Muslims, Great Britain announces plans to divide the subcontinent into India and Pakistan. Hinduism prevails in India, Islam in Pakistan.

Islamic scholar and politician Maulana Sayyid Abul Ala Mawdudi, though pleased by Pakistan's independence from Britain, is unhappy with the country's new secular rulers. He endeavors to make Pakistan a genuinely Islamic state.

Joseph Martin Dawson helps organize Protestants and Other Americans United for the Separation of Church and State, which evolves into Americans United for the Separation of Church and State.

1948   Mahatma Gandhi, India's religious and political leader, is assassinated by a Hindu fundamentalist who is angered by Gandhi's overtures of accommodation toward the Muslims.

The Jewish nation of Israel is founded, carved out of Palestine over the objections of the neighboring Muslim states of Lebanon, Syria, Jordan, Iraq, and Egypt.

1949   Hasan al-Banna is assassinated in Cairo, Egypt. His followers suspect the Egyptian government of complicity.

1950   On the pretext of ending feudalism, the People's Republic of China seizes control of Tibet, a predominantly Buddhist country.

1951   The People's Republic of China and the Vatican break diplomatic ties.

Egyptian Sayyid Qutb joins the Muslim Brotherhood and becomes a vigorous advocate of Islamic conservatism.

1954   Reflecting the growing religiosity of Americans during the Cold War, "under God" is added to the pledge of allegiance to the U.S. flag.

The Muslim Brotherhood attempts to assassinate Prime Minister Gamal Abdel Nasser, an Egyptian secularist who will soon become the nation's president.

Sayyid Qutb is arrested for the Muslim Brotherhood's attempt on Nasser's life and spends the next decade in jail where he develops a rationale for opposing nominal Muslim leaders.

Sun Myung Moon founds the Holy Spirit Association for the Unification of World Christianity (better known simply as the Unification Church) in Seoul, Korea.

1955   "In God We Trust" is inscribed on American currency, and the following year it becomes the national motto.

By refusing to move to the rear of the bus, Rosa Parks sets in motion the Montgomery bus boycott, which advances Reverend Martin Luther King Jr. to the forefront of the civil rights movement in the United States.

1956   The young pastor of the Dexter Avenue Baptist Church in Montgomery, Alabama, Martin Luther King Jr. leads a successful boycott against the city's segregated bus lines. This not only establishes King as a major voice in the civil rights movement, but also inspires church leaders to organize similar boycotts in other southern cities.

1957   Emerging as a dominant figure in the American civil rights movement, Martin Luther King Jr., along with a number of allies, founds the Southern Christian Leadership Conference in Atlanta, Georgia. Through this organization, King, relying on nonviolent means, spearheads the movement for racial justice in the

1957, United States, frequently and eloquently pointing to
cont.   the discrepancy between discriminatory practices and
        America's democratic and religious ideals.

        Sun Myung Moon writes *Divine Principle,* an interpreta-
        tion of the Bible filtered through Eastern thought. Re-
        flecting Buddhist influences, Moon makes little
        distinction between the sacred and profane and fore-
        tells of another messiah who will complete the ministry
        of Jesus.

1959   Tibet's fourteenth Dalai Lama flees to India, where-
        upon China replaces Tibetan Buddhist institutions with
        ones directed by Beijing. To the irritation of China,
        meanwhile, India allows the Dalai Lama to establish a
        government in exile.

        Upon seizing power in Cuba, Communist dictator
        Fidel Castro expels all foreign missionaries, especially
        Americans.

1960   Pat Robertson launches the Christian Broadcasting Net-
        work (CBN) in Portsmouth, Virginia, thus beginning
        the increased media influence of the religious right.

1961   Burma, in southeastern Asia, establishes Buddhism as
        the state religion.

1962   Igniting a storm of protests, the U.S. Supreme Court in
        Engel v. Vitale declares it unconstitutional to recite a
        brief, nondenominational prayer in America's public
        schools.

        Algeria, an overwhelmingly Muslim country in north-
        ern Africa, achieves its independence from France.
        Since the first government of the new nation is secular
        in outlook, there will follow a tug-of-war between sec-
        ularists and religionists for political control, a struggle
        that continues to this day.

        Some 2,300 bishops from seventy-nine countries gather
        for the Second Vatican Council (Vatican II). Before they
        adjourn in December 1965, they will issue sixteen doc-

uments that revolutionize Roman Catholicism. In *Dignitatis Humamae* ("Declaration on Religious Freedom"), for instance, the church accepts the reality of religious pluralism and aligns itself with political democracy.

1963   In *Abington Township v. Schempp* the U.S. Supreme Court proscribes required Bible reading in the nation's public schools. This decision, along with *Engel* of the previous year, touches off a debate that continues in the United States to this day.

Martin Luther King Jr. electrifies an estimated crowd of 250,000 in Washington, D.C., with the "I have a dream" speech, appealing to all Americans to live up to the nation's religious and democratic ideals.

Four young black girls are killed in a bombing at the Sixteenth Street Baptist Church in Birmingham, Alabama. The brutality of this act stands in sharp contrast to the subsequent appeal of Martin Luther King Jr. for forgiveness.

Martin Luther King Jr. is *Time*'s Man of the Year, the first African American to be so honored, and his image will grace the magazine's cover on January 3, 1964.

1964   The U.S. Congress, pressured by the civil rights movement, which draws considerable support from the nation's churches, white as well as black, passes the Civil Rights Act. This measure outlaws discrimination in hotels, motels, restaurants, theaters, and other public accommodations and requires equal and impartial application of voter application requirements.

Because of his ongoing criticism of the shah, Ayatollah Ruhollah Khomeini is forced into exile.

The American Black Muslim leader Malcolm X visits Mecca and other sites in the Middle East where he meets white Muslims who seemingly have no prejudice toward blacks. This prompts him to soften his hostility toward whites and to adopt a more racially inclusive policy.

1964,   Because of his nonviolent efforts in behalf of civil
cont.   rights, Martin Luther King Jr. becomes the youngest recipient of the Nobel Peace Prize.

1965   The U.S. Congress enacts the Voting Rights Act, which
empowers the attorney general to appoint federal
examiners to supervise voter registration in states that
have traditionally used various means to disqualify
certain voters. Within five months of the law's passage
the number of African American voters in the Deep
South increases by 40 percent. The churches, through
the civil rights movement, support this legislation.

American atheist Madalyn Murray O'Hair founds the
American Atheists and supports a rigid policy of separation of church and state in the United States.

Burma adopts a policy of religious freedom, but the following year, driven more by nationalistic than religious
sentiment, expels all foreign missionaries.

Indonesia requires its citizens to espouse either Islam,
Protestantism, Catholicism, Hinduism, or Buddhism.

American Black Muslim leader Malcolm X is assassinated in the Audubon Ballroom in New York City's
Harlem.

A California evangelist, Rousas John Rushdoony, founds
the Chalcedon Ministries and initiates an effort to "reconstruct" American society in accordance with God's
laws, a society comparable to that of the seventeenth-
century Puritans in Massachusetts.

Martin Luther King Jr. publicly opposes American military involvement in southeast Asia, believing it de-
tracts from problems at home.

1966   China's Communist Party chairman, Mao Tse-tung, initiates a Cultural Revolution to eradicate all vestiges of
the old order. Among the victims will be thousands of
believers of all religious faiths.

Sayyid Qutb is hanged for his alleged role in a conspiracy to topple President Gamal Abdel Nasser of Egypt.

1967   Responding to an attack by its Muslim neighbors, Israel, in what will be known as the Six-Day War, defeats Egypt, Jordan, and Syria. Israel subsequently occupies the Gaza Strip and the Sinai peninsula of Egypt, the Golan Heights of Syria, and the West Bank and east Jerusalem of Jordan.

Martin Luther King Jr. delivers a major address against the war in Vietnam at Riverside Church in New York City.

1968   Martin Luther King Jr. is assassinated in Memphis, Tennessee. This eliminates the movement's most powerful voice for nonviolent resistance.

Rabbi Meir Kahane founds the militant Jewish Defense League, which champions pride in Jewishness.

1971   In *Lemon v. Kurtzman* the U.S. Supreme Court sets forth a three-pronged test for determining whether a statute violates either the free exercise or establishment clauses of the First Amendment to the Constitution. To be constitutional, a statute must have a secular legislative purpose, neither promote nor retard religion, and avoid excessive entanglements with religion.

Rabbi Meir Kahane organizes the Kach (Thus!) Party and seeks to build an Israeli nation based on the Torah.

1973   In *Roe v. Wade* the U.S. Supreme Court rules that laws restricting abortion during the first six months of pregnancy are unconstitutional. This decision infuriates many religious conservatives and ignites a debate that continues to the present.

1974   Gush Emunim, meaning "Bloc of the Faithful," is established in Israel. Its objective is to secure Jewish sovereignty over what it considers to be the Holy Land, which includes all of the ancient biblical lands of Judea and Samaria. The movement, intensely Zionist, will ebb in the 1980s.

1974,   Peruvian priest and scholar Gustavo Merino Gutierrez
cont.   writes *Liberation Theology—Perspectives*, which aligns
        the gospel message with the struggle of the poor to im-
        prove their status in this life.

1975   Radical Communist revolutionaries known as the
        Khmer Rouge seize control of Cambodia and immedi-
        ately embark upon a campaign, similar to China's Cul-
        tural Revolution, to eradicate the country's Buddhist
        heritage. Some 2 million Cambodians subsequently
        perish.

1976   China's Cultural Revolution officially ends when a
        more moderate element in the Communist Party gains
        power, thus easing the hostility toward religion.

        Americans elect a "born again" Southern Baptist,
        Jimmy Carter of Georgia, as president. However, be-
        cause of his positions on matters of church and state, he
        is soon at odds with many fellow religionists from the
        American South.

1977   Police in South Africa kill student leader Stephen Biko,
        prompting Bishop Desmond Tutu to denounce the gov-
        ernment's repressive racial policies.

1978   President Anwar Sadat of Egypt and Prime Minister
        Menachem Begin of Israel receive the Nobel Peace Prize
        for their efforts to bring peace to the Middle East.

        Cardinal Karol Joseph Wojtyla of Poland becomes Pope
        John Paul II, the first non-Italian elevated to the papacy
        in over 450 years.

1979   Inspired by Ayatollah Ruhollah Khomeini, Islamic fun-
        damentalists in Iran topple the secular regime of Reza
        Shah Pahlavi.

        The exiled Ayatollah Khomeini returns to Iran in
        triumph.

        Egypt signs a peace treaty with Israel, the first Arab
        state to do so.

Vietnamese forces drive the Khmer Rouge from Cambodia and establish a new government that is more hospitable to Buddhism.

The prominent American televangelist from Lynchburg, Virginia, Jerry Falwell, founds the Moral Majority, Inc., and embarks on a crusade to politicize religious conservatives and restore America's presumed religious heritage.

1980   War erupts between Iraq and Iran, both Islamic nations, but of different varieties. Shi'ism prevails in Iran, whereas most other Muslim nations, including Iraq, practice Sunni Islam.

In a pamphlet entitled *Armageddon and the Coming War with Russia*, American televangelist Jerry Falwell voices the belief that a Russian invasion of Israel will precipitate a nuclear war, the battle of Armageddon, in which the world will be destroyed.

1981   President Anwar Sadat of Egypt is assassinated by Islamic fundamentalists belonging to Islamic Jihad, an extremist group angered by the president's signing of the peace treaty with Israel.

A Turkish terrorist fails in an attempt to assassinate Pope John Paul II, although the pope is seriously wounded.

1982   China's Communist Party guarantees the right of religious *belief*, but still maintains strict limits on religious *practice*.

The Reverend Sun Myung Moon is convicted of tax evasion in the United States and sentenced to jail for eighteen months.

U.S. President Ronald Reagan, in obvious deference to religious conservatives, becomes the first incumbent president to endorse a school prayer amendment, informing Congress it is time to "allow prayer back in our schools."

1982,   Pope John Paul II meets privately with Yasser Arafat to
cont.   discuss prospects for peace in the Middle East.

1984   President Ronald Reagan establishes diplomatic rela-
          tions with the Vatican, an objective long opposed by
          many American Protestants.

          Pope John Paul II denounces apartheid in South Africa.

          Anglican priest Desmond Tutu of South Africa receives
          the Nobel Peace Prize for his daring opposition to
          apartheid in his country.

1985   Desmond Tutu, a strong supporter of blacks' rights, be-
          comes the first black South African to serve as bishop of
          Johannesburg.

1986   Bishop Desmond Tutu becomes archbishop of Cape
          Town.

          Pope John Paul II makes an unprecedented visit to
          Rome's main synagogue and prays with the president
          of the city's Jewish community.

1987   The Dalai Lama presents a plan to the U.S. Congress
          calling for, if not full independence, autonomy for Tibet
          within China.

          The first Buddhist in American history becomes a chap-
          lain to the armed services.

          The American Buddhist Congress is founded.

          U.S. President Ronald Reagan has an official visit with
          Pope John Paul II.

          Arabs rise in rebellion, called an *intifada,* against Israeli
          occupation of the West Bank and Gaza Strip.

1989   Bearing similarities to Iran, an Islamic revolution oc-
          curs in Sudan, inspired in part by a sixty-nine-year-old
          Sorbonne-educated Islamic ideologue, Hasan al-Turabi.
          Described by some observers as a Sudanese version of

Ayatollah Khomeini, Turabi quickly imposes strict Islamic law on this east African nation of 34 million inhabitants.

Ayatollah Ruhollah Khomeini of Iran issues a *fatwa* (religious decree) condemning Salman Rushdie to death for publishing the novel *The Satanic Verses,* a work considered insulting to the Islamic faith.

President Mikhail Gorbachev is the first Soviet head of state to be received at the Vatican.

American televangelist Pat Robertson founds the Christian Coalition. With headquarters in Chesapeake, Virginia, this organization opposes abortion, pornography, condom distribution, waiting periods for hand-gun purchases, and tax and welfare programs that allegedly discriminate against mothers who stay home with their children.

The Dalai Lama wins the Nobel Peace Prize for seeking greater freedom for Tibet, a Buddhist country, from China.

1990   American-born Rabbi Meir Kahane, who founded in Israel the now-outlawed Kach movement, which advocated the forcible removal of Palestinians from the West Bank and Gaza Strip, is gunned down following a speech in New York City.

The Vatican and the Soviet government exchange official representatives.

1991   In an effort to avert war, Pope John Paul II appeals to both U.S. President George H. W. Bush and Iraqi President Saddam Hussein.

On the centennial of *Rerum Novarum,* Pope John Paul II issues *Centesimus Annus* ("The Hundredth Year"), a celebration of Leo's earlier statement and a fresh declaration of the church's social doctrine. Central to John Paul's announcement is the assertion of the moral and cultural primacy of humans over political and economic systems.

1992   Hindus destroy the Babri Mosque in Ayodhya in India.

1993   Disciples of Sheik Omar Abdel-Rahman (the "Blind Sheik"), who was implicated in the 1981 assassination of Egyptian President Anwar Sadat, detonate a 1,500-pound truck bomb in the underground garage of the World Trade Center in New York City. Although this effort to topple the famed twin towers fails, six people are killed and more than 1,000 injured. At least one of the plotters, Ramzi Yousef, has some ties to Osama bin Laden, a wealthy Muslim fundamentalist increasingly linked to terrorist activities around the globe.

A standoff near Waco, Texas, between the Branch Davidians and agents of the U.S. Bureau of Alcohol, Tobacco, and Firearms ends in a fiery conflagration that leaves eighty-eight cult members, including many children and leader David Koresh, dead.

At a secret meeting in Oslo, Norway, Israel and Yasser Arafat's Palestine Liberation Organization agree to commence peace talks.

Following the fall of the Soviet Union, a portion of the new Russian constitution reads: "The Russian Federation is a secular state. No religion may be established in a state or mandatory capacity." The succeeding paragraph adds that "religious organizations are separate from the state, and equal before the law."

The U.S. Congress passes and President Bill Clinton applauds the Religious Freedom Restoration Act. Its purpose is to make government interference in religious matters more difficult.

Israel and the Vatican establish formal diplomatic ties.

1994   A follower of Rabbi Meir Kahane, who was assassinated in 1990, kills twenty-nine Muslims as they worship at the Shrine of the Cave of the Patriarchs in Hebron.

Taliban rebels gain control of about two-thirds of

Afghanistan and establish a rigidly theocratic Islamic regime, perhaps the most conservative in the world, in which schools for girls are closed, men are compelled to grow full beards, adultery is punished by stoning, and mutilation is the penalty for thievery. The Taliban's success inspires Muslim fundamentalists elsewhere to strive to establish Islamic states.

Archbishop Desmond Tutu delivers the prayer at the inauguration of Nelson Mandela as president of South Africa.

Pope John Paul II receives the first Israeli ambassador to the Holy See.

Pope John Paul II is *Time*'s Man of the Year because of his efforts for world peace.

1995   Angered by U.S. government action against the Branch Davidians in Waco, Texas, Timothy McVeigh bombs the federal building in Oklahoma City, Oklahoma, killing 168 people, including many children. The attack comes on the second anniversary of the destruction of the Branch Davidian compound.

The Dalai Lama recognizes a young Tibetan boy as the reincarnation of the Panchen Lama, who had died in 1989.

Israeli Prime Minister Yitzhak Rabin is assassinated by a Jewish fanatic opposed to any peaceful overtures toward Muslims.

1996   Former Russian leader Mikhail Gorbachev has an audience with Pope John Paul II.

Osama bin Laden, who apparently had established Al Qaeda, meaning "the base," in 1989 to provide logistical, financial, and religious support to Muslim terrorists around the globe, proclaims it the duty of Muslims everywhere to kill American soldiers, a duty he broadens two years later to include all Americans.

1996,   Cuban leader Fidel Castro has an audience with Pope
cont.   John Paul II, and the pope accepts an invitation to visit
           Cuba in January 1998.

1997   Mohammad Khatami, a moderate, is elected president
           of Iran, giving hope to many Iranians, especially the
           young, that the country's strict Islamic rules will be
           softened somewhat.

           Russia enacts the Law on Freedom of Conscience and
           Religious Association, which recognizes Judaism, Bud-
           dhism, Islam, and Christianity as the nation's tradi-
           tional religions. All other faiths must undergo a
           complicated registration process. Critics inside and
           outside Russia fear the law, believing it jeopardizes re-
           ligious freedom and, without saying as much, virtually
           establishes Russia's Orthodox Church as a state reli-
           gion. And, in fact, Orthodox Church leaders now rou-
           tinely look to the state to proscribe, or least control, the
           activities of Jehovah's Witnesses, Pentecostals, Mor-
           mons, and Roman Catholics. The United States and the
           Vatican criticize the law.

1998   Pope John Paul II visits Fidel Castro's Cuba.

           After thirty-two years of authoritarian rule, dictator
           Suharto of Indonesia, who had maintained a tight rein
           on Islamic fundamentalists, falls from power amid
           charges of corruption.

           Resulting in a loss of 224 lives, the U.S. embassies in
           Kenya and Tanzania in eastern Africa are bombed. Sus-
           picion immediately falls on Osama bin Laden.

           In November and December four Iranian intellectuals,
           critics of their country's Islamic regime, are murdered.
           Followers of reform-minded President Mohammad
           Khatami attribute the slayings to high-ranking mili-
           tants in the government who oppose the social reforms
           of the new president.

           Congress passes and President Bill Clinton signs the In-
           ternational Religious Freedom Act, which establishes a

bipartisan and multireligious panel, the U.S. Commission on International Religious Freedom. Nations the commission determines to be guilty of religious persecution will be subject to sanctions by the U.S. government.

1999   American televangelist Pat Robertson endorses assassinations, arguing it makes more sense "to take out" someone like Yugoslav President Slobodan Milosevic or Iraqi President Saddam Hussein than to spend "billions of dollars on a war that harms innocent civilians."

China outlaws Falun Gong, a spiritual health movement, declaring it "an evil cult."

The U.S. National Conference of Catholic Bishops, in a document entitled *Faithful Citizenship: Civic Responsibility for the New Millennium,* calls for a "new kind of politics." The bishops implore all Americans to be more civil in political debate, more concerned about impoverished children, and more alert to a "growing culture of death"—abortion, capital punishment, and euthanasia.

British author John Cornwell, in *Hitler's Pope: The Secret History of Pius XII,* accuses the pope of ignoring the plight of the Jews during World War II because of anti-Semitism. The Vatican rejects the claim, yet establishes a commission to research the charges.

The U.S. Congress passes a resolution accusing China of persecuting followers of Falun Gong and other religions. A spokesperson for the Chinese embassy in Washington expresses disappointment in the American action, calling Falun Gong "a criminal cult" responsible for at least 1,000 deaths.

Pope John Paul II angers India's Hindu nationalists by refusing to apologize for alleged atrocities committed by Portuguese Catholics over 400 years ago in the subcontinent and by encouraging Indian Christians to continue evangelistic efforts to convert Hindus.

2000   The Vatican signs an agreement with the Palestine Liberation Organization, which guarantees religious free-

2000,
cont.

dom and the legal status of Christian churches in a Palestinian state. Pope John Paul's sympathy for the Palestinian cause is a matter of longstanding, to the chagrin of the Israelis, who express displeasure with this latest Vatican announcement.

Religion figures prominently in the American presidential race, as Republican hopeful John McCain, campaigning in Virginia, levels a stinging attack on conservative televangelists Pat Robertson and Jerry Falwell, dubbing them "agents of intolerance." It is unfortunate, says McCain, that his opponent, Texas Governor George W. Bush, has identified himself with men such as these who practice the "political tactics of division and slander." The televangelists allegedly take part in a smear campaign against McCain in Virginia.

In the most sweeping papal apology ever, Pope John Paul II, seventy-nine years old and visibly ailing, asks forgiveness for the errors of the church over the past 2,000 years. "We cannot not recognize the betrayal of the Gospel committed by some of our brothers, especially in the second millennium," the pope declares in a Sunday Mass in March inside St. Peter's Basilica.

Republican presidential nominee George W. Bush tells a B'nai B'rith gathering in Washington, D.C., of his support of Israel.

Elliott Abrams, chair of the U.S. Commission on International Religious Freedom, complains that the Clinton administration has imposed either trivial or no penalties at all on several nations regarded by the commission as among the worst offenders of religious freedom. Abrams cites as an example the administration's response to conditions in China, Saudi Arabia, Laos, and North Korea.

The U.S. Commission on International Religious Freedom reports that it has reliable information from Anglican and Roman Catholic bishops in Sudan that the Muslim-dominated government there is trying to force Christians to convert to Islam by refusing them food and other aid provided by the United Nations and the United States.

When President Bill Clinton meets with President Vladimir Putin in Moscow, the American leader stresses the importance of religious freedom.

Democratic presidential hopeful Al Gore picks an Orthodox Jew, Senator Joseph Lieberman of Connecticut, as his vice presidential running mate, the first Jew put forth in an American presidential campaign by a major party.

On the campaign trail U.S. vice presidential candidate Joseph Lieberman talks openly about religion, calling America "the most religious country in the world" and heralding all Americans as "children of the same awesome God."

Declaring it a violation of the teachings of Islam, Mullah Mohammed Omar, the Taliban leader of Afghanistan, outlaws the cultivation of poppy, the plant from which opium is derived. Accordingly, Taliban authorities destroy drug laboratories used to covert opium to heroin and arrest farmers who proceed to plant poppy. As a result of these measures, a United Nations committee subsequently concludes that opium production in Afghanistan, once the world's largest supplier to major markets in Europe and the United States, has been virtually eliminated. Officials in the United States are more skeptical, agreeing that poppy cultivation has been decreased but not eliminated.

President Bill Clinton's effort at Camp David to keep the peace talks between Israelis and Palestinians alive collapses. At issue, among other things, is a seemingly irreconcilable dispute over control of the Temple Mount, or Haram al-Sharif, in Jerusalem. The Temple Mount is Judaism's holiest shrine, believed to be the site of the first of two temples built by King Solomon some 3,000 years ago. However, known to Muslims as Haram al-Sharif, or Noble Sanctuary, the site is the third-holiest place of Islam. From that spot Muslims believe the Prophet Muhammad ascended to heaven, and

2000,
cont.

today it is home to two mosques, Al Aqsa and Dome of the Rock. Given its profound religious significance to both sides, Israelis and Palestinians each demand sovereignty over the site, which Israel captured in the Six-Day War of 1967.

Israeli opposition leader and hard-liner Ariel Sharon visits the Temple Mount. To Muslims, Sharon's visit is seen as provocative, thus precipitating violence that quickly escalates into what Palestinians call the Al Aqsa Intifada, recalling a similar conflict of the late 1980s.

Palestinians in Nablus, located in the Israeli occupied West Bank, attack with hammers and pickaxes and destroy one of Judaism's holier sites, Joseph's Tomb, the burial place of the biblical patriarch. In the escalating clash between Palestinians and Israelis, Arab youths throw rocks at Jews praying at the Western Wall in Jerusalem, Judaism's holiest site.

The U.S.S. *Cole*, at anchor in Aden harbor in southern Yemen, is attacked by two suicide bombers, resulting in considerable damage to the vessel and the death of seventeen American sailors. Osama bin Laden is the principal suspect.

The United States and Russia, in a rare show of cooperation, sponsor a United Nations resolution, which the Security Council passes, imposing broad sanctions on Afghanistan's Taliban rulers. The United States and Russia both accuse Afghanistan, which provides a safe haven for international terrorist Osama bin Laden, of operating terrorist training camps. The Russians believe that Chechen rebels, who are seeking independence from Russia, are schooled in such camps.

In a show of support for Palestinians, Muslims throughout the Islamic world join in protests, a "day of rage," against Israel for the violence in the Gaza Strip and West Bank. In Lebanon, effigies of Israeli Prime Minister Ehud Barak and the U.S. secretary of state are burned; in Indonesia and Sudan, the U.S. embassies are stoned; in Egypt, there is a call for a holy war; and in

New York City, local Muslim leaders pray near the Is-raeli consulate.

An Egyptian television soap opera, *Awan al-Ward*, or *Time of Roses*, featuring a Coptic Christian woman mar-ried to a Muslim man, angers conservatives of both faiths. To Coptic Christians, comprising about 10 per-cent of the population, interfaith marriages are prohib-ited; to Muslims, the show's frank discussion of sex and exposure of female flesh are offensive.

A team of three Jewish and three Catholic scholars urge the Vatican to open its wartime archives for further re-search, hoping to resolve once and for all the role of Pope Pius XII and the church during the Holocaust.

On Christmas Eve a series of church bombings across Indonesia kills fifteen people. Although no one claims credit, Muslim militants are suspected. President Ab-durrahman Wahid, a respected Muslim scholar of mod-erate views, condemns the attacks, which he contends are calculated to divide the nation religiously.

Binyamin Kahane, the thirty-four-year-old son of Rabbi Meir Kahane, an extremist who was shot and killed in 1990 after a speech in New York City, is ambushed and killed, along with his wife, in the West Bank. After the assassination of his father, the younger Kahane had founded an anti-Arab movement, Kahane Chai, or Ka-hane Lives, which is subsequently banned in Israel. Militant Israelis vow to avenge Kahane's death.

2001   By imposing extraordinarily tight security measures, Chinese authorities frustrate a planned protest by Falun Gong at Beijing's Tiananmen Square.

In an act of defiance, about 1,200 Falun Gong followers from around the world hold a conference in Hong Kong, where the religious group is legal and where free speech is guaranteed. Expressing the Chinese govern-ment's view, the *Beijing Daily* denounces anew Falun Gong and its leader Li Hongzhi, asserting: "Li Hongzhi's claim that he doesn't take part in politics and doesn't oppose the government is a cheap lie."

2001,   Hasan al-Turabi, upon orders from his former protégé,
cont.   President Omar al-Bashir, is imprisoned in Sudan.

George Tenet, head of the Central Intelligence Agency, tells the U.S. Senate's Intelligence Committee that Osama bin Laden is "the most immediate and serious threat" to the United States.

Culminating a two-year court battle focusing on Russia's Law on Freedom of Conscience and Religious Association, the Jehovah's Witnesses win an important victory when a Moscow judge refuses to liquidate the group's Moscow communities. An elated spokesperson for the Witnesses proclaims, "You can now say freedom of belief really still exists in Russia." On the other hand, a spokesperson for the Orthodox Church defends the 1997 law as a way of stopping the proliferation of dangerous sects, concluding that the Witnesses are "quite dangerous," the judge's ruling notwithstanding.

Former general and noted hard-liner Ariel Sharon defeats incumbent Ehud Barak to become Israel's prime minister. Although President Hosni Mubarak of Egypt urges fellow Muslims to refrain from making premature judgments, elsewhere in the Arab world Sharon is condemned for his hawkish ways and encouragement of Jewish settlements on Palestinian soil.

Mullah Mohammad Omar, the Taliban ruler of Afghanistan, orders the destruction of non-Muslim symbols. Hence, some two-thirds of all statues in Afghanistan, deemed idolatrous and contrary to the teachings of Islam, are destroyed, including two ancient Buddhas, one standing 175 feet, the other 120 feet, about 90 miles from Kabul. Hewn from a cliff face in the third and fifth centuries, these two statues are regarded as priceless cultural treasures. Even so, Taliban leaders ignore the pleas of much of the world to save the ancient relics. Says Taliban's foreign minister: "They are against Islam." Adds the supreme leader Omar: "All we are breaking are stones."

In its second annual report the U.S. Commission on International Religious Freedom informs the new Bush administration on the status of religious freedom in North Korea, India, Iran, Indonesia, Sudan, Vietnam, Russia, China, Nigeria, and Pakistan. The report faults China for intensifying its attack on the Falun Gong, destroying some 3,000 unregistered religious buildings and sites in southeastern China, interfering in the training and selection of religious leaders and clergy, and tightening its control over Tibetan Buddhists and Uighur Muslims. Likewise, the report raises concern about a 1997 Russian law that requires religious groups to register with the government before they can operate. According to the report, this requirement could jeopardize the existence of some 1,500 religious groups in Russia.

In the ongoing political tug-of-war in Iran, Islamic hard-liners arrest forty opposition leaders belonging to the Freedom Movement, which the Teheran Revolutionary Court, composed of fundamentalists, had earlier outlawed and now accuses of wanting to "overthrow the Islamic establishment." Moderates dispute the court's position, convinced the real purpose of the arrests is to intimidate the backers of President Mohammad Khatami's social reforms.

Thousands of radical Muslim men from the world over gather in Peshawar, Pakistan, to pay tribute to a brand of Islam known as Deoband Dar-ul-Uloom. This is a staunchly conservative and intensely anti-Western variety of Islam taught at the 143-year-old seminary in Deoband, India. It holds that men are innately smarter than women, music is evil, and education for girls beyond the age of eight is a waste, and it considers the West immoral, decadent, and anti-Islam. Male followers are not allowed to shave, and women are required to wear a burqa, an all-enveloping gown. It is this kind of Islam that undergirds the Taliban movement in Afghanistan.

In response to a Palestinian suicide attack at a mall in the Israeli coastal town of Netanya, Israeli F-16 warplanes strike Palestinian targets in the West Bank and Gaza Strip. This is the first such air attack by Israel since the 1967 Six-Day War. Since the beginning of hos-

2001,
cont.

tilities the previous September, 463 Palestinians have been killed, 84 Israelis.

Angered by the recent air attack on Palestinian targets, members of the twenty-two nation Arab League, meeting in Cairo, call on all Arab states to sever contact with Israel until the military action against the Palestinians ceases.

President George W. Bush welcomes the Dalai Lama to the White House. Although the visit takes place in the residence rather than the Oval Office, China nonetheless condemns the meeting.

Recalling memories of Nazi Germany's policy of requiring European Jews to wear the yellow Star of David, Afghanistan's Taliban rulers announce plans to require the nation's Hindus to wear labels on their clothing distinguishing them from Muslims. India and the United States promptly denounce the proposal, but the head of the Taliban's religious police defends the measure, asserting: "Religious minorities living in an Islamic state must be identified."

Indonesian Christians in certain areas of the country report being forced to convert to Islam to escape violence from their Muslim neighbors. Many of the Christian women endure circumcision, actually a form of genital mutilation often performed with crude instruments and believed to suppress the sex drive and ensure chastity. Although outlawed in some places and decried by human rights groups, the practice persists.

Taliban officials accuse international aid groups in Afghanistan of promoting Christianity. Eight Westerners, including two young American women who work for Shelter Now International, a German-based Christian organization, are arrested. "Under the cover of humanitarian assistance," asserts a ranking Taliban official, the eight foreigners "are offering bread to our poor people and then asking them to convert to a religion that was canceled out by the advent of Islam." Efforts to secure the release of the imprisoned workers fail.

On September 11, in the deadliest attack ever on American soil, nineteen Islamic terrorists hijack four American commercial airliners and crash two of them into the World Trade Center, reducing New York City's twin towers to smouldering rubble and killing an estimated 3,000 people; a third plane slams into the Pentagon, adding nearly 200 to the death toll; and the fourth plunges into the Pennsylvania countryside, brought down by heroic passengers who fight back against the hijackers. All aboard are killed.

"We're at war," proclaims President George W. Bush, vowing to firefighters who sustain over 300 losses in the collapse of the towers: "The people who knocked these buildings down will hear from us all soon."

Two days after the attack Reverend Jerry Falwell, appearing on Pat Robertson's *The 700 Club*, points an accusing finger at the American Civil Liberties Union, People for the American Way, the National Organization for Women and other abortion and gay rights activists, and the federal courts. "God has protected America from her inception," declares the Virginia preacher, but these groups have successfully thrown religion "out of the public square, out of the schools." Consequently, God "lifted the curtain of protection," thereby permitting the deadly assault. "And I believe," Falwell adds, "that if America does not repent and return to a genuine faith and dependence on him, we may expect more tragedies, unfortunately." As on many prior occasions following intemperate remarks, Jerry Falwell subsequently apologizes for any hurt caused by his accusations, but Pat Robertson does not.

Convinced of Osama bin Laden's guilt in the recent attack, the Bush administration demands that Afghanistan's Taliban regime surrender the exiled Saudi terrorist to "responsible authorities." Attempting to save face for the Taliban and to satisfy the United States, ranking Islamic clerics in Afghanistan urge bin Laden to leave the country voluntarily. Explains one cleric: "We wanted to find a solution that would save our country [from a U.S. air strike] and solve the problem of our guest."

2001,
cont.

Some Arab Americans are taunted and beaten and mosques vandalized in the wake of September 11, prompting an effort on several fronts to disassociate an extremist such as Osama bin Laden from mainstream Islam. In a show of religious unity, a Muslim cleric shares the stage with Reverend Billy Graham and other spiritual leaders for a service at the National Cathedral, while two other Muslims assist in a Boston vigil. A Muslim chaplain at the University of Georgetown in reference to the violence of September 11 asserts: "It violates the very foundation of Islamic law." And a thirty-year-old Egyptian who has made the United States his home gives assurance and makes a plea. "We [Muslims] are part of the community as much as anyone else," he states. "We just hope to be part of the rebuilding." President George W. Bush makes clear that bin Laden does not exemplify the basic values of Islam, which the president calls a peaceful religion.

Because of the Taliban's refusal to surrender Osama bin Laden, the United States and Great Britain, America's staunchest ally, begin bombing key targets in Afghanistan. The objective is to topple the Taliban and capture bin Laden.

In the face of a concerted air attack by the United States and an offensive by the Northern Alliance, Taliban forces are routed. The capital city of Kabul falls to the Northern Alliance, and Taliban forces are in retreat throughout the country. Mullah Mohammed Omar and Osama bin Laden continue to elude capture.

The eight foreign aid workers are rescued from the Taliban. The two American women tell reporters they have been treated humanely by their captors.

The United States offers a $25 million reward for the capture of Osama bin Laden.

3

Biographical Sketches

The following biographical sketches are intended as a representative sample of individuals whose careers intersected religion and politics in significant ways. Some of the individuals were primarily thinkers, some doers, some both. The inclusion of some requires no explanation, for their significance is obvious. How could one talk about religion and politics in the twentieth century, for instance, without discussing Mohandas Gandhi or Ayatollah Ruhollah Khomeini? In other cases the reason for inclusion is not so apparent. Why Joseph Martin Dawson and Will Campbell, for instance, two rather obscure Baptist preachers from the American South who were minor players on the international stage? Dawson's contribution was to religious lobbying, helping forge an organization that evolved into Americans United for the Separation of Church and State, the group most vigilant today to perceived transgressions of the First Amendment to the U.S. Constitution. Campbell, who surveyed the American landscape from the perspective of the political left, exemplifies religious figures who eventually became disenchanted with all institutional approaches to social change. One presently sees this disenchantment in the United States among certain prominent voices on the religious right who have concluded that politics offers false hope. Syndicated columnist Cal Thomas and political strategist Paul Weyrich, both formerly involved in Jerry Falwell's Moral Majority, readily come to mind. Some individuals are noteworthy for bringing the moral suasion of their religious convictions to bear on politics, such as Archbishop Desmond Tutu and Islamic scholar Maulana Sayyid Abul Ala Mawdudi, while others were secularists whose public policies had profound effects on the religious community, as in the case of Mustafa Kemal Atatürk. Almost all the personalities discussed

59

here reached their peak after World War II, a notable exception being Atatürk, who nonetheless merits inclusion for having created a secular regime that still exists in a country that has always been overwhelmingly Muslim. And, taken collectively, these biographies call attention to the diversity of religion and politics.

Ralph David Abernathy (1926–1990)

Ralph David Abernathy was a Baptist preacher who sought political remedies to end racial discrimination in the United States, particularly in the South. Though neither as eloquent nor as internationally acclaimed, Abernathy was just as committed to the cause of civil rights as his close friend and colleague Dr. Martin Luther King Jr. Born in Marengo County, Alabama, and reared on his father's 500-acre plantation, Abernathy proudly boasted on occasion that he had "never worked for a white man." He served in the army during World War II, then obtained a bachelor's degree from Alabama State College in Montgomery, Alabama, and pursued graduate work at Atlanta University. As first a student, then as pastor of the First Baptist Church, a position assumed in early 1953, Abernathy occupied a place of prominence in the African American community of Montgomery. When King took the helm at Dexter Avenue Baptist Church in late 1954, the two young pastors became fast friends, although in many ways they were quite different. Whereas King would soon have a doctorate from a major university, Abernathy's intellectual accomplishments were more modest. Both were rousing speakers, but whereas one would go to Dexter Avenue to hear about Aquinas, Hegel, or Socrates, one would go to First Baptist for more exuberant services.

Abernathy and King would soon become major figures in the civil rights movement, but it was the quiet defiance of Mrs. Rosa Parks that catapulted them to the forefront. By refusing to move to the rear of the bus on December 1, 1955, she set in motion events leading to the Montgomery bus boycott. At the outset Abernathy was more prominent than King among local blacks. Always combative, he readily supported the boycott. The Montgomery Improvement Association (MIA), which spearheaded the boycott, organized car pools, and tutored blacks on nonviolent resistance, was his idea. Nevertheless, Abernathy nominated King to head the MIA, believing a capable newcomer to Montgomery, one who had not been around long enough to anger any of the various elements of the African American community, would be in a better position to unite blacks for a confrontation with the white establishment. King was elected unanimously, and from that point forward Abernathy was overshadowed by the Dexter Avenue preacher. This eventually aroused some jealousy in Abernathy, particularly following the "I have a Dream" speech in the nation's capital in August 1963, which considerably heightened King's national standing.

The success of the Montgomery bus boycott in December 1956 prompted Abernathy, King, and some sixty other black pastors to gather in Atlanta in January 1957. The upshot was the formation of the Southern Christian Leadership Conference (SCLC), headed by King until his assassination in April 1968. As King's right hand, Abernathy endured continual abuse. His home and church were bombed, and he was regularly harassed, arrested, and jailed. In 1961 Abernathy left Montgomery for Atlanta, becoming pastor of the West Hunter Street Baptist Church, where he remained until his death. As King's successor at the SCLC he focused on the plight of the poor, as exemplified by the Poor People's Campaign in Washington, D.C. This effort landed Abernathy in jail for twenty days for refusing to remove Resurrection City, a disheveled collection of huts in the heart of the nation's capital. Thereafter he organized Operation Breadbasket, whose primary purpose was to exert pressure on companies derelict in according equal opportunities to African Americans.

Although Abernathy was a competent leader, the SCLC declined in membership and influence during his tenure. He could never fill the void left by King's death, and in 1977 he stepped down as head of the SCLC to run for the congressional seat previously held by Andrew Young. Defeated in this bid, he turned away from civil rights and devoted more attention to his church and world peace. Published shortly before his death, Abernathy's autobiography, *And the Walls Came Tumbling Down* (1989), gives a good assessment of the civil rights movement from an insider's viewpoint.

Mustafa Kemal Atatürk (1881–1938)

As the founder and first president of modern Turkey, Mustafa Kemal Atatürk turned an Islamic country into a secular nation based upon Western culture. For this he is revered to this day by secular Turks and despised by contemporary Islamic fundamentalists. Born into a middle class family in Salonica, then a city of the Ottoman Empire, now the Greek metropolis of Thessalonica,

Atatürk was educated primarily in military schools. In 1905 he graduated from the War Academy in Istanbul. As the Ottoman Empire disintegrated from 1910 to 1920 because of growing internal resistance to the caliphate and the sultan's pro-German stance in World War I, Atatürk's career steadily advanced. His role in frustrating the invasion of the British in the Dardanelles in 1915 and of the British-backed Greeks in Izmir in 1919 made him a national hero, while his defiance of the sultan made him a leader of the insurgents. In 1920 Atatürk was chosen to head the newly fashioned Grand National Assembly, and in November 1922 he abolished the sultanate, causing Mohammed VI to flee. Turkey secured its borders by the Treaty of Lausanne in July 1923, and in October 1923 the nation became a republic with Atatürk as president.

Under Atatürk, Turkey became a parliamentary-style republic, the first Muslim nation to move in this direction, but it was never a full-fledged democracy. Only one political party existed, thereby diminishing the ability of dissenters to make themselves heard. In fact, it was risky to criticize Atatürk's policies, and to this day journalists and historians probe at their own peril Atatürk's problem with alcohol and alleged irreligion. Many of Atatürk's sweeping reforms were accomplished at the expense of Muslim traditions. Islam was no longer the state religion, education became secular and coeducational, polygamy was abolished, and women obtained the suffrage in national elections and the right to serve in parliament. Additional changes were the elimination of Arabic and Persian in schools, adoption of the Latin alphabet and Western calendar, implementation of new civil and penal codes patterned respectively after the Swiss and Italian models, and prohibition of such traditional dress as fezzes and veils. In economic matters the state became an active participant with private enterprise in fostering agricultural and industrial growth. For his vast accomplishments the National Assembly in 1934 bestowed on Kemal the honorary title "Atatürk," meaning "Father of the Turks."

Not all Turks applauded the secular trends initiated by Atatürk, and since 1946, when a multiparty system evolved, opposition voices have been heard. In Turkey today there is a growing tug-of-war between the secularists and Islamic conservatives.

Hasan al-Banna (1906–1949)

As the founder of the Muslim Brotherhood, Hasan al-Banna was the spiritual and intellectual leader of those Egyptians, and later of Muslims throughout the Near and Middle East, who wanted to purge their land of foreign influences, resist the trend toward secularization, and rebuild society around Islamic ideals. He was born into a well-educated and deeply religious family. An Islamic scholar, his father was a teacher and a prayer leader, or imam, at a mosque near Alexandria. Schooled in both religious and secular institutions, Banna graduated in 1927 from a college in Cairo, Dar al-Ulum, and promptly took a teaching position with a state school in Ismailiyya, located in the Suez Canal Zone.

Although nominally independent since 1922, Egypt was still controlled by the British, a fact made inescapable in Ismailiyya by the presence of British troops and constant reminders that foreigners owned the Suez Canal Company. This was fertile soil for Islamic nationalism, and in spring 1928 Banna, his brother, and a handful of followers forged the Muslim Brotherhood. Broadly, the Brotherhood aimed at reversing secular trends and restoring Islamic ways. Toward that end, Banna specifically objected to Christian missionaries, Western culture, and British occupation forces. Particularly disturbing to him were Egyptians who emulated westerners, for Banna saw in this the eventual elimination of Muslim culture.

Upon taking a teaching job in Cairo in 1932, Banna moved the Brotherhood's offices to that city. Within two years the organization had over fifty branches across Egypt, and within a few more years it had spilled into several neighboring Muslim countries. Banna coupled efforts to re-educate Egyptians in traditional Muslim ways with the Brotherhood's programs in behalf of the poor and less fortunate. Although no one, including the British, questioned the worthiness of social welfare and economic reforms, Banna's Brotherhood, with its growing network of schools, mosques, and factories, appeared to critics as an emergent state within a state, a potential threat to the established political order. Banna never intended for the Brotherhood to be a political organization, but political involvement became unavoidable as the tumultuous events of the 1930s and 1940s unfolded. Compounding the economic pain of the Great Depression was the humiliation of the Muslim world by the Israeli victory of 1948.

Creation of the Jewish state in Palestine, a major defeat for Egypt, undermined the authority of King Farouk's government and threw the nation into turmoil. The police chief of Cairo was assassinated in December 1948, followed shortly by the assassination of Prime Minister Mahmud Fahmi Nuqrashi. Although an advocate of jihad, meaning in this case resistance to British and other foreign influences, Banna did not endorse violence and he condemned the killing of the prime minister. Still, the assassin of Nuqrashi had been a student member of the Brotherhood, and, Banna's denials notwithstanding, suspicion of the secret society persisted. On February 12, 1949, Banna was shot to death in Cairo. Although never proven, his followers were convinced high-ranking government officials had ordered the slaying. Banna's teaching and martyrdom have given inspiration to contemporary religious conservatives who desire a society based on the Qur'an.

Daniel Berrigan (1921–) and Philip Berrigan (1923–)

During the 1960s Daniel and Philip Berrigan, brothers who were Roman Catholic priests and archetypes of Christian political activism, saw in politics a way of bettering the condition of the less affluent and rectifying the plight of those suffering from injustice. Believers at first in civil disobedience, they moved beyond passive resistance to active opposition to the United States government, which they believed was involved in an unjust and illegal war in Vietnam. The brothers committed their most daring act in 1968 when they joined seven others in breaking into the draft-board office at Catonsville, Maryland, and destroying several hundred files. Their complicity in this act landed Daniel and Philip in prison.

From their father, a Roman Catholic and a socialist, the brothers acquired a concern and compassion for the disadvantaged. In 1939 Daniel entered the Jesuit order of priests, enrolling in a seminary near Poughkeepsie, New York. In 1941 Philip went to St. Michael's College in Toronto, Canada, but was drafted into the armed forces in 1943. Stationed in the American South for basic training, he was troubled by the unjust treatment of African Americans. Following military service, Philip's education continued at Holy Cross College in Worcester, Massachusetts, where he majored in English. Additional schooling followed at the seminary for the Society of Saint Joseph, an order dedicated to service to the African American community.

The brothers believed their primary duty was not so much to convert the secular world to Roman Catholicism as to engage the church actively in the fight for social, economic, and political justice. Accordingly, wherever the brothers served, they worked to improve the condition of the disadvantaged and those they considered victims of injustice. In 1954, when Daniel began teaching French and theology at the Jesuits' Preparatory School in New York City, he initiated assistance activities among laborers and the black and Puerto Rican communities. Ordained in 1955, Philip served in a Washington, D.C., ghetto parish from 1955 to 1956, then taught at a New Orleans high school from 1957 to 1962, where he took part in the struggle for integration and racial justice. By 1964 Daniel and Philip had become more extreme politically, moving beyond passive protest to more militant strategies.

The brothers shared the frustration of Martin Luther King Jr., who believed the war in Vietnam diverted resources and attention from this nation's impoverished citizens. The solution was to end the conflict in southeast Asia. Hence, Daniel founded the Catholic Peace Fellowship and, along with a rabbi and a Lutheran pastor, formed Clergy Concerned About Vietnam, an ecumenical antiwar organization. Daniel's superior, Francis Cardinal Spellman, attempted to transfer the troublesome priest to Latin America, but withdrew the order following a public outcry from Catholic clergy and lay people. Although Daniel and Philip often criticized the church's failure to speak out against American policy in Vietnam, they remained loyal to their calling as priests. In 1966 Philip, along with members of the Baltimore Interfaith Peace Mission, focused attention on U.S. congressmen who supported government policy in Vietnam, holding vigils on the front lawns of those congressmen's homes. In April 1968 Daniel and historian Howard Zinn traveled to Hanoi, where they successfully negotiated the release of three American pilots held captive by the North Vietnamese government.

Participation in the 1968 Catonsville affair troubled some of the brothers' supporters, who recognized the priests had now moved beyond the principles of passive resistance. For involvement in this event, as well as for a raid at a Baltimore draft board where he and three others had splattered files with blood, Philip received a six-year prison sentence. He served thirty-nine months of his sentence. Daniel served nineteen months for the Catonsville raid. Released from prison, Philip married Elizabeth McAlister, a nun. Both renounced their vows, and together they established a commune in Baltimore called Jonah House. Daniel remained a Jesuit priest, exploring in his writings and teachings such topics as ecumenism and religious consciousness and spirituality in the contemporary world.

Will Campbell (1924–)

Through the National Council of Churches (NCC), Will Campbell was involved in virtually all the major civil rights developments of the late 1950s and early 1960s in the United States. His actions offer proof that it is possible to rise above one's culture and religious heritage. Here was a rural Mississippian reared in a Southern Baptist church who championed the causes of labor and African Americans and challenged the righteous to practice the ideals of their faith. Ultimately disenchanted with organized religion, Campbell turned increasingly to writing after 1977. The Campbells, who had lived in southwestern Mississippi for five generations, were Baptists of longstanding. Will joined the church at an early age, resolved to become a preacher, and was ordained while in high school.

Although an unusual academic choice inasmuch as a Mississippi youngster with ministerial ambitions normally would have gone to one of the Magnolia State's Baptist colleges, Campbell enrolled in Louisiana College in Pineville, Louisiana, in 1941. World War II intervened, and he served in the army from 1943 to 1946. This was a broadening experience, for it exposed him to the diversity of American culture. He met Jews and Cajuns, encountered Marxism and the neo-orthodoxy of Reinhold Niebuhr, and witnessed racial discrimination. He emerged from the military determined to be a social activist. Instead of the usual pietistic platitudes, his ministry would come to grips with race, labor, and poverty. This new goal guided his subsequent education. To complete undergraduate schooling, Campbell attended Wake Forest College, a nontraditional Baptist institution in North Carolina; spent one year at Tulane University in New Orleans taking graduate courses in philosophy, sociology, and labor law; then in 1949 headed to Yale Divinity School, which in the 1950s attracted numerous young southerners interested in Christian ethics.

After leaving Yale in 1952, Campbell served successively as a pastor in Taylor, Louisiana, 1952–1954, a chaplain at the University of Mississippi, 1954–1956, and a field agent for the Department of Racial and Cultural Relations of the National Council of Churches, 1956–1963. Each of these positions was different, but none was fulfilling for Campbell. The Taylor congregation simply disregarded his pronouncements on labor and race, the Supreme Court's 1954 decision in *Brown v. Board of Education* notwithstanding. Although not fired as campus chaplain, his efforts to desegregate Ole Miss aroused such fury that he was forced to leave. The job with the National Council of Churches seemed ideal, for it allowed Campbell to devote all his energy to the racial issue. Working out of headquarters in Nashville, Tennessee, he traveled the South in the late 1950s and early 1960s assisting civil rights activists and adding moral pressure to the cause. He escorted black youngsters past the angry mobs in Little Rock, Arkansas, in 1957; was the only white minister to attend the first organizational meeting of the Southern Christian Leadership Conference, founded by Dr. Martin Luther King Jr.; and discussed racial justice in the South with Attorney General Robert F. Kennedy.

Campbell left the NCC in 1963 because of growing disenchantment with all institutionalized approaches to social activism. As a Baptist preacher convinced of the universality and tenacity of human sin, Campbell could imagine the possibility of today's oppressed becoming tomorrow's oppressors, of whites being marched into gas chambers by a "black Eichmann." Such a theological perspective made it increasingly difficult for him to portray one side in the civil rights struggle as entirely evil and the other as entirely pure. As his sentiments became known, Campbell discovered that the liberal NCC was just as intolerant of dissenting views as the reactionary segregationists at Ole Miss. This realization led Campbell to the conclusion that all institutions, regardless of ideology, were concerned ultimately with their own preservation. "In my experiences," he observed, "[institutions are] all after your soul, your ultimate allegiance, and they get it one way or another or you're out."

Campbell remained a preacher after leaving the NCC, but one without a pulpit; he remained a Baptist, but no longer a *Southern* Baptist; he remained a social activist, but no longer worked within any organizational framework; and he befriended African American radicals and Ku Klux Klansmen, but also rebuked both. From 1963 to 1972 Campbell belonged to the Committee of Southern Churchmen, a loose affiliation of like-minded men that paid him a salary and supported his anti-institutional variety of social activism. Campbell's writings afford the best insight to his current thought. In *Race and the Renewal of the Church* (1962), he reproached the church for surrendering to secular politicians the leadership of the civil rights movement, a moral struggle in which religious institutions should have been in the forefront. Many of his subsequent works have been well-received, such as *Brother to a Dragonfly* (1977), which won the Lillian Smith Prize and the Christopher Award and earned a National Book Award nomination, and *The Glad River* (1982), which received a first-place award from the Friends of American Writers. Campbell's varied career caught the attention of cartoonist Doug Marlette, whose syndicated strip *Kudzu* features an eccentric preacher, the Reverend Will B. Dunn.

William Sloan Coffin Jr. (1924–)

William Sloan Coffin Jr., a Presbyterian minister and chaplain at Yale University, became politically active in the 1960s, protesting U.S. military policy in Vietnam. Along with other prestigious Americans, Coffin objected on moral grounds to American involvement in Southeast Asia. In his opinion, young Americans should not be forced to fight for a cause they believed immoral. But Coffin did more than preach against the conflict. He helped plan antiwar strategy and appeared at rallies where draft-age Americans were encouraged to resist service in the armed forces. Along with four others, including Dr. Benjamin Spock, the noted pediatrician and author, Coffin was indicted for conspiring to advise young men to violate draft laws.

Coffin was born in New York City to an affluent family. He attended Phillips Academy in Andover, Massachusetts, and graduated from Yale University. He studied at Union Theological Seminary for a year, spent three years during the Korean War at the Central Intelligence Agency working on Russian affairs, and then entered Yale Divinity School. He graduated in 1956 and was ordained a Presbyterian minister.

Deeply offended by racial discrimination and segregation, Coffin joined the 1961 Freedom Rides to Alabama. Like so many other activists of the 1960s, the Yale preacher moved easily from the civil rights struggle at home to the growing protest against war abroad. Thus, in 1966 he collaborated with socialist leader Norman Thomas in a campaign to have voters pledge support only for congressional candidates who advocated an end to the Vietnam conflict. In cooperation with Democratic leaders unhappy with President Lyndon Johnson's foreign policy, Coffin organized Americans for a Reappraisal of East Asian Policy, which advocated official U.S. recognition of the People's Republic of China, the admission of that country to the United Nations, and a negotiated peace in Vietnam. In addition, Coffin became executive secretary of a National Emergency Committee of Clergy Concerned about Vietnam. At a Boston rally in October 1967 Coffin publicly defended draft resistance as an act of civil disobedience. Over 900 individuals turned over their draft cards, and on October 20 Coffin, Spock, Marcus Raskin, codirector of the Washington-based Institute for Policy Studies, and Mitchell Goodman, a novelist, delivered the cards to the Justice Department in Washington, D.C.

In January 1968 Coffin, Spock, Raskin, Goodman, and Harvard graduate student Michael Ferber were indicted for conspiring to counsel draft-age men to violate federal draft laws. Believing that civil disobedience involved the challenging of statutes of dubious constitutionality, Coffin attempted to focus the trial on the government's policy. The trial judge maintained strict control of the proceedings, however, and refused to permit a defense based on the legality or morality of American involvement in Vietnam. In June the jury found all defendants except Raskin guilty of conspiring to counsel evasion of the draft. The four were sentenced to two years in federal prison. A U.S. Court of Appeals subsequently overturned the convictions of Spock and Ferber. A new trial was ordered for Coffin and Goodman, but the Justice Department declined to take further action.

That the trial had failed to gain much publicity disappointed Coffin. He continued to participate in antiwar demonstrations, but became increasingly frustrated with the lack of visible results and with the more radical tactics of other members of the antiwar movement, such as the Students for a Democratic Society. On returning from a trip to Hanoi in fall 1972, he voiced dismay over the continuing violence in Vietnam and the apparent disinterest shown by many U.S. citizens. Even so, he trudged onward, opposing the war and speaking in favor of legal amnesty for those who violated the draft.

From 1977 to 1987 Coffin was the senior minister at the Riverside Church in New York City, an interdenominational congregation of varied national, ethnic, and cultural backgrounds. In 1997, while serving as a visiting professor of religious studies at Lawrence University in Appleton, Wisconsin, he reflected on his participation in the antiwar protests. Although "confession is good for the soul," remarked Coffin, no high government officials from the 1960s had admitted that the Vietnam War was a mistake.

Dalai Lama (1934–)

The "Dalai Lama," a title that originated with the Mongolian ruler Altan Khan in 1578, is the supreme religious and political leader of Tibetan Buddhism. The current, fourteenth Dalai Lama is Tenzin Gyatso (1934–), who has lived in exile in northern India since 1959. In keeping with Buddhist beliefs and traditions, Gyatso, who was born in northeastern Tibet, was recognized while still a child as the reincarnation of the previous Dalai Lama. As such, he was also considered the embodiment of the Tibetan deity of compassion. In 1950 troops representing the new

Communist regime of Mao Tse-tung marched into Tibet on the pretext of liberating it from feudal slavery and incorporated the small Himalayan country into the People's Republic of China. Aside from other political and cultural differences, the official atheism of Mao's government put the Chinese at sharp odds with the followers of the Dalai Lama, who looked upon the intruders as foreign invaders. The Dalai Lama subsequently escaped and formed a government in exile in India. Over 100,000 Tibetans have since followed their spiritual leader into exile.

From the 1950s to the early 1980s the Chinese government in Beijing sought to suppress Buddhism by eliminating Tibet's religious-political institutions and destroying thousands of shrines and monasteries and murdering numerous monks. Mao's Cultural Revolution of the late 1960s was particularly harsh. Through it all the Dalai Lama was a source of unity and strength for oppressed Tibetans, who were finally permitted in the early 1980s to resume practicing their faith. If the Chinese expected this new policy of moderation to satisfy the Tibetans, they were sadly mistaken. Instead, Tibetans, spurred on by the Dalai Lama, demanded greater independence. In 1987, for instance, a year in which Tibetans in Lhasa and other areas of the country defiantly protested Chinese rule, the Dalai Lama presented the U.S. Congress a five-point plan for Tibet. He proposed the cessation of Chinese immigration to Tibet, the protection of Tibet's natural environment, respect for the human rights of Tibetans, the creation of Tibet as a neutral "zone of peace," and the initiation of talks leading, if not to full independence, to autonomy for Tibet within China.

Although the Dalai Lama's efforts won him the Nobel Peace Prize in 1989, that same year the Chinese, annoyed by continuing Tibetan protests, imposed martial law in Lhasa. Even so, the Dalai Lama continued to work toward a peaceful resolution of the problems in his country. As a Buddhist monk, he was committed to the kind of nonviolent resistance advocated by Mohandas Gandhi and Martin Luther King Jr. One familiar with this aspect of the Dalai Lama's thought would not have been surprised by his remarks in Cape Town, South Africa, in December 1999. Addressing the Parliament of the World's Religions, a Chicago-based organization composed of religious people around the globe, he asserted that it would take more than prayer to make the world a better place to live. "Change only takes place through action," he declared. "Frankly speaking, not through prayer or meditation, but through action."

Joseph Martin Dawson (1879–1973)

Joseph Martin Dawson, a prominent Southern Baptist from Texas, contributed to the formation of two contemporary religious lobbying groups, the Baptist Joint Committee on Public Affairs and Protestants and Other Americans United for the Separation of Church and State. Somewhat liberal in his approach to scripture and rather progressive on many social issues, Dawson was a rarity among conservative Baptists in Texas. Born in the cotton belt south of Dallas near Waxahachie, he was reared in the small community of Italy, Texas. Torn between journalism and the ministry, Dawson entered Baylor University in Waco, Texas, in 1898 to prepare for a preaching career. While in college he served several small congregations and upon graduation in 1904 pastored in the Texas communities of Lampasas (1905–1906), Hillsboro (1908–1912), and Temple (1912–1915).

It was in Temple in 1914 that Dawson preached perhaps the first formal series of sermons by a Texas Baptist on the social applications of the "good news." He touched on child labor, the exploitation of immigrants and women, labor conditions, capitalism, and women's rights and disclosed a familiarity with such leading figures of the social gospel movement as Washington Gladden, Josiah Strong, and Walter Rauschenbusch. Though liberal by Texas Baptist standards, Dawson at this stage still espoused a fundamentally conservative solution to social ills—individual salvation. Not until the Great Depression of the 1930s did he fully grasp that salvation, although a private experience, involved a commitment to social regeneration. Institutions as well as individuals had to change.

In 1915 Dawson became pastor of the First Baptist Church, Waco, a position he held until 1946. This was a momentous time for the new preacher and the nation. The brutal killing of a seventeen-year-old black male in front of the Waco city hall on May 15, 1916, forced Dawson to face the issue of race. The criticism by the National Association for the Advancement of Colored People (NAACP) of Waco ministers for their timidity in responding to this barbarous act was not altogether justified. One week after the incident Dawson condemned it in a strongly worded resolution before the Waco Pastor's Conference. Thereafter he openly rebuked the Ku Klux Klan, which was powerful in central Texas in the 1920s; he attempted to shame the South for its disgracefully low appropriations for black schools; he sought to prick the conscience of his own denomination by suggesting that the South, despite the preponderance of Baptists, still harbored what he saw as the worst prejudices; and in 1957 the elderly preacher appeared before a hostile state senate committee in Austin, Texas, to oppose pending legislation detrimental to blacks.

Increasingly of concern to Dawson after World War II were matters of church and state, particularly transgressions of the First Amendment to the Constitution. Thus, in 1946 he left Waco for Washington, D.C., to become the first full-time director of the newly fashioned Baptist Joint Committee on Public Affairs (BJCPA), a lobbying agency supported originally by four national Baptist bodies. The following year Dawson was instrumental in organizing Protestants and Other Americans United for the Separation of Church and State (POAU). Both organizations initially were stridently anti-Catholic, objecting vigorously to the appointment of an ambassador to the Vatican, the usage of public buses to transport children to parochial schools, and efforts to secure public funds for sectarian school construction. Although Dawson retired in 1953, he remained alert to First Amendment issues until his death. Significantly, these two Dawson-inspired agencies still exist, although POAU has become simply Americans United for the Separation of Church and State, and in recent years they have devoted considerable attention to actions of the religious right that they claim violate the First Amendment.

Dorothy Day (1897–1980)

Dorothy Day was an American radical who condemned child labor, discrimination against African Americans, and anti-Semitism in the 1930s and protested against the treatment of migrant workers, the war in Southeast Asia, and the nuclear arms race in the 1960s and 1970s. As a university student she discarded religion because of its lack of social concern, but later embraced Roman Catholicism, which satisfied a spiritual hunger and provided a fresh rationale for her lifelong opposition to war and violence.

Although born in Brooklyn, New York, Day grew to maturity in Chicago during the heady days of the progressive era. At the University of Illinois, socialism displaced religion, and it subsequently informed Day's commentaries as a left-wing journalist in New York City. She objected to U.S. involvement in World War I, protested the draft, and marched for women's suffrage. Although the nation turned rightward in the 1920s under presidents Warren Harding and Calvin Coolidge, Day and her common-law husband found continuing support for their left-wing views among friends and associates in Greenwich Village. It was also in the 1920s that Day turned to Catholicism, and soon thereafter French philosopher Peter Maurin helped her find a religious underpinning for political radicalism. Together, Day and Maurin founded the radical Catholic Worker Movement in 1933, and Day thereafter published the *Catholic Worker,* a monthly newspaper. The objective of the movement was to remake society in accordance with Day's new understanding of the gospel message. Accordingly, the movement faulted both capitalism and Marxism.

A genuine Christian pacifist, Day and her movement consistently objected to warfare, whether it was the Spanish Civil War in the 1930s, World War II, the Cold War, or Vietnam in the 1960s. Through the Association of Catholic Conscientious Objectors, she and her associates advocated alternative service to military combat in the 1940s; they campaigned for nuclear disarmament in the 1950s; and they supported the protests against American involvement in Vietnam in the 1960s and 1970s. Day was even arrested on one occasion in the 1950s for refusing to take part in mandatory air-raid drills.

But Day and her allies did more than protest. They also engaged in practical programs to feed and clothe the needy and to promote interracial justice. Specifically, they established about forty "houses of hospitality" across the United States, shelters through which they labored in a personal way to ameliorate the plight of the destitute. Much like Mother Teresa in Calcutta, India, Day actually lived among the poor on the Lower East Side of New York City. She thereby knew from personal experience their impoverished conditions, and she demonstrated on a daily basis genuine Christian compassion and respect for society's least fortunate. But unlike Mother Teresa, who generally eschewed direct political involvement, Day actively worked through the political process, frequently challenging public policies she considered wrongheaded, to uplift humanity's outcasts.

Jerry Falwell (1932–)

The religious right's most prominent spokesman in the United States by the early 1980s, Jerry Falwell demonstrated that fundamentalist Christians could be effectively involved in the political process. Raised among rowdy bootleggers in the hill country of central Virginia, his formative years gave no hint of later religious stature. After becoming a Christian in 1952, he attended Bible Baptist College in Missouri. Four years later he returned home to Lynchburg, Virginia, established an independent Baptist church in a vacant bottling plant, and promptly took to the airwaves with a thirty-minute radio program. Within six months he aired his first telecast. The smoothly articulate pastor quickly became an institution. From only 35 members in 1956, his Thomas Road congregation numbered almost 20,000 by the early 1980s, and his Sunday service, *The Old-Time Gospel Hour,* was carried to an estimated 21 million faithful listeners via 681 radio and television stations. Falwell's fundraising capacity was impressive. By 1980 he was generating about $1 million per week, enough to sustain a college, Liberty Baptist (now Liberty University), with approximately 3,000 students, a home for alcoholics, a children's day school, a seminary, 62 assistant pastors, and 1,300 employees.

As noteworthy as these church-related achievements were, Falwell was becoming better known to the American public because of his venture into politics. Assisted by the capable conservative political strategist Paul Weyrich, the popular preacher launched Moral Majority, Inc., in 1979. The purpose was to give political voice to a growing tide of disenchanted Christian fundamentalists, religionists who, like Falwell himself, had traditionally abstained from the political process. By the late 1970s Falwell was convinced that America's moral decline, as presumably exemplified by Supreme Court decisions on prayer in the public schools and abortion, the pervasiveness of "smutty" television, the assertiveness of the gay community, and the push for the Equal Rights Amendment, could be reversed only by vigorous political activism from the religious right. Ironically, it was disappointment with another "born again" Christian, President Jimmy Carter, a Southern Baptist layman, that prompted Falwell to political action.

The extent to which Moral Majority contributed to the success of conservative Republicans in the 1980s is open to debate, but there is no denying the organization's efforts. It hastily established local chapters in all the states, conducted voter registration campaigns and educational seminars, and targeted liberal Democrats for defeat. Claims of nonpartisanship notwithstanding, Moral Majority clearly was more at ease with a conservative Republican agenda. The organization was never very successful in attracting nonfundamentalists, and so in an effort to broaden its support, Falwell renamed it Liberty Federation in 1987. That same year Falwell's ministries, like those of many other televangelists, suffered serious economic losses in the wake of the scandal involving Jim Bakker, another prominent televangelist. A

Gallup Poll disclosed that 62 percent of the American public now viewed Falwell unfavorably. Consequently, in 1989 he dissolved Moral Majority, devoted more attention to his local congregation and college, and assumed a lower profile. Even so, Falwell continues to be strident in his criticism of American society, and he has been challenged in recent years for his harsh statements about homosexuals. He played a relatively minor role in the 2000 presidential race, but supported Republican George W. Bush.

Most recently Falwell saw in the terrorist attacks of September 11, 2001, evidence of God's displeasure with a sinful society. Appearing on Pat Robertson's *The 700 Club* two days after the assault, he blamed longstanding adversaries—homosexuals and feminists who had been spurred on and abetted by the American Civil Liberties Union, People for the American Way, the National Organization for Women, and permissive federal judges for "throwing God out" of the public schools, legalizing abortion, and promoting gay rights. He claimed God had "lifted the curtain of protection" from America. These remarks brought a sharp rebuke. The dean of the Wake Forest Divinity School, a Baptist institution in Winston-Salem, North Carolina, dismissed Falwell's comments as "a travesty," "a mistaken effort to sound prophetic." Somewhat chastened, Falwell, as he has done on prior occasions following such outbursts, apologized.

Louis Farrakhan (1933–)

Often accused of being antiwhite and anti-Semitic, Louis Farrakhan, the controversial leader of the Nation of Islam since 1977, appeals to prison inmates and youthful gang members as well as college educated and middle-class African Americans with a message of black nationalism, economic independence, and racial separation and a puritanical lifestyle that eschews drinking, smoking, and drugs. Born Louis Eugene Walcott in Roxbury, Massachusetts, he was reared by his mother, a seamstress and housekeeper who made him aware of the African American struggle for equality. Showing early an aptitude for music, Farrakhan received a violin and began formal training by age six. He performed with the Boston Civic Symphony and Boston College Orchestra by age thirteen, winning the following year the popular Ted Mack Amateur Hour. A track scholarship allowed the sixteen-year-old youngster to attend Winston-Salem Teacher's College in North Carolina, where he studied English. In September 1953 he married his childhood sweetheart and soon thereafter left college.

Returning to Boston, Farrakhan took to the stage. Billed variously as "Calypso Gene" and "The Charmer," the young singer, dancer, and violinist seemed destined for show business stardom. This all changed in early 1955. While performing in Chicago in February, Farrakhan attended a Nation of Islam convention. This brought him into contact with the charismatic Malcolm X, then a devoted follower of Elijah Muhammad, head of the Nation of Islam. Farrakhan promptly put aside music, took the name Louis X, changed later to Louis Haleem Abdul Farrakhan, and dedicated himself to the teachings of Elijah Muhammad. A brief stint with Malcolm in Harlem was followed by a lengthy, successful tenure from 1956 to 1965 as minister of Boston's Temple Number Eleven. In May 1965, just three months after Malcolm's assassination, Elijah Muhammad made Farrakhan minister of Malcolm's Harlem temple, a particularly difficult assignment given widespread rumors of Muslim complicity in Malcolm's death. Nevertheless, through hard work Farrakhan turned the situation around in New York.

With the death of Elijah Muhammad in 1975, the Nation of Islam underwent dramatic changes. Wallace Deen Muhammad, the son of Elijah and the new leader of the faith, opened the Nation's doors to white members, rejecting his father's preachments as racist and out of character with true Islam. Alienated by this trend, Farrakhan bolted in 1977, forming the rival Original Nation of Islam (referred to now, along with about six other groups, as the Nation of Islam) and returning to the separatist teachings of Elijah Muhammad. Farrakhan's harsh rhetoric over the years about Jews, Israel, whites, Christianity, and so-called mainstream blacks has drawn sharp criticism. Still, his efforts in behalf of underprivileged blacks have been noteworthy, particularly programs to rehabilitate drug addicts, prisoners, and gang members. Through its own restaurants, bakeries, bookstores, and farms, Farrakhan's Nation offers jobs and training.

To Farrakhan's traditional message of economic empowerment of African Americans has been added in recent years a new political emphasis, a development spurred in part by a growing conservative trend seen as hostile to minorities. Citing the 1994 Republicans' "Contract With America" and recent Supreme Court decisions regarding affirmative action, Farrakhan feared for gains made in civil rights since the 1950s. Hence, he called "for one million disciplined, committed, and dedicated Black men, from all walks of life in America, to march in Washington, D.C." in October 1995 and urged all eligible African Americans to register to vote. Declared Farrakhan: "We shall emphasize in our actions and in the written word that the Black community shall not give our vote to anyone who is against, or is not willing, to represent the best interest of our people." If Farrakhan's Million Man March improved his image and offset somewhat his fiery anti-Semitic rhetoric, his world tour the following year quickly erased it all. In Libya, Iran, Iraq, Sudan, and Syria, Muslim countries hostile toward the United States, Farrakhan apparently pleased his hosts with attacks on Jews and the U.S. government, allegedly calling it while in Iran "the Great Satan." Small wonder that Muammar al-Qaddafi of Libya offered $1 billion to Farrakhan to fund Muslim activities in the United States, an offer never accepted.

In late 1999 Farrakhan announced a change of heart, a metamorphosis allegedly brought on by a near-death encounter with prostate cancer. Preaching to about 200 followers in Chicago, the Nation of Islam leader called for the unity of all races and religions in the next millennium. Said Farrakhan: "Only through our act of atonement can we be forgiven for what we have said or done to injure other human beings—a member of another race or a member of another religious group, another nation or another ethnic group." Given Farrakhan's history, other religious leaders were understandably wary, including the elder statesman of American evangelicalism, the Reverend Billy Graham, who doubted that the Muslim minister could be a unifying figure.

With mosques in cities across the United States, Farrakhan's group is easily the more vigorous of today's various branches of the Nation of Islam. Yet, for all the attention Farrakhan has drawn, the Nation of Islam probably numbers no more than 20,000.

Mohandas Gandhi (1869–1948)

One of this century's more important religious and political leaders, Mohandas Gandhi made fasting a form of political protest. He was born into an influential family in Probandar, a city in western India. His relatives belonged to a Hindu sect that stressed nonviolence, and his father was prominent in local politics. In accordance with a family arrangement, Gandhi married at age thirteen. This union lasted sixty-two years and produced four children, but Gandhi came to oppose such youthful, prearranged nuptials. In 1888 young Gandhi jumped at the chance to study law in England, where he remained until 1891. A friend remarked in jest that Gandhi, already a vegetarian, would never fit into British society without eating meat. There was something prophetic in the observation, for Gandhi and the British Empire certainly did not fit together.

In 1893 Gandhi took a job with an Indian trading firm in Natal, South Africa, a British crown colony on the Indian Ocean. This was a turning point in Gandhi's life, for the discrimination and humiliation he encountered in this British province politicized him. To expose mistreatment of the Indian population in South Africa, he organized the Natal Indian Congress in 1894 and peppered the newspapers with letters, drafted petitions, and published pamphlets. To this point Gandhi's method of protest was typically liberal and British. Nonviolent civil disobedience, characterized by marches, strikes, boycotts, and noncooperation with authorities, did not evolve until about 1906, and the immediate provocation was a new South African law requiring Indians to carry identification cards. During this encounter Gandhi coined the term *satyagraha*, meaning the power of love and truth, to describe his kind of peaceful defiance. This struggle lasted seven years, during which hundreds of Indians were imprisoned, including Gandhi, who considered it noble to be jailed for a just cause. Altogether Gandhi would spend almost seven years behind bars for his political activities. On November 25, 1913, Natal police fired into a crowd of demonstrators, killing two and wounding twenty. Shortly thereafter Gandhi negotiated an agreement ending the struggle.

In 1914, when Gandhi returned home to India from South Africa, a South African official reportedly observed, "The saint has left our shores; I hope forever." To reverse the old adage, in this instance South Africa's gain was Great Britain's loss, inasmuch as Gandhi would soon be at the heart of India's quest for independence. The movement began in 1919 when Gandhi encouraged a nationwide boycott of British manufactured goods. Consistent with the principles of *satyagraha*, Gandhi insisted upon peaceful protests. The British had little patience with such an open challenge to their rule and responded harshly, arresting Gandhi and beating many of his followers. Some of Gandhi's supporters met violence with violence. They not only killed several policemen in 1922 but also fell out among themselves. Gandhi dreamed of a united India composed of Hindus and Muslims, but religious differences proved too deep to sustain political cooperation.

The eruption of violence prompted Gandhi not only to end the boycott in 1922, but also to begin a fast in behalf of Hindu-

Muslim unity in 1924. Fasting added another dimension to Gandhi's method of peaceful protest, for he infused this fundamentally religious exercise with political meaning. Gandhi's many fasts always had political objectives, calculated usually to draw attention to British mistreatment of Indians or to shame Hindus and Muslims into cooperation. Although not always successful, this peaceful revolutionary's preference for fasting over fighting won the admiration of fellow Indians, who accorded him the title *Mahatma*, meaning great soul.

At the behest of the All-India Trade Congress, Gandhi initiated a concerted campaign of civil disobedience against British authority in spring 1930. Central to this effort was a 165-mile march to the Gujarat Coast on the Arabian Sea to protest Britain's monopoly on salt production. Some 60,000 Indians were arrested and rioting occurred, but a truce was reached in 1931. This was the occasion when Winston Churchill described Gandhi as "this seditious fakir . . . striding half-naked up the steps of the Viceroy's palace," an indiscreet remark that played into the hands of the Indians. In 1932 Gandhi began another fast, this time protesting British policies toward the "untouchables," members of India's lowest caste. The British moderated their position.

Another push for Indian independence begun during World War II finally succeeded, but not to Gandhi's full satisfaction. The Muslim leader Mohammad Ali Jinnah, never optimistic about a united India of Hindus and Muslims, proposed separate nationhood in 1940 for those parts of the continent composed primarily of Muslims. Accordingly, the creation of Pakistan, a Muslim country, accompanied India's independence from Great Britain in August 1947. Although *satyagraha* had prevailed against the British, it failed to overcome the deep suspicions dividing Hindus and Muslims. In the wake of independence, these two groups clashed violently, bringing another round of fasts by Gandhi. On January 30, 1948, just days after Hindu and Muslim leaders agreed to end the bloodshed, Gandhi, on his way to an evening prayer meeting, was assassinated by a young Hindu fanatic.

Gustavo Merino Gutierrez (1928–)

Widely recognized as the founder of liberation theology, Gustavo Gutierrez, a Roman Catholic priest, has worked for over twenty-five years to improve the social, economic, and political status of the poor in Latin American. In *Liberation Theology—Perspectives,* first published in 1974, Gutierrez abandoned the traditional notion of two realities, one temporal and the other transcendent, and two histories, one worldly and the other sacred. The Kingdom of God, he claimed, was to be realized to some extent in this world, and it could be achieved through political efforts. Redemption, to be sure, ultimately belonged to God, but salvation was of this world as well as the next, and worldly redemption served as an approximation of the complete salvation to be effected by God. Gutierrez believed salvation, rather than being a private, individual experience, was communitarian and public. As seen in the Book of Exodus, the liberation of the Israelites applied to an entire nation, not simply to individual persons. A step toward salvation in this life could be taken, Gutierrez argued, when the more affluent fulfilled their obligation to share wealth with the poor.

As the son of a mestizo born in Lima, Peru, Gutierrez shared the dual heritage of the conquering Spaniards and the conquered Incas. During his teens he was bedridden and confined to a wheelchair with osteomyelitis, an inflammation of the bone marrow that left him with a permanent limp. A bright young man, Gutierrez entered San Marcos University, intending to receive a degree in psychiatry. Instead, he became a priest and began studying philosophy at the seminary in Santiago de Chile. Additional studies took him to Belgium, France, and Rome. He was ordained in 1959. Returning to Peru in 1960, Gutierrez began to teach part-time at the Catholic University in Lima. He emphasized the interaction of God with the present world, comparing his faith with systems such as Marxism thought to be critical of Christianity.

Rejecting the standard model of development that emphasized a capitalistic market economy, Gutierrez focused instead on transforming the ownership system, granting the lower class political and economic power, and ending the poor's dependency on the rich. His criticism of prevalent notions of modernization in no way reflected a yearning for traditional social relationships. Uppermost for Gutierrez was the social liberation of the poor, and in pursuit of this objective he rebuked the left almost as sharply as the right. He faulted liberal theology because it usually emphasized the private demands of a middle-class society, and, while using the language of Marxism, he and other adherents of liberation theology rejected the Marxist view of religion as simply a means of subjecting the people to the existing social and economic order. The poor of Latin America, he believed, should create their own path to socialism.

Gutierrez knew that the church in Latin America had traditionally supported and benefited from the established capitalistic system, and he has rebuked the more conservative elements within the church. For its part, the church has been just as quick to criticize the affinity of Gutierrez's theology to Marxism. Significantly, Gutierrez has commended more recent trends within the church, such as Vatican II, which indicate an acceptance of the more contemporary values of human rights, freedom, and social equality.

Recently Gutierrez has been criticized for failing to include feminism in liberation theology, neglecting the distinct needs of Native Americans, and ignoring Protestant groups that support liberation theology. In response, Gutierrez in his most recent writings has included women as an exploited social group in need of liberation and he has broadened the focus of liberation theology to include races and cultures as well as classes.

Jesse Jackson (1941–)

In the 1960s Jesse Jackson became a noted African American political leader and prominent figure in the civil rights movement. As do many other preachers, he easily combines religion and politics. Like Pat Robertson, Jackson is a Baptist minister who has had presidential aspirations, although the two men have little else in common. Whereas Robertson is a conservative Republican, Jackson is a liberal Democrat, one who shares the dream of such other African American religious political leaders as Martin Luther King Jr. and Ralph David Abernathy. Jackson has never pastored a congregation. His public career began in the 1960s with the civil rights movement. In the 1970s he continued the struggle for racial equality in Chicago, and in the 1980s he entered national politics, vying for the Democratic presidential nomination in 1984 and 1988. He has remained a national political figure, advocating political action for the disadvantaged and minorities.

Jackson was born in Greenville, South Carolina, the son of an unwed mother. Two years after his birth, Jackson's mother married Charles Henry Jackson, who adopted Jesse. In 1959, after graduating from high school, Jackson was offered a professional baseball contract, but decided instead to attend the University of Illinois on a baseball scholarship. After a year he transferred to North Carolina Agricultural and Technical State University in Greensboro. While a student, Jackson took part in sit-in demonstrations and the Freedom Rides conducted by the Congress for Racial Equality (CORE). In 1962 he married Jacqueline Lavinia Brown, who participated with her husband in civil rights demonstrations.

After graduating in 1963, Jackson worked for North Carolina Governor Terry Sanford as an organizer for the Young Democrats. In 1965 he decided to become a minister, enrolling in the Chicago Theological Seminary. Once in Chicago, he joined a branch of the Southern Christian Leadership Conference (SCLC) and organized students to take part in the civil rights movement in the South. Working through Chicago's black churches, he sought to activate African Americans in support of social programs and jobs for minorities and the poor. In 1966 King, as head of the SCLC, appointed Jackson director of Chicago's Operation Breadbasket, a program designed to find employment for poor people, encourage blacks to purchase goods from black-owned businesses, and get stores to stock goods made by blacks. Jackson organized boycotts against stores that failed to hire minorities. His involvement in the organization left him little time to pursue a divinity degree, so he left the seminary.

In March 1968 Jackson was with King when the civil rights leader was shot and killed in Memphis, Tennessee. Later that year he took part in the Poor People's March on Washington, D.C. In 1969 Jackson was granted an honorary degree from the Chicago Theological Seminary and was ordained a minister. In 1971, following conflicts with the SCLC leadership, Jackson resigned from the organization and formed a new group, Operation PUSH (People United to Serve Humanity), and established a related program, EXCEL (short for "excellence"), which focused on service to youth.

In 1972 Jackson decided to enter politics directly, running against Richard Daley for mayor of Chicago. Jackson lost, but he challenged Daley once more at the Democratic National Convention over the selection of convention delegates from Illinois. Jackson won this time, as the Daley delegates were unseated and a new slate was certified. In 1984 Jackson established the Rainbow Coalition as part of his bid for the Democratic presidential nomination. An unfortunate reference to New York City as "Hymietown" and his association with Louis Farrakhan, leader of the Nation of Islam (Black Muslims), created the perception that Jackson was anti-Semitic, which the candidate strongly denied. Although Jackson had little chance of winning the nomination, his candidacy gave him greater influence over the party's national platform. In 1988 he sought the nomination again, but lost to Michael Dukakis. Even so, he was able once more to influence the Democratic platform.

In 1989 Jackson moved his family and the offices of the Rainbow Coalition to Washington, D.C. This encouraged speculation that a run for mayor of the nation's capital was in the offing, but Jackson so far has shown no interest in such a race. Instead, he has been a frequent commentator on national politics, often interjecting his views on major political issues. In 1999, during the NATO operation in Kosovo, Jackson traveled to eastern Europe and successfully negotiated the release of three captured American soldiers. His reputation was tarnished somewhat in early 2001 when it was disclosed that he had recently fathered an illegitimate child by a staff worker.

Pope John Paul II (1920–)

As head of the Roman Catholic Church since 1978, almost everything Pope John Paul II says has political repercussions, whether criticizing communism in Eastern Europe or U.S. economic sanctions of Cuba, opposing abortion, or pleading for peace in the Middle East. Born Karol Joseph Wojtyla in Wadowice, Poland, the future pope seemed an unlikely prospect for the holy office. His mind was on mountain climbing, literature, and an acting career. In 1938 he became a student at Jagellonian University in Krakow, but his education and career aspirations were changed by the Nazi invasion of his country in September 1939. As a member of a Christian democratic underground group, he helped Jews flee the Nazis, sensed God's call to service, and secretly studied for the Catholic priesthood. He became an ordained priest in November 1946 and two years later obtained a doctorate in theology at the Angelicum in Rome, Italy. He was a parish priest in Krakow from 1948 to 1951, studied an additional year at Jagellonian University, taught social ethics at Krakow Seminary from 1952 to 1958, and joined the faculty at the University of Lublin in 1956.

Despite determined efforts by the post–World War II Communist regime, Catholicism in Poland, the faith of over 90 percent of the populace, remained vigorous. Wojtyla steadily advanced within the Polish church. In July 1958 Pope Pius XII, whose alleged wartime dealings with the Nazis have sparked controversy, named Wojtyla an auxiliary bishop in Krakow, and in December 1963 Pope Paul VI elevated him to Archbishop of

Krakow. While resisting communism in Poland, Wojtyla, as a participant in all four major sessions of Vatican II (October 1962–December 1965), labored to update Catholicism. He joined American bishops, for instance, in drafting the Declaration of Religious Freedom, which acknowledged religious pluralism and repudiated totalitarian regimes. In June 1967 Pope Paul VI made him a cardinal.

In October 1978 a deadlock between two Italians led to Wojtyla's election by the college of cardinals to the papacy, making him the first non-Italian pope in over 450 years, the only Polish pope ever, and the youngest pope of the twentieth century. Although Pope John Paul's strong opposition to abortion, homosexuality, and the ordination of women make him a conservative, one at times at odds with segments of the church, his efforts to move the church into the modern world make him a progressive. Reflecting a new openness, he has participated in prayer services with both Lutheran and Jewish congregations in Rome. In behalf of world peace, he has either met with or appealed to virtually all the major international figures—Yasser Arafat, King Hussein of Jordan, prime ministers Yitzhak Rabin and Benjamin Netanyahu of Israel, President George H. W. Bush of the United States, and President Saddam Hussein of Iraq. His endeavors for peace made him *Time*'s Man of the Year in 1994.

Over the opposition of many American Protestants, the administration of President Ronald Reagan established diplomatic relations with the Vatican in 1984. In 1989 President Mikhail Gorbachev was the first Soviet head of state to be received by the pope, and the following year the Holy See and the Soviet government exchanged official representatives. Although in frail health, hastened by an assassination attempt by a Turkish terrorist in 1981, Pope John Paul II continues to be an influence on the world's religious and political stages, as seen in his celebrated visit to Fidel Castro's Cuba in January 1998 and to India, the world's only predominantly Hindu country, in November 1999. This latter trip sparked controversy when some Hindus demanded that the pope not only apologize for alleged atrocities committed by Portuguese Catholics in India over 400 years ago but also discourage recent attempts by Christian missionaries to convert Hindus. Unfazed, Pope John Paul II ignored the call for an apology and told Indian Christians in New Delhi to continue evangelistic efforts.

Meir Kahane (1932–1990)

An American-born rabbi whose reading of scripture shaped his political outlook, Meir Kahane ridiculed the American Jewish establishment for allegedly fostering intermarriage and assimilation, founded the Jewish Defense League to counter anti-Semitism, and called for the expulsion of all Arabs from Israeli-held territory. Contemptuous of those who wanted Israel to be a Western-style democracy, Kahane asserted: "Judaism is not Thomas Jefferson and the Middle East is not the Mid West." The son of a rabbi, Kahane was born in New York City, studied at Mir Yeshiva in Brooklyn, and became an ordained rabbi in 1956. That same year he obtained a law degree from New York Law School, followed somewhat later by a masters degree in international relations from New York University.

From the early to mid-1960s Kahane served as a congregational rabbi in the Howard Beach area of New York City, and in 1961 he began a lifelong association with the *Jewish Press*, perhaps the most widely read English-speaking Jewish newspaper in the world. Incensed by growing acts of violence against Jews in some American inner cities and the plight of Russian Jews, he created the militant Jewish Defense League in 1968. This organization not only met violence with violence but also championed pride in Jewishness, strength, love of Jews everywhere, and cultural solidarity. Particularly galling to the rabbi was "the curse and cancer of intermarriage and assimilation," a condition in the United States he attributed to the Jewish establishment that sought acceptance in the broader society, public schools that regularly exposed Jewish youngsters to Gentiles, temple rabbis who watered down the unique faith of Judaism, and Jewish parents who sacrificed their heritage for material success. An effective speaker, Kahane spoke frequently on American campuses, imploring Jewish students to learn about and return to the faith of Abraham.

With his wife and four children, Kahane migrated to Israel in 1971, residing in Jerusalem. Immediately involved in politics, he formed the Kach (Thus!) Party and worked doggedly toward the creation of an Israeli state based upon the religious laws of the Torah. This brought Kahane into sharp conflict with secular Jews and intensified the debate within Israel over the character and nature of the Jewish nation itself. Was Israel to be a secularized democracy, providing a refuge for Jews of varied persuasions from around the globe, or was it to be a theocracy, a home only to those who shared Kahane's brand of the true faith? Kahane's position on this was unswerving, and in a confrontational manner he mocked fellow Jews who failed to embrace his vision, labeling them as "demented" and "besotted with Gentilized concepts." Kahane wanted Israel to keep all the territory it conquered from neighboring Arabs in the 1967 war, settle that land with Jews, and expel all Arabs. "To expel an Arab is moral," he declared. "To allow him to stay as a potential murderer of a Jew is to be an accomplice to that murder."

Defeated for the Knesset in 1976 and 1980, he won a seat in 1984. His violent rhetoric and behavior angered both the Likud and Labor parties, which joined forces to exclude Kahane from the 1988 elections. His assassination two years later in New York City by members of a fringe group associated with the Egyptian Muslim Brotherhood did not cancel Kahane's violent legacy. It was one of his disciples who killed Muslim worshipers in Hebron in 1994 and another who assassinated Prime Minister Yitzhak Rabin in 1995.

Ayatollah Ruhollah Khomeini (1900–1989)

Ayatollah Ruhollah Khomeini, an Iranian Shi'ite Muslim cleric, successfully led a revolt against the regime of Shah Mohammed Reza Pahlavi in the late 1970s. Upon taking power he and his Islamic fundamentalist followers set about eliminating Western influences in Iran, particularly that of the United States, the so-called Great Satan. Prevailing over those Iranians who wished to establish a democratic society, Khomeini forged a theocratic state. Women were compelled to wear traditional veils and long gowns, called *chadors,* and music was banned from television and radio. In November 1979 Iranians overran the American embassy in Teheran, ultimately holding embassy personnel hostage for 444 days. Although creating a crisis in American politics that contributed to the defeat of President Jimmy Carter in 1980, the hostage situation helped solidify Khomeini's support among Iranians.

Khomeini was just a child when his father, a mullah, was killed in a dispute over irrigation rights. Khomeini's own religious studies began in Khomein, his birthplace, and continued at various Iranian schools, including the Marvi Theological School in Teheran. After becoming a teacher Khomeini continued his own intellectual development, studying subjects such as Islamic mysticism. Married twice, a son from his second marriage became one of his close aides.

Khomeini was an early critic of Reza Shah Pahlavi (1877–1944) and his son Shah Mohammed Reza Pahlavi. In 1941 his book *Unveiling the Mysteries* condemned the ruling monarchy for oppressing the clergy and contributing to the subversion of Islamic culture by embracing foreign influences. Khomeini believed Islam offered the only legitimate basis for government, and his ongoing opposition to the secular regime of the shah steadily earned him prestige with the Iranian people. His followers granted him the title Ayatollah, meaning Reflection of Allah, and he was honored with the designation Grand Ayatollah in 1962. That same year Khomeini initiated a general strike when the government declared that court witnesses no longer had to swear on the Qur'an. His anger toward the shah deepened the following year as a result of government efforts to modernize the country, efforts that included granting rights to women and seizure of lands held by the clergy. In 1964, after he was arrested for encouraging opposition to the shah, the Iranian government exiled Khomeini, who went first to Turkey, then to Iraq, where he continued to issue antigovernment diatribes.

Massive demonstrations by Khomeini's supporters in Iran in January 1978 forced Iraq to expel the ayatollah, who took up residence in France. Opposition to the Iranian government reached a fever pitch by the end of 1978, and the shah was forced to leave the country in January 1979. Khomeini returned to Iran in triumph on February 1. At first Khomeini hinted that he would defer to the secular government that had been established in the wake of the shah's collapse, but he instead opposed more moderate political figures and steadily increased his own involvement in government affairs, ultimately consolidating power through such mullah-dominated groups as the Islamic Revolutionary Council.

Claims were made that Khomeini, not content to establish an Islamic state in one country, gave financial support to insurgent groups in such Persian Gulf countries as Kuwait and Saudi Arabia. There was internal opposition to the ayatollah, but he repelled all challenges to his power, including rebellions by Kurdish and Baluchi minorities and an assassination campaign initiated by the political left. Even the disastrous war with Iraq from 1980 to 1988, in which both sides suffered high casualties and economic exhaustion before agreeing to a truce, could not shake Khomeini's hold over the Iranian people. Until his death in 1989, the ayatollah strenuously opposed any suggestion, within or outside the clergy, to moderate his vision of an ideal theocracy.

Martin Luther King Jr. (1929–1968)

Perhaps no single religious figure did more to energize the civil rights movement of the 1960s than Martin Luther King Jr. From the cadence and rhythmic pattern of speech to the genuine belief that the oppressed must forgive and thereby redeem the oppressors, King disclosed the influence of his religious upbringing. His maternal grandfather, Alfred Daniel Williams, had founded the Ebenezer Baptist Church of Atlanta, Georgia, and his father, Martin Luther King Sr., had made it one of the city's larger and more prestigious African American congregations. It was in these exuberantly evangelical services that King Jr. began to learn the oratorical skills for which he would later become famous. If middle-class origins provided material security and opened opportunities for young King, they did not shelter him from the pain of racial prejudice. White playmates were forbidden as they grew older to associate with him; at age eleven a white woman slapped him in the face and called him "a nigger," apparently for stepping on her foot; and on a return trip from a high school debating tournament, he was forced to give his bus seat to a white passenger and stand in the aisle for ninety miles. "It was a night I'll never forget," King recalled. "I have never been so deeply angry in my life." But instead of lashing out in rage at such abuses, King followed a more constructive path, drawing upon the examples of his grandfather and father. Williams was a charter member of the NAACP in Atlanta and King Sr. a charter member of the Atlanta Voters League and an active Republican. To the political activism of his relatives King would add nonviolent resistance.

Without finishing high school, King entered Morehouse College, a respectable black institution in Atlanta, in September 1944, intent on becoming a doctor or lawyer. The decision to become a preacher was not made until his junior year, whereupon he was ordained and joined his father as an associate pastor at Ebenezer in February 1948. Additional schooling followed at Crozer Theological Seminary (B.D., 1951) in Chester, Pennsylvania, and Boston University (Ph.D., 1955). Intellectually, socially, and professionally this was a crucial decade in King's life. He read Henry David Thoreau's *On Civil Disobedience* and studied the tactics of Mohandas Gandhi, thereby sharpening his understanding of passive resistance; he married Coretta Scott, the talented daughter of a prosperous Marion, Alabama, store owner whose skepticism of ministers was overcome by Martin's commitment to civil rights; and in late 1954 he became pastor of the Dexter Avenue Baptist Church in Montgomery, Alabama, which soon placed him at the center of the bus boycott.

King had been in Montgomery only a year when Mrs. Rosa Parks defied law and tradition on December 1, 1955, by refusing to move to the rear of a city bus. His ideas on civil disobedience were not yet fully crystallized, and at the outset he was not yet the leader of the boycott. Yet King emerged from this year-long confrontation with the white community a figure of national stature. Dependent on black passengers for about 75 percent of its revenue and faced with an unfavorable Supreme Court ruling, Montgomery's city bus line capitulated in December 1956. Segregated seating was eliminated, and throughout the struggle the black community, despite the hostility of whites, had followed the advice of its leaders: "If cursed, do not curse back. If struck, do not strike back, but evidence love and goodwill at all times."

Civil disobedience had worked in Montgomery, and King moved promptly to keep the momentum going. Meeting in Atlanta in January 1957 with more than sixty black ministers, including Ralph David Abernathy, King forged what would soon become the Southern Christian Leadership Conference, an organization dedicated to the achievement of racial equality through nonviolent resistance. As president of this group, King was at the forefront of the civil rights struggle until his assassination in April 1968. In cities across the South—Atlanta and Albany, Georgia, Birmingham, Montgomery, and Selma, Alabama, and Jackson, Mississippi—he challenged segregation laws with marches, sit-ins, and freedom rides. He appealed to Vice President Richard Nixon in 1957 to tour the South in behalf of racial justice, met with Senator John F. Kennedy in 1960, electrified the estimated crowd of 250,000 that marched on Washington, D.C., in August 1963 with his "dream" for America, and witnessed President Lyndon B. Johnson's signing of the Civil Rights Act in 1964 and the Voting Rights Act in 1965. Sadly, King's appeal to the conscience of white southerners, his plea that they practice the principles of their religious faith and uphold the ideals of the American dream in matters of race, was all too frequently met with vicious police dogs, fire hoses, arrests on dubious charges, dynamite bombs, and murder. Few acts shocked Americans more than the bombing that killed four young black girls at Birmingham's Sixteenth Street Baptist Church in September 1963, and the stark contrast between the violence of this act and King's subsequent appeal to forgiveness was especially telling.

For his efforts in behalf of racial justice King was *Time*'s Man of the Year in 1963, the first African American so honored, and in November 1964 he was the youngest recipient to that time of the Nobel Peace Prize. Of growing concern to King by this time was the nation's involvement in Vietnam, a conflict that he thought diverted resources from problems of race and poverty at home. In August 1965 he publicly opposed the fighting in southeast Asia, and in April 1967 gave a major antiwar address at the Riverside Church in New York City, noting how inconsistent it would be to oppose violence at home and condone it abroad. A strike by sanitation workers took him to Memphis, Tennessee, in March 1968. A few days later, on April 4, the country's best known apostle of nonviolence was shot and killed by a sniper. In eulogies across the land mourners were reminded of the prophecy in King's famous "I Have a Dream" speech, when "*all* God's children, black men and white men, Jews and Gentiles, Protestants and Catholics, will be able to join hands and sing in the words of the old Negro spiritual, 'Free at last! Free at last! Thank God Almighty, we are free at last!'"

Osama bin Laden (1955–)

With a personal fortune estimated at $200 to $400 million, Osama bin Laden, often cited in the Western press as the banker of Islamic terrorism, was unknown to most of the world until the deadly attacks in August 1998 on the American embassies in Nairobi, Kenya, and Dar Es Salaam, Tanzania, killing 224 and injuring thousands. Assuming near mythological stature since then, bin Laden has been suspected of complicity in violent activities around the globe, from the bombing of the World Trade Center in New York City in February 1993, to the lethal attack on the USS *Cole* in October 2000, and finally to the attacks that damaged the Pentagon and destroyed the World Trade Center on September 11, 2001. Confident of Allah's blessing, bin Laden quickly deflects such charges with countercharges that the world's worst terrorist is the United States, whose bombing of Hiroshima and Nagasaki with nuclear weapons and Iraq with sophisticated conventional weapons killed thousands of innocent men, women, and children. Born into one of Saudi Arabia's wealthier and more prominent families, bin Laden was the youngest son of some fifty children. Although a Saudi Arabian national, his familial roots lay elsewhere. His father, a Yemeni immigrant to the Arabian kingdom, forged a construction company into a financial empire, the

Bin Laden Group; his mother, the fourth and last of his father's wives, was a Syrian, and Osama was her only son. Such parentage made bin Laden, wealth and privilege notwithstanding, something of an outsider in a land that prizes deep ancestral connections. When his father died in a plane crash in 1968, bin Laden inherited approximately $80 million.

Though reared a Wahhab Muslim, the dominant and rather puritanical branch of Islam in Saudi Arabia, bin Laden's formative years were hardly straitlaced. He had a stable of horses at age fifteen and reportedly spent much of the early 1970s enjoying Beirut's nightlife, earning a reputation as a fun-loving, hard-drinking, free-spending pursuer of attractive dancers and barmaids. In 1974 he entered King Abdul-Aziz University in Jidda, completing a civil engineering program five years later. Politics to this point had held little interest for him, but that changed with the far-reaching events of 1979: Egypt and Israel signed a peace agreement, to the dismay of much of the Muslim world; Ayatollah Ruhollah Khomeini toppled the shah in Iran, inspiring Islamic fundamentalists elsewhere; and the Soviet Union invaded Afghanistan, a costly and unsuccessful venture that prompted comparisons to U.S. involvement in Vietnam.

There was some irony in the Afghanistan situation. It not only enraged Muslims such as bin Laden, but also brought about a momentary coalescence of interests between the resistance fighters and the United States—both wanted the Soviet Union out of Afghanistan. For its part, the United States, through the Central Intelligence Agency, funneled weapons and approximately $3 billion to the various Afghan fighters; for his part, bin Laden promptly set about raising money and providing equipment, much of it coming from the Bin Laden Group, for the jihad. More fund-raiser than warrior, bin Laden enhanced his operations by establishing a base in 1984 at Peshawar, a Pakistani town near the Afghan border.

By the time the Russians pulled out in 1989, bin Laden had come to a broader view of the conflict as a struggle between heretics and faithful Muslims. He had cultivated ties with some of the region's harsher anti-American critics, including Sheik Omar Abdel-Rahman, the Egyptian cleric now imprisoned in the United States in conjunction with the 1993 attack on the World Trade Center, and so it was easy to transfer anger from the Soviet Union to the United States. If nothing else, America's allegedly pro-Israeli policies were sufficient cause for bin Laden's contempt. But what of Saudi Arabia? It infuriated bin Laden when his homeland permitted U.S. troops not only to use its territory in the 1991 Persian Gulf War but also to remain there after the conflict. For openly criticizing the Saudi royal family as corrupt and as traitors to Islam, bin Laden was expelled from the country and renounced by his family in 1991, then stripped of citizenship in 1994.

Living in Sudan from 1991 to 1996, bin Laden pursued both economic interests and the jihad against the West. Apparently legitimate agricultural, banking, construction, and charitable activities commingled with support of military training camps and the so-called Afghan Arabs, those who had earlier fought with bin Laden against the Russians. Pressured by the U.S. and Saudi governments, Sudanese authorities asked bin Laden to leave in May 1996. Afghanistan became home to bin Laden and his four wives and numerous children, who enjoyed close ties to the Taliban rebels who seized power in 1996. A symbiotic relationship quickly emerged between Mullah Muhammad Omar, an Islamic fundamentalist and Taliban leader, and bin Laden. Whereas Omar needed money, bin Laden needed a safe haven. Since 1996 bin Laden has poured millions in cash and equipment into Afghanistan, shoring up Mullah Omar's Taliban regime. In return, Mullah Omar not only gave bin Laden safe haven, but also allowed him to use Afghanistan as a training ground for international terrorism. Further strengthening the bond between the two men was the marriage of one of bin Laden's daughters to Mullah Omar.

Although known to authorities in the United States and the Arab world, it was the 1998 attack on the embassies in Kenya and Tanzania that lifted bin Laden from relative obscurity to international renown. Since then his name, rightly or wrongly, has been linked to terrorist activities and plots around the world, including one scheme to assassinate then President Bill Clinton while on a trip to the Philippines. Islamic fundamentalists in Egypt, Algeria, Yemen, Somalia, Saudi Arabia, Chechnya, Kosovo, Kashmir, Bosnia, and elsewhere have received his financial help. In June 1999 he was added to the Federal Bureau of Investigation's (FBI) Ten Most Wanted list, and the U.S. government offered a $5 million reward. Such concern certainly seemed warranted, as two individuals suspected of having ties to bin Laden were arrested in December 1999 and February 2000 attempting to slip into the United States from Canada. In May 2001 a New York city jury convicted four of bin Laden's alleged followers for the 1998 embassy bombings in Africa.

On September 11, 2001, nineteen Islamic terrorists carried out the deadliest attack ever on American soil. They hijacked four American commercial airliners, successfully crashing two into the World Trade Center, reducing New York City's twin towers to rubble, and one into the Pentagon. On the fourth airplane passengers fought the terrorists, causing it to plunge into the Pennsylvania countryside, killing all aboard. Including scores of policemen and over 300 firemen, the death toll was estimated at more than 3,000. Suspicion immediately fell on bin Laden, and President George W. Bush issued an ultimatum to the Taliban—surrender the terrorist or face the military wrath of the United States. Given the intimate ties between bin Laden and the Taliban, it was implausible to think Afghanistan's current rulers would comply. Accordingly, in early October the United States and Great Britain, America's most steadfast ally, commenced bombing in Afghanistan to topple the Taliban and to destroy bin Laden. President Bush said in a televised speech to the nation: "We will not waiver, we will not tire. We will not falter and we will not fail." A taunting and defiant bin Laden was unfazed. In a tape made *before* but not released until *after* the attack, he thanked Allah for the destruction of September 11 and vowed that American citizens would never know security until "all the infidel armies leave the land of Muhammad." Taliban forces in Afghanistan collapsed in November in the face of the U.S. air assault and Northern Alliance offensive. To date, efforts to capture bin Laden have been fruitless.

Malcolm X (1925–1965)

Malcolm X, a convert to Islam and a member of the Black Muslims until shortly before his violent death, contributed to the development of racial self-esteem among African Americans while at the same time alienating more moderate black leaders and much of the white population. Malcolm preached a doctrine of African identification and black control of politics and economics in their own communities. He rejected nonviolence as a policy and called for the formation of a separate black nation in North America.

Malcolm X was born in Omaha, Nebraska, the son of Earl Little, a Baptist minister who became involved in Marcus Garvey's Universal Negro Improvement Association. This black separatist movement brought the elder Little into conflict with the local Ku Klux Klan. Angry whites burned the Little home in 1929, and two years later Little was murdered. Malcolm, embittered by his early experience with racial violence, was sent to a detention home in Mason, Michigan. Although a bright student, he did not receive encouragement from teachers. After moving to Boston to live with a half sister, he dropped out of school in the eighth grade. Working first in railroad dining cars, then as a waiter in a Harlem nightclub, Malcolm became involved in various illegal activities, including using and selling drugs, gambling, and procuring prostitutes for white visitors to Harlem.

An arrest in Boston in 1946 for burglary, which brought a ten-year sentence, changed Malcolm's life dramatically. In prison he learned of Elijah Muhammad's Lost-Found Nation of Islam (the Black Muslims) and converted to the group's strict moral teachings. Upon his release from prison in 1952, he changed his last name to X and joined the Black Muslims as a recruiter. In 1953 he became assistant minister of Temple Number One in Detroit, and in 1954 he was appointed a minister in Harlem's Temple Number Seven. In 1958 Malcolm married Betty X Shabazz. The couple had six children. Although Malcolm's popularity contributed greatly to the increasing strength of the Black Muslims in the African American community, other leaders in the movement criticized him, claiming he was attempting to assume control of the organization. By 1961 Malcolm had begun to have reservations about the movement. He questioned the Muslim strategy of nonengagement with white society and was dismayed by rumors of Elijah Muhammad's sexual escapades with secretaries. In 1964 Malcolm left the organization.

On a 1964 tour of the holy city of Mecca and other locations in the Middle East, including Egypt, Lebanon, Morocco, and Algeria, Malcolm met white members of the Islamic faith who appeared to be racially unprejudiced. This prompted him to modify his racial views upon returning to the United States. Recent experiences, he explained, had taught him that racism was not inherent in whites, but rather was a result of Western culture. In June 1964 he established the Organization of Afro-American Unity, patterned after the Organization of African Unity. Malcolm, who began calling himself El-Hajj Malik El-Shabazz, called for unity among black leaders, but achieved few positive results in a movement fragmented by widely varying beliefs and tactics. In February 1965 his home was fire-bombed, and soon thereafter he was shot and killed at the Audubon Ballroom in Harlem. Three individuals, including two members of the Black Muslims, were convicted and sentenced to life terms for the assassination.

Evidence did not indicate whether these individuals were members of a larger conspiracy.

Maulana Sayyid Abul Ala Mawdudi (1903–1979)

A noted journalist, charismatic leader, superb orator, skilled politician, and renowned scholar, Abul Ala Mawdudi was determined to make Islam the ultimate code of conduct for social, economic, and political behavior. More than any other twentieth-century Muslim thinker, he found in Islam rules for virtually all aspects of life, as seen in numerous terms of his minting: "Islamic politics," "the Islamic system of life," "the economic system of Islam," "the political system of Islam," "the Islamic constitution," and "Islamic ideology." Best known today as an author, he wrote on the Qur'an, the sayings and actions of the Prophet Muhammad, and Islamic law, philosophy, economics, social relations, and political theory. In essence, Mawdudi was an indefatigable promoter of Islam as an alternative to Western culture and Soviet-style Marxism.

Born in India, educated primarily at home by tutors and his father, a British-trained lawyer who detested English schooling, Mawdudi studied Islam mainly on his own and had learned by age sixteen to read Arabic, Persian, and English. A career in journalism began in 1920, and he soon became the editor of Delhi's most outspoken anti-British Muslim daily, *Jamiyat*. Like Mohandas Gandhi, the noted Indian Hindu leader, Mawdudi sought an end to British colonialism in the subcontinent, but he was unenthusiastic about Gandhi's dream of a united Hindu-Muslim nation. So when *Jamiyat* identified itself too closely with Gandhi's position, Mawdudi left that paper and in 1933 took the helm of a monthly publication, *Tarjuman-al-Qur'an*, an editorial post he held for the rest of his life. Mawdudi had already attracted considerable attention by this time with a work entitled *Al-Jihad fil Islam*, a forthright expression of Islamic teaching on war and peace. Now, through the *Tarjuman-al-Qur'an*, he aggressively proclaimed Islam's superiority to all Western thought. Becoming a major voice for what Westerners would call Islamic fundamentalism, Mawdudi increasingly called for a society based upon the divine laws of the Qur'an, a society in which all economic, social, and political institutions would be subordinate to and in harmony with the sovereign principles of Islam.

Mawdudi not only offered an intellectually respectable rationale for a Muslim social order but also founded in August 1941 the Jamaat-e-Islami to assist in bringing it about. This organization coincided with the emergence of a popular nationalistic movement headed by Mohammad Ali Jinnah, Gandhi's nemesis, to make Pakistan an independent Muslim state. Although Mawdudi did not oppose, neither did he applaud the creation of a Pakistani nation. He had serious misgivings about, first, the would-be secular rulers of the new country and, second, Pakistani nationalism, viewing it as a corruption of the universalism of Islam. Significantly, it was at this time that Mawdudi began his most notable study, *Toward Understanding the Qur'an*, which emphasized the universal character of Islam.

After Pakistan became an independent nation in August 1947, Mawdudi moved to Lahore, a city in the western part of the country, and from there launched a vigorous drive to make Pakistan a genuinely Islamic state. Toward that end, Mawdudi wanted an Islamic constitution, one that would empower religious leaders to determine whether legislation was in accord with the Qur'an. This put Mawdudi at odds with Pakistan's more secular, Western-oriented political leaders, Muslims whose faith was tempered somewhat by Western notions of separation of religion and state. In the resulting tug-of-war Mawdudi was arrested at one point and held without trial for over a year, and for an extended period in the 1960s his party was banned. Even so, Mawdudi's followers were a force to be reckoned with, as evidenced by their dogged resistance to the secularism of General Mohammad Ayub Khan in the 1960s and to the socialism of Zulfikar Ali Bhutto in the 1970s. Although never able to gain political control of Pakistan, the Jamaat-e-Islami nevertheless gave powerful expression to the nation's more religious elements and forced the state to be more accommodating. Significantly, however, Mawdudi and the Jamaat-e-Islami, unable to have their way at the polls and never enamored of democracy anyway, had no qualms about using undemocratic means to achieve desired religious-political objectives.

Benjamin Elijah Mays (1895–1984)

A respected Baptist preacher, a distinguished educator, and a vigorous civil rights activist, Benjamin Mays was an inspiration to Martin Luther King Jr. Of humble origins, he was born to tenant-farming parents in Epworth, South Carolina. In 1920 he graduated Phi Beta Kappa from Bates College in Lewiston, Maine. While studying religion and sociology at the University of

Chicago, from which he obtained a masters degree in 1925 and eventually a doctorate, Mays became an ordained Baptist minister. As president of the Tampa Urban League, he spent two years in Florida, 1926–1928; and as the national student secretary of the Young Men's Christian Association, he went to New York in 1928. In 1930 Mays began scrutinizing African American church history for the New York Institute of Social and Religious Research. This led to publication of a major sociological study, *The Negro's Church* (1933). As dean of the Howard University School of Religion, Mays moved to Washington, D.C., in 1934. Four years later *The Negro's God*, his second important book, was published.

By the time Mays became president of Morehouse College in Atlanta, Georgia, in 1940, he was a nationally recognized scholar. Theologians Reinhold Niebuhr and Paul Tillich held him in such high regard that they included him in a group to discuss contemporary issues of God and mankind. In twenty-seven years at the helm, Mays transformed Morehouse from an acceptable black school into a highly respected academic institution. The percentage of faculty members holding doctoral degrees increased from 8 to 25 percent; the number of international students rose significantly; the Southern Association of Colleges and Schools awarded full accreditation in 1957; and a Phi Beta Kappa chapter was established in 1968, crowning a fourteen-year effort.

While seeking to provide a first-rate education for students at Morehouse, Mays simultaneously endeavored to expand opportunities for African Americans in all areas of life. Segregation offended him, and he criticized it frequently. Chapel attendance was compulsory at Morehouse, and Mays addressed students at these services each Tuesday morning. One youngster particularly impressed by the president's remarks was Martin Luther King Jr., who enrolled in September 1944. Mays became a mentor of sorts to the serious-minded King, whose father, Martin Luther King Sr., was not only pastor of the prestigious Ebenezer Baptist Church in Atlanta but also a Morehouse trustee. After King Jr. decided to enter the ministry, he wanted to follow in President Mays's footsteps by obtaining advanced degrees. King Sr. saw no need for additional schooling, preferring instead that his talented son join him as copastor at Ebenezer. Mays interceded, persuading the elder King to acquiesce in his son's academic aspirations.

King's subsequent prominence in the civil rights movement added stature to Morehouse and Mays. Becoming something of an unofficial adviser to his former student, Mays often shared the stage with King. It was Mays who offered the benediction after

King's "I Have a Dream" speech in the nation's capital and who stood with King in efforts to desegregate Atlanta. And, appropriately, it was also Mays who delivered the eulogy at King's funeral in April 1968. Some of his remarks were particularly barbed, taking the public to task for creating an atmosphere of hate. "We all pray that the assassin will be apprehended," he said. "But make no mistake, the American people are in part responsible for Martin Luther King Jr.'s death. The assassin heard enough condemnation of King and of Negroes to feel that he had public support. He knew that millions hated King." Mays concluded that "Morehouse College will never be the same because Martin Luther came here; and the nation and the world will be indebted to him for centuries to come." Continuing his own efforts to desegregate Atlanta, Mays eventually became the first African American president of that city's school board.

Sun Myung Moon (1920–)

A Korean evangelist and founder of the Holy Spirit Association for the Unification of World Christianity, popularly known as the Unification Church, Sun Myung Moon has supported right-wing political causes around the globe, particularly those seeking to stem the growth of communism and to enhance free enterprise. Born in what is now North Korea, Moon grew to maturity during the tumultuous era of World War II. His family converted to Christianity, becoming Presbyterians, and in 1935 the youthful Moon allegedly had a vision instructing him to fulfill the unfinished ministry of Jesus. At that time Korean Pentecostals anticipated the appearance of a Korean Messiah, thus adding significance to Moon's claim. Politics momentarily took precedence over religion, however, as Moon joined efforts to free Korea from Japan. He was subsequently arrested by the Japanese in 1944, then by the North Korean communist regime of Kim Il Sung for much of 1946–1950. Disagreement shrouds this latter period of incarceration. Whereas Moon supporters point to courageous resistance of communism, critics allude to immoral behavior. The one certainty to emerge from the decade commencing in 1945 was Moon's growing religious involvement.

Beginning his ministry with a few followers in 1945, Moon established the Broad Sea Church two years later, about the time he changed his name from Yong Myung Moon to Sun Myung Moon, meaning one who clarified truth. In 1954 he founded the Unification Church in Seoul and three years later published *Di-*

vine Principle, an interpretation of the Bible filtered through Eastern, primarily Buddhist, thought. Making little distinction between heavenly and earthly spheres, Moon easily foresaw the possibility of achieving perfection in this life. Because of disobedience, Adam and Eve had lost their opportunity to bring about worldly perfection; and Jesus, whose resurrection made possible spiritual perfection in a life to come, was killed before he could create a temporal paradise. Thus, another Messiah was yet to come who would complete God's mission on earth. This would be a perfect world, one without sin or evil, one where humans would live in peace. Moon found in the Lord's Prayer scriptural basis for such belief: "Thy Kingdom come on earth as in Heaven." The return of Christ was expected to occur in Korea, for that country, divided at the thirty-eighth parallel between the democratic South and communist North, symbolized the confrontation between good and evil. Is Moon the new Christ who will bring this about? He has never expressly claimed to be, but many of his followers have made the claim for him.

Since coming to the United States in 1971, Moon has pursued his religious and political objectives through a multitude of organizations. To reach college students, for instance, he founded the Collegiate Association for the Research of Principles, which has been especially active in Latin America; to battle communism, the Freedom Leadership Foundation; to promote what he calls "true families," the Family Federation for World Peace and Unification and the True Family Values Ministry; to foster religious unity and world peace, the International Cultural Foundation, the International Religious Foundation, and the Inter-Religious Federation for World Peace; and to sway public policy, the Washington Institute for Values in Public Policy, a right-wing think tank that organizes seminars and publishes materials on contemporary issues. Moon aggressively advances his numerous causes through several church-owned newspapers, among them: the *Washington Times,* said to have been a favorite of President Ronald Reagan and other influential conservatives; *Noticias del Mundo,* a Spanish daily aimed at Hispanics in the New York–New Jersey area; and *Sekai Nippo,* a national daily published in Japan, where the Unification Church has been quite successful. Through such agencies and newspapers, Moon's critics insist, the Korean evangelist attempts to shape and influence politics.

Moon and his followers, contemptuously called "Moonies," have sparked considerable controversy in the United States, coming to exemplify to many Americans cultic behavior. This image is buttressed by the frequent presence of church members at airports and on street corners soliciting donations and by those mass marriage ceremonies over which Moon and his wife preside, in which thousands of young couples are wed. This popular impression notwithstanding, members of the Unification Church in the United States, though not numerous, have tended to be intelligent and well educated. Still, the church has been at the center of numerous lawsuits. Whereas it has consistently lost cases against the press for alleged libel, notably the *New York Times*, Moon himself was convicted in 1982 of income tax evasion and sentenced to eighteen months in jail. Because of such hostility, Moon has turned increasing attention to Latin America, where the church is currently building a major center in southwest Brazil.

Elijah Muhammad (1897–1975)

Elijah Muhammad, leader of the Nation of Islam (also known as the Black Muslims) from 1934 until his death in 1975, preached the precepts of black pride and personal self-discipline. He advocated black separation, encouraging the development of Muslim-owned businesses. The organization's ideology encompassed black nationalism, a belief in capitalism for African Americans, and a variety of socialism that emphasized community solidarity. By 1970 Black Muslims constituted the largest economic influence in the black community. The movement that Elijah led was able to reform drug addicts and criminals, bringing them into productive membership in the Black Muslim organization. The movement opposed the use of alcohol, tobacco, and drugs, and renounced extramarital sex, dancing, gambling, and all but religious music.

Elijah was born Elijah Poole on a Georgia tenant farm, the son of a sharecropper and part-time Baptist minister. Leaving school in the fourth grade, Elijah went to work in the fields. At sixteen he left home, working at various jobs around the country. In 1919 he married Clara Evans, and in 1923 they and their two children moved to Detroit, where for six years he worked for an automobile manufacturer and briefly became a Baptist preacher. In 1929, with the onset of the Great Depression, Elijah lost his job. At this time he met W. D. Fard, the founder of the Temple of Islam and the secret religious group, The Lost-Found Nation of Islam in the Wilderness of North America. Converting to Islam, Elijah changed his surname to Karriem, became a disciple of

Fard, and ultimately became the leader of the Detroit temple. In 1934, when Fard fled Detroit under considerable pressure from white law enforcement, Elijah announced that Fard had named him "Messenger of Allah" and changed his name to Muhammad. Since others in the organization refused to accept his leadership, Elijah moved to Chicago and ultimately to Washington, D.C., where he lived from 1935 to 1941.

Following the Japanese attack on Pearl Harbor, Elijah openly criticized government treatment of Japanese Americans and urged African Americans to refuse to serve in the armed forces. Charged with sedition in 1942, he was tried and acquitted. However, he was retried for draft evasion, found guilty, and given a five-year prison sentence. Following his release in 1946, Elijah returned to Chicago and became the unchallenged leader of the Nation of Islam. His religious doctrine included the claim that Allah had created nonwhite people, called the tribes of Shabazz. Allah then granted the white race, or "blue-eyed devils," the opportunity to rule for 6,000 years. Corrupt and inferior to nonwhite peoples, the white race would soon lose its domination.

In the 1950s Elijah and Malcolm X became close allies in the steady expansion of the Black Muslim community, but the two began to have differences in the early 1960s. Elijah disassociated himself from his heir apparent after Malcolm commented during a public presentation that President John F. Kennedy's assassination was an example of "the chickens coming home to roost." In March 1964 Malcolm left the Nation of Islam over disagreements with the organization's policy of excluding whites and refusal to take a stand on civil rights. After Malcolm's assassination in 1965 by men identified as Black Muslims, Elijah strongly denied any role in the murder. In the following years dissident groups challenged Elijah's authority, leading to disputes that sometimes resulted in violent confrontation. Elijah, in ill health, failed to end the conflict. He died of heart failure in Chicago.

Marvin Olasky (1950–)

To some Americans, Marvin Olasky is "the godfather of 'compassionate conservatism'"; to others, "a leading thinker and propagandist of the Christian right," or, more harshly, an overly zealous Presbyterian fundamentalist whose "historical judgements are so crude and pinched" they will most likely "buttress the stereotypes of those who are prejudiced against religious conservatives." One thing is certain, Olasky has the ear of President

George W. Bush, who said of the University of Texas-Austin journalism professor: "Marvin offers not just a blueprint for government, but also an inspiring picture of the great resources of
decency, caring, and commitment to one another that Americans
share." One detects in this remark the nebulous outlines of the
president's compassionate conservatism. So, who is Olasky?

An intellectual vagabond, Olasky has embraced at different
times sharply divergent philosophical and religious expressions.
His search for a worldview governed by explicit and discernable
laws led him from Judaism to atheism to Marxism-Leninism to
Christian fundamentalism. Born in Massachusetts of second-
generation Russian Jewish immigrants, Olasky, as he put it, "was
bar mitzvahed at thirteen and an atheist at fourteen." Entering
the American Studies program at Yale in 1968, coincidentally just
as Bush was leaving, he was soon immersed in left-wing politics,
protesting the war in Vietnam and championing the causes of
labor. He graduated from Yale in 1971, and from that point to late
1973 his life veered radically from one direction to another. He
married his first wife, took a job as a reporter in Oregon, joined
the Communist Party, and made a pilgrimage to Russia. By the
end of 1973 he had divorced his wife, abandoned communism,
and entered the graduate program at the University of Michigan
in American Culture. Not long afterward he met Susan North-
way, an undergraduate at Michigan, who would become his second wife in 1976. From 1973 to 1976 Olasky moved to the
political and religious right. Because his doctoral dissertation,
"Clean Pictures with Red Blood? American Popular Film and the
Adversary Intention," dealt with politics and American films, he
studied the classic westerns and was impressed by their strong
sense of right and wrong. He prepared a course on early American literature, reading numerous Puritan sermons in the process,
and he studied the Christian existentialists. In 1976 Olasky became a Christian. John Wayne and Jonathan Edwards had displaced Marx and Lenin.

A one-year stint as a lecturer at San Diego State in 1976–1977
was followed by five and a half years in public relations for
DuPont Corporation in Delaware. By 1983, when Olasky arrived
at the University of Texas as an assistant professor of journalism,
he had matured as a Calvinist, a Presbyterian fundamentalist,
and an outspoken critic of abortion and welfare. A prolific writer,
authoring some 200 articles and numerous books, Olasky perhaps would have remained an obscure journalism professor and
right-wing polemicist but for the opportune publication of *The*

Tragedy of American Compassion. Released in 1992 on the cusp of the "Republican revolution of '94," this work expressed the sentiment of many conservatives. Specifically, Olasky offered a rationale for slashing welfare and downsizing government, and doing it all in the name of family values and compassion. Instead of the "false compassion" of the existing welfare state, which doled out material aid without providing spiritual guidance or imposing discipline on the poor, true compassion nourished the soul as well as the body. "Faith-based" institutions, presumably having proven their superiority to secular governmental agencies, should receive tax support in order to advance programs for the needy.

Former Secretary of Education William Bennett pronounced *The Tragedy of American Compassion* the "most important book on welfare and social policy in a decade" and sent a copy to Republican Newt Gingrich, the new Speaker of the House. Addressing the nation as Speaker for the first time in 1995, Gingrich proclaimed: "Our models are Alexis de Tocqueville and Marvin Olasky. We are going to redefine compassion and take it back." That was a heady moment, and all of a sudden Olasky was a celebrity to the religious and political right, a frequent guest on television talk shows and a favorite of newspaper reporters. Of course, critics (and there were many) argued it would be impossible for private, religious-based charities to meet all the needs of destitute Americans. After all, government programs to help the poor had emerged earlier in the century in part because of the inability of private charity to meet such vast needs. Critics therefore believed Olasky's ideas were being used by cynical conservative politicians primarily to dismantle various social programs. If such censure bothered him, it was not apparent in Olasky's most recent book, *Compassionate Conservatism* (2000), for which Bush wrote the foreword. Although Olasky is much more intensely evangelistic than Bush, always seizing the opportunity to proselytize, the two men hold comparable views on welfare and the relative importance of religion and government in helping the poor. That alone ensures Olasky's continued prominence for the near future.

Adam Clayton Powell Jr. (1908–1972)

Pastor of the Abyssinian Baptist Church in Harlem from 1937 to 1971 and U.S. representative from 1945 to 1967, Adam Clayton Powell Jr. was a flamboyant African American religious leader and highly controversial politician. He became active in politics at a time when segregation was still accepted in many parts of the country, including the nation's capital. His position as a religious leader provided him a strong political base from which to challenge a discriminatory social, economic, and political system and to advocate social and political reform.

Born in New Haven, Connecticut, in 1908, Powell moved with his family to New York, where his father became pastor of the Abyssinian Baptist Church. Following an unproductive year at City University of New York, he transferred to Colgate University. Graduating in 1930, he spent a year at Union Theological Seminary. This was a dissatisfying experience, and so he moved on to the Teachers College of Columbia University and received a masters degree in 1932. After succeeding his father as pastor of Abyssinian Baptist, Powell entered politics, becoming New York's first black city councilmember in 1941. Reapportionment created a majority black congressional district, and he was elected as the first African American representative from the northeast. Having already led protests against discrimination in Harlem in the 1930s, Powell began speaking out for equal rights and fighting segregation laws in the nation's capital. For several years the Harlem Democrat insisted on adding a provision to social legislation, called the "Powell Amendment," which would deny federal funding to any agency or district that practiced racial discrimination. Liberals favoring social legislation tried unsuccessfully to get Powell to withdraw his amendment, which was finally enacted as part of Title VI of the Civil Rights Act of 1964. Powell was at the height of his influence by the early 1960s, deserving much of the credit for maneuvering President Lyndon Johnson's civil rights legislation through the House.

During most of his tenure in the House of Representatives, Powell won reelection with little effort, mounting huge majorities against opponents. A careless remark in 1960, however, created problems for the representative. A woman in his district filed a libel suit against him for calling her a "bag woman" for illegal gamblers. She won a judgment of over $200,000, but Powell refused to pay the award and avoided all court summonses. Adding to his legal and political difficulties was a tattered private life. In 1933 he had married a divorced nightclub singer, whom he divorced in 1944 and replaced the next year with a jazz pianist. Chair of the Committee on Education and Labor, Powell gave his third wife, Yvette Diago, a staff position on the committee, even though she spent much of her time in Puerto Rico.

Yvette's paychecks were deposited in Powell's congressional bank account.

In September 1966 the members of the Education and Labor Committee limited Powell's authority as chair. He was reelected in November, but in January 1967 the House of Representatives refused to seat him. Although Powell was elected once more in a special election, he did not attempt to take his seat, turning instead to the courts. In 1969 the U.S. Supreme Court ruled that the House had acted unconstitutionally in excluding Powell from Congress. It was a hollow victory. Powell had regained his seat, but lost most of his power, having been stripped of seniority and chair of the Education and Labor Committee. In 1970 Powell was narrowly defeated in the Democratic primary. In 1971, in ill health, he resigned as pastor of the Abyssinian Baptist Church and moved to the island of Bimini, where he died a year later.

Sayyid Qutb (1906–1966)

A school teacher, a respected literary figure, and an intellectual leader of the Muslim Brotherhood, Sayyid Qutb has given inspiration to many of today's more militant Muslim groups in the Near and Middle East. Born in upper Egypt, he learned early from his father, who subscribed to a nationalist newspaper, to resent the British colonials who dominated the country until the 1950s. He attended a state primary school, then later enrolled at Dar al-Ulum, a college in Cairo that trained future teachers. During his student days Qutb breathed deeply of liberal ideals and joined the nationalistic Wafd Party, which sought greater independence from the British. He graduated in 1933 and throughout the 1930s was essentially a secular reformer. His stance changed in the 1940s, as Qutb became increasingly disenchanted with the West, a sentiment deepened by a two-year stint in the United States to work on a masters degree from 1948 to 1950. The technological and material success of the United States, Qutb believed, was more than offset by racism, licentiousness, and spiritual bankruptcy. Adding to this negative impression was Qutb's conviction that his host country was ignorant of and unfriendly toward Islam and much too supportive of the new Israeli state. So, given its own decadence, the West was hardly a suitable guide for the Muslim world.

Upon returning to Egypt in 1951, Qutb gave up his teaching career with the Ministry of Education, joined the Muslim Brotherhood, an organization left adrift by the murder of its founder

Hasan al-Banna in 1949, and pointed Egypt toward Islamic conservatism. Qutb and the Brotherhood at first applauded the Egyptian officers who in 1952 deposed the king, established a republic, and endeavored to expel the British from the Suez Canal Zone. It was a brief honeymoon. Colonel Gamal Abdel Nasser, who emerged from the coup as Egypt's dominant political figure, becoming prime minister in 1954 and president in 1956, was a secularist who had no intention of sharing authority with Islamic conservatives. A failed attempt by the Brotherhood to assassinate Nasser in late 1954 brought swift retribution. Qutb spent the next decade in prison, where he formulated an Islamic rationale for opposing nominally Muslim regimes such as Nasser's.

Although it had always been easy to attack the British, as well as the Egyptian monarchy, Nasser was another matter. Here was a popular nationalist hero, a Muslim who had freed the nation from the grip of foreign infidels. What objection could there be to a leader who had restored a measure of Egyptian pride? To Qutb, faced with torture in Nasser's jails and increasingly conservative in religious thought, the colonel, along with his socialist policies, was actually more pernicious than the British. Instead of creating a godly society based upon the teachings of the Qur'an, as Qutb believed a true Muslim would have done, Nasser had established a secular state in which sovereignty rested in the nation rather than Allah. This made Nasser guilty of *jahiliyya,* or rebellion against God, and justified jihad, or holy struggle by true believers, against his regime. Such an argument, expressed by Qutb in *Milestones* and other writings, furnished Islamic fundamentalists a rationale for identifying (*takfir*) and attacking false Muslims (*kafir*).

Although freed from prison in 1964, Qutb was arrested again in 1965 in the wake of another alleged antigovernment conspiracy. Qutb's own words in *Milestones,* practically calling for the overthrow of Nasser's regime, were certainly damning, and in 1966 Qutb and two brothers were hanged. However, his writings continue to influence Islamic fundamentalists, some of whom found in Qutb justification for the 1981 slaying of another *kafir* leader, President Anwar Sadat.

Ralph Reed (1961–)

From 1989 to 1997 Ralph Reed was executive secretary of the Christian Coalition, the most politically influential religious organization at that time in the United States. Reed was born in

Biographical Sketches **107**

Portsmouth, Virginia, and his early years were interrupted by frequent moves. His father was a navy doctor, and by the time Reed entered high school the family had lived in seven towns in five states. Upon graduation from high school in Toccoa, Georgia, he entered the University of Georgia. In the summer of 1981 a U.S. Senate internship took him to Washington, D.C., where he remained through the fall working with the National College Republicans. He returned to the University of Georgia in spring 1982, completed his degree, and then resumed his efforts in the nation's capital with the National College Republicans. With the approach of the 1984 senatorial race in North Carolina between Jim Hunt and Jesse Helms, the outspoken Republican incumbent whose political and religious conservatism made him a favorite of the religious right, Reed left Washington for Raleigh. He promptly founded Students for America and joined the fray in behalf of the North Carolina senator. Reed unquestionably loved politics; even so, he entered the graduate program at Emory University on a scholarship, obtained a Ph.D. in history in 1986, and anticipated a career in academia. Three years later he was the executive secretary of Pat Robertson's new Christian Coalition, a position he held until 1997.

Reed's fondness for conservative politics and causes was longstanding. As a youth he read biographies of the presidents, as well as William L. Shirer's *The Rise and Fall of the Third Reich*, which impressed upon him the power of politics. At the University of Georgia he was a College Republican, debater, and columnist for the school paper, *Red and Black*, a position he eventually lost because of his act of plagiarism. Always on the political right of every issue, Reed was a leader among campus conservatives by 1982. Shortly thereafter he discovered religion. This nominal Methodist smoked and drank until the early 1980s, whereupon he promptly put away cigarettes and alcohol and became a born-again, charismatic Christian. God and Caesar now became allies, as Reed discovered the so-called true meaning of politics. "I now realize," said the new convert, "that politics is a noble calling to serve God and my fellow man." Appropriately, his dissertation at Emory, which focused on the early history of church-related colleges, criticized some sectarian schools for sacrificing their religious heritage for endowments.

Although Reed supported Jack Kemp over Pat Robertson in the 1988 presidential primaries, the Virginia televangelist admired the young man's organizational talent and religious commitment. When Robertson formed the Christian Coalition in

1989, Reed became its executive secretary. Despite his affable nature and disarming good looks, Reed is a shrewd political strategist. One admirer aptly described him as "the Christian Lee Atwater," that hardball political strategist of the Ronald Reagan era, while another considered him "one of the main people responsible for the Republicans taking Congress." Friends and foes acknowledge Reed's determination to win, evidenced by an effort to broaden the base of the Christian Coalition, to make it more inclusive. To accomplish this task Reed has occasionally downplayed the primary concerns of many staunch religious conservatives—abortion, homosexuality, and prayer in public schools—in favor of matters calculated to reach moderates—taxes, crime, and education. The risk in such a strategy was that in attempting to be more centrist, Reed would offend the Coalition's hardcore base.

In striving to reach out to Catholics, Jews, and African Americans without alienating staunch religious conservatives, Reed has appeared at times to vacillate. While urging Republicans to tone down their harsh rhetoric on cultural concerns, for instance, he has at the same time given assurances that the Coalition's positions on abortion and school prayer have not changed. A measure of Reed's success at this difficult balancing act has been the growing strength of the Christian Coalition. When Reed resigned in September 1997 to form his own consulting agency, the Coalition was a formidable grassroots organization with a $27 million budget, chapters in all fifty states, and approximately 2 million members, although some critics consider this last figure greatly inflated. Century Strategies, Reed's new Atlanta-based firm, appeals to both religious and secular conservatives, supporting the election of "pro-family, pro-faith, pro–free enterprise" candidates to Congress. Numerous politicians promptly hired Reed, and results of the 1998 elections were encouraging but not altogether successful. Several of his candidates won, but the defeat of incumbent Republican Governor Fob James of Alabama by Democrat Don Siegelman was a major setback. Even so, Reed met with Governor George W. Bush in Austin, Texas, in 1999, and he played a major role, albeit behind the scene, in Bush's victory over John McCain in the nasty Republican primary in South Carolina in 2000.

Marion Gordon "Pat" Robertson (1930–)

A successful televangelist who aspired to the presidency of the United States, Pat Robertson has been this country's most prominent religious lobbyist. He was born and reared in Lexington, Virginia. The son of a prominent politician, Senator A. Willis Robertson, and a devoutly religious mother, the intelligent and charming Robertson seemed marked for success. A Phi Beta Kappa graduate of Washington and Lee University, he subsequently studied at the University of London, served as a noncombatant with the marines in Korea (1951–1952), and enrolled in Yale Law School, graduating in 1955. Although reared a Baptist, the youthful Robertson was not particularly religious, as evidenced by a fondness for women, whiskey, and poker. His habits would change in 1956.

Following a religious experience that was helped along by a staunch fundamentalist whom his mother respected, Robertson entered the Biblical Seminary, later rechristened the New York Theological Seminary, in New York City. It was at this conservative enclave from 1956 to 1959 that he became a charismatic evangelical. In 1959 Robertson returned to Virginia, purchased a television station in Portsmouth, and launched the Christian Broadcasting Network (CBN) in January 1960. Three years later, seeking to raise funds to cover monthly costs of $7,000, he sought to enlist 700 listeners who would pay $10 per month. From this emerged The 700 Club and later *The 700 Club* program, which deliberately copied the format of *The Johnny Carson Show.* Jim Bakker, a religious fund-raiser par excellence who later established the PTL complex at Charlotte, North Carolina, joined CBN in 1965. Bakker deserves considerable credit for the success of Robertson's telethons. By 1975 CBN had an estimated 110 million viewers, and in 1979 Robertson opened an impressive International Headquarters Building and CBN University at Virginia Beach. By 1987 his empire extended over 380 acres and employed more than 4,000 people.

Robertson's social concerns were virtually identical to those of other figures on the religious right. He opposed abortion, homosexuality, pornography, and the Equal Rights Amendment for women, and he encouraged prayer in the public schools and tuition tax credits for private schooling. Failing miserably in the 1988 presidential campaign to translate television celebrity into political success, Robertson nevertheless quickly regrouped. His pro-family, "values oriented politics" were institutionalized by the new Christian Coalition (CC), created in 1989. Heir to Jerry Falwell's Moral Majority, the CC embarked upon an aggressive grassroots campaign to defeat politicians, from school board elections on up, whose values were not sufficiently pro-family.

Reaching its peak in late 1997, the CC, following the resignation of its astute executive director Ralph Reed, has since declined rather sharply. In December 2001 Robertson stepped down from his leadership position.

Positions taken at times by Robertson have surprised if not astonished friends and foes. Two cases illustrate the point. In 1999 the televangelist, speaking on *The 700 Club*, announced that it was all right to assassinate certain roguish heads of state, a practice not only at odds with the preacher's professed reverence for life but also banned by U.S. policy. "I know it sounds somewhat Machiavellian and evil," Robertson confessed, but added: "Isn't it better to do something like that, to take out [Yugoslav President Slobodan] Milsosevic, to take out [Iraqi President] Saddam Hussein, rather than to spend billions of dollars on a war that harms innocent civilians and destroys the infrastructure of a country?" In October 1999 Robertson urged the CC to support Governor George W. Bush of Texas for the presidency in 2000. Practical politics more so than moral principle appeared central to this decision, inasmuch as Bush was much less forthright than someone like Gary Bauer on concerns dear to the religious right. According to Robertson, Bush was a winner, Bauer a "lost cause." With Robertson, as with many secular politicians, it would seem that pragmatism sometimes takes precedence over morality.

Randy Tate (1965–)

Critics once described Randy Tate, an intensely religious political conservative and successor to Ralph Reed as executive director of the Christian Coalition, as "the poster boy of the radical right" in the United States, a perception seemingly bolstered by the ratings of several special-interest groups. Whereas Tate's congressional voting record earned a zero from the Sierra Club and League of Conservation Voters, it scored a 100 from the Christian Coalition and National Rifle Association. Born in Puyallup, Washington, Tate attended Tacoma Community College and in 1988 obtained a baccalaureate from Western Washington University. Something of a political junkie, he was elected to the state legislature while in his senior year at the university, and in 1988 he supported the presidential bid of televangelist Pat Robertson. After three terms in the state legislature, where he became the Republican caucus chair, Tate was elected to the U.S. House, swept into office by the so-called Republican revolution of 1994.

Tate only narrowly defeated his Democratic opponent in

1994, but he acted as though he had received an overwhelming mandate to pursue the objectives of religious and social conservatives. He was a true believer who quickly caught the eye of House Majority Whip Tom Delay (R-TX), as well as Speaker Newt Gingrich. He worked to restrict abortion rights, eliminate the National Endowment for the Humanities and the Corporation for Public Broadcasting, repeal the assault weapons ban, prevent any increase in the minimum wage, establish English as the nation's official tongue, prohibit flag burning by a constitutional amendment, provide vouchers for students to attend private schools, and weaken environmental restrictions. Tate made the mistake of attempting to impose a narrow agenda lacking in broad public support. Most Americans, whether Republicans or Democrats, did not want a woman's right to an abortion eliminated, or environmental regulations rolled back, or the ban on assault weapons repealed. Opposed by labor unions and environmental groups, Tate, despite strong backing from the Christian Coalition and other conservative organizations, was defeated in 1996. The assessment of Tate's Democratic opponent was discerning: "Randy Tate will do a very good job of representing the Republican Party in the Ninth District. I'll do a good job of representing everybody in the district."

In August 1997 Tate, prematurely bald and looking older than his thirty-one years, took the helm of the Christian Coalition. Another run at Congress was an option, he explained, but concluded "after much prayer" that "this position affords an even greater opportunity to shape the future of America." Making family issues a top priority, the Coalition under Tate has opposed late-term abortions, sought the repeal of the marriage-tax penalty, objected to legislation according "special rights based on sexual behavior," urged the defeat of state gay-adoption laws, and supported efforts to allow inner-city parents to send their children to the best school of their choice. In 1998 Tate praised the U.S. House for its vote to impeach President Bill Clinton, then urged the president to spare the country more turmoil by resigning. Polls in late 1998, as well as the outcome of the midterm elections, showed that most Americans did not share Tate's opinion on impeachment and resignation.

Mother Teresa (1910–1997)

Of Albanian descent, Agnes Gonxha Bojaxhiu was born in Skopje, Yugoslavia. The youngest of three children, she joined the

Irish Sisters of Loreto in 1928 and took the name Teresa. This religious society had a mission in Calcutta, India, where Teresa assumed a teaching position at the prestigious St. Mary's High School in 1929. A capable young woman who served with distinction, she eventually became principal of the school. Teresa's years at St. Mary's were successful by the world's standards, and her reward for a job well done was material comfort. But she felt spiritually unfulfilled, perhaps even somewhat guilty, and in the later 1940s her life took a radically new departure.

In 1946 Teresa became ill, and while journeying by train to convalesce in the mountain village of Darjeeling she experienced a call to abandon material possessions and serve Christ in the Calcutta slums. She did precisely that, leaving the convent and turning her attention to Calcutta's slum children, who dubbed her Mother Teresa. But it was an experience with a dying woman in 1948 that led Mother Teresa to the labor for which she became world renowned—serving all the disinherited elements of Calcutta. From this point to the end of her life Mother Teresa's tireless efforts for the poor found reinforcement in a simple theology. She saw in all people a reflection of Jesus, and so by helping the needy she was helping Jesus. Put somewhat differently, Mother Teresa believed one served God by serving God's people, and serve God's people she did.

Supported by a small group of women who shared her convictions, Mother Teresa first organized the Missionary Sisters of Charity. Then in 1952 she began the Nirmal Hriday (Pure Heart) Home for the Dying, essentially a hospice where dying people could end their lives in dignity. Her selfless toil on behalf of the world's "throw aways" brought international acclaim, and in 1979 she received the Nobel Peace Prize. Although always an effective fund-raiser, this kind of recognition enhanced her ability to generate revenue for an expanding network of orphanages, hospitals, schools, youth centers, and shelters for lepers and the terminally ill. By the time of Mother Teresa's death in 1997 the Missionary Sisters had increased from twelve women in India to a worldwide organization consisting of more than 3,000 sisters in 517 missions in 100 nations. Small wonder many in the church regard Mother Teresa as a saint.

In one sense Mother Teresa was not politically engaged. Although assisting downtrodden individuals, for instance, she generally avoided political causes on behalf of the poor. In another sense she was quite political. A good friend of Pope John Paul II, she joined him in defending many of the church's traditional positions. Abortion was a case in point. Mother Teresa considered it an evil, and she condemned it as such. So, somewhat like the pope himself, her words did have political impact.

Desmond Mpilo Tutu (1931–)

Desmond Tutu, Anglican priest and archbishop, worked diligently to destroy the system of apartheid and to achieve civil rights and liberties for black Africans in South Africa. Although not an unconditional pacifist, believing instead that Christian theology sanctions force as a last resort, Tutu continuously preached a doctrine of understanding, compassion, and nonviolence. He received the Nobel Peace Prize in 1984 for his activities in support of democracy in South Africa. During the final years before his country approved a new constitution, Tutu joined other priests and bishops in efforts to create a just and stable multiracial society. They labored to curb violence between not only blacks and whites but also among differing black political factions.

Tutu was born in Klerksdorp in the Transvaal and grew up in a rigidly segregated society in which black South Africans were disfranchised, a society dominated by whites of Boer and British descent. Tutu first chose education as a career, but when the minister of black education in the mid-1950s declared that Africans should be limited to labor professions, he decided to enter the Anglican priesthood. Following his ordination in 1961 Tutu engaged in a number of activities, serving as curate in the Diocese of Johannesburg, studying in London, lecturing on theology in South Africa, and returning to London to work for the Theological Education Fund of the World Council of Churches. After returning to South Africa in 1975, Tutu became dean of St. Mary's Cathedral in Johannesburg. Rather than request government permission to live in the official residence, which was located in a white suburb, he stayed in the black-populated section of the city called Soweto.

In 1977, when police killed student leader Stephen Biko while he was in their custody, Tutu, then Anglican bishop of Lesotho, spoke out at the funeral against the repressive actions of the government. The following year Tutu became general secretary of the South African Council of Churches (SACC), holding the position until 1985. In 1979 he supported a SACC resolution advocating civil disobedience against racist laws. Because organized African political opposition was outlawed, the churches served as an important conduit for political protest. The white regime of P. T.

Botha responded with a dual strategy. To maintain authority, it strengthened the military; to appease black South Africans, it instituted minor reforms, including a new constitution.

In the mid-1980s guerilla activity increased, as did attacks by blacks on blacks who were considered collaborators with the white regime. Tutu deplored such actions, stating that if violent methods continued to be used, "I am going to collect my family and leave a country that I love very deeply." Tutu continued to rise in the Anglican hierarchy, in 1985 chosen the first black to serve as bishop of Johannesburg, and in 1986 elected Archbishop of Cape Town. He lived, without official government permission, in Bishopscourt, a suburb of Cape Town. Tutu and other clergy continued to protest the restrictive measures taken by the government, placing the church in the front lines of the protest against apartheid. In 1987 he was chosen president of the All Africa Conference of Churches, a position that added to his stature as a human rights advocate. He had become a world-renowned figure, promoting embargoes on trade with South Africa.

In 1990, after the government lifted the ban against liberation movements and allowed the release of antiapartheid leader Nelson Mandela, church leaders initiated a new role for themselves, attempting to promote peace among rival factions, particularly between the African National Congress and the Inkatha Freedom Party. Tutu appealed to all sides to seek a peaceful elimination of apartheid and to reach agreement on a new constitution. In May 1994 the African National Congress, under the leadership of Mandela, won the election, forming the first democratically elected legislature in the history of South Africa. At Mandela's presidential inauguration, Tutu prayed, "Bless this beautiful land with its wonderful people of different cultures and languages so that it will be a land of laughter and joy, of justice and reconciliation, of peace and unity, of compassion, caring and sharing." Appropriately, Tutu subsequently rendered invaluable service to his country's Truth and Reconciliation Commission, which gathered testimony from the perpetrators and victims of atrocities. The commission concluded its work in 1998, and throughout the process Tutu, true to his vision for "justice and reconciliation," labored to create an atmosphere of forgiveness.

Jim Wallis (1949–)

Preacher, writer, and activist Jim Wallis is an example of a person driven by religious conviction to use all his talents for the betterment of America's least fortunate citizens. Toward that end, religion has always informed and guided his political activism. To Wallis, religion and politics are inseparable. Reared in Detroit, Michigan, he grew up in a devout Plymouth Brethren family, one that took biblical teachings seriously. Yet, as a teenager Wallis discovered that his church was sadly lacking when it came to racism. "Why didn't" whites and blacks "go to church together?" he wondered, and why did the races live "completely divided from one another?" The failure of "the little church that had nurtured and raised" him to answer such questions pushed Wallis toward "a new home in the civil rights movement and the black community. There I learned," Wallis remarked, "from the illuminating oratory of Martin Luther King Jr. and the other preacher-activists of the movement, about the intimate relationship between religious conviction and political activism."

As a student at Michigan State University from 1966–1970, then at Trinity Evangelical Divinity School in Deerfield, Illinois, Wallis's passion for racial justice coalesced with the growing protests against the Vietnam War. Accordingly, he organized prayer vigils for peace and invoked forgotten biblical texts, activities that rankled some administrators and brought threats of Wallis's expulsion from school. In 1971 he and several other seminary students founded an international community committed to social justice and launched a magazine, *The Post American*, forerunner of *Sojourners*. In 1975 the Sojourners Community and magazine moved to Washington, D.C., where both remain.

With a current readership of about 80,000, the magazine, of which Wallis is editor-in-chief, focuses regularly on issues of faith, politics, and the American poor. But Wallis is no ivory-tower analyst proclaiming to others what they *ought* to do. Indeed, he lives out his religious faith among the destitute in one of the capital city's impoverished neighborhoods. "Jim Wallis, along with his family," noted one observer, "has spent the bulk of his life living in one of the poorest neighborhoods in the most violent city in the country—Washington, D.C. He is a white man in a mostly black world." And through the Sojourners Community, which offers tutoring and mentoring services, a summer Freedom School, and parental support activities, Wallis, as one admirer commented, "serves up meals, hope, and activism" for residents of the inner city.

Wallis's work has attracted international attention, and he spends considerable time today traveling, preaching, teaching, debating, and imploring pastors, business and civic leaders, and elected officials to join the cause of social justice and to give greater prominence to values in politics. Indeed, he spent the academic year 1998–1999 at Harvard Divinity School as a Fellow at the Center for the Study of Values. This afforded him an opportunity to lecture at the divinity school, the Kennedy School of Government, and elsewhere around the university on such topics as economic inequality as a religious issue, faith and politics, and ethics and public life. Wallis echoes many of these same themes in his books, most notably *The Soul of Politics: A Practical and Prophetic Vision for Change* (1994), *Who Speaks for God? An Alternative to the Religious Right—A New Politics of Compassion, Community, and Civility* (1996), and *Faith Works: Lessons from the Life of an Activist Preacher* (2000).

Looking upon poverty amid this nation's vast wealth as a serious religious issue, Wallis recently initiated Call to Renewal, a national coalition of churches, denominations, and faith-based organizations from across the religious spectrum—mainline Protestants, Catholics, Pentecostals, Evangelicals, and African Americans. Its ultimate objective is the elimination of poverty in the United States, and pursuant to that it calls for living wages for families, quality health care, educational opportunity, and affordable housing regardless of income. Although a Democrat who opposed George W. Bush's presidential bid in 2000, Wallis nonetheless endorsed the Texan's "charitable choice" proposal, seeing it as a helpful step toward the goals of Call to Renewal. Wallis was encouraged by the new president's inaugural address, saying, "I thought it was a great speech, both in tone and content," for it kept returning to the notion that "persistent poverty" was "unworthy of the nation's promise." If the president's deeds subsequently match his words, the Democrat Wallis will have no difficulty working with the Republican Bush to uplift America's needy.

4

Data and Quotations

Data

The following tables reflect the approximate number of adherents to, as opposed to confirmed membership of, the world's major religious groupings. This is a significant distinction. Among Baptists of the Christian faith, for instance, *members* are those who have experienced conversion and been baptized; *adherents* include not only such members but also their unbaptized children and an estimated number of other fairly regular participants who have not been baptized. Hence, adherents to a religious body always exceed, sometimes substantially, actual membership. Table 4.1 offers an overview of the world's largest religious groupings. It is easy to understand the evangelical and missionary zeal of various Christian groups, considering that some 918 million people are either atheists or nonreligious.

By percentages of a nation's total population, Table 4.2 shows the relative numerical strength of several major religious bodies in a selected group of countries. Such figures shed some light on politics, but they do not tell the full story. Islamic nationalism and religious fundamentalism are likely to be more intense, for example, in those countries whose populations are overwhelmingly Muslim. But one must be wary of easy generalizations. Afghanistan and Turkey, each having populations composed of 98 percent Muslims, present strikingly different faces of Islam. Afghanistan's former Taliban rulers created a rigid theocracy, whereas Turkey has been a secular state since the early twentieth century. Given India's overwhelming preponderance of Hindus, it would seem that Indians had no cause to fret over the relatively small numbers of Muslims and Christians. Yet, Hindu nationalists have voiced deep resentment toward Christians in recent years, particularly regarding missionary activity, and acts of violence toward Muslims have punctuated the subcontinent since the 1940s. In some ways the United States is the most paradoxical nation of all. It is a secular state composed of a towering majority of Christians in which public officials devote an inordinate amount of time to religious issues. Yet from prominent pulpits on the religious right the nation is regularly portrayed as something of a modern Sodom in which sin reigns and the righteous endure persecution. So, while the data in Table 4.2 are illuminating, it is necessary to probe more deeply to grasp the subtleties of religion and politics.

The value of Table 4.3 is that it depicts shifts in the religious composition of a nation's population over time. And politics has obviously been a causal factor in much of this realignment. In the area of the Levant now occupied by Israel, for example, the Muslim population was 83.3 percent in 1900. That figure plummeted after the creation of Israel in 1948, so that in 1970 Muslims comprised only 10.6 percent; and by 2000, 12 percent. Conversely, Jews in the same area represented only 8.7 percent in 1900, but 85.4 percent by 1970, and by 2000, 77.1 percent. It is likewise reasonable to assume that the decline of the Jewish population in countries such as Iraq, admittedly always quite small, has been due to the formation of the Jewish state and the resulting hostility between it and its Arab neighbors. It is also worth noting that the Christian community in India, while still minute in comparison to that of the Hindus, has grown in the twentieth century, a fact obviously disturbing to Hindu nationalists. And in Russia, the Revolution of 1917 and subsequent Communist rule took a heavy toll on the church, as Christians dropped from 83.4 percent in 1900 to 38.4 percent in 1970, and by 2000, 57.4 percent. It will be interesting to chart the effect of the collapse of the Soviet regime on future religious developments in Russia. As for China, Christianity, numerically speaking, has never amounted to much in that country.

Table 4.1
Major Religions with Adherents Estimated Over One Million

Christianity	2 billion
Islam	1.2 billion
Nonreligious/Atheist	918 million
Hinduism	811 million
Chinese folk religion	384.8 million
Buddhism	360 million
Ethno-Religionists	228.4 million
Asian New-Religionists	102.4 million
Quasi-Religionists	80 million
Sikhism	23.3 million
Judaism	14.4 million
Non-Christian Spiritism	12.3 million
Baha'i	7.1 million
Jainism	4.2 million
Cao Dai	3.2 million
Tenrikyo	3 million
Shinto	2.8 million
Yoruba	1 million

Source: World Christian Encyclopedia: A Comparative Study of Churches and Religions in the Modern World AD 1900–2000. David B. Barrett, ed. Oxford: Oxford University Press, 1982.

Table 4.2
Religious Adherents in Selected Countries, 2000
(Estimated percentage of total population)

	Muslims	Hindus	Christians	Buddhists	Tribal (Folk) Religionists	Jews	Non-religious, Atheists
Afghanistan(1)	98.1	0.4	–	–	–	–	–
China	1.5	–	7.1	8.4	28.5	–	50.3
Egypt	84.4	–	15.1	–	–	–	0.1
India(2)	12.1	74.5	6.2	0.7	3.4	–	1.5
Indonesia(3)	54.7	3.4	13.1	0.9	1.8	–	2.1
Iran	95.6	–	0.5	–	–	–	–
Iraq	96.0	–	3.2	–	–	–	0.2
Israel	12.0	–	5.8	–	–	77.1	0.7
Japan(4)	–	–	3.6	55.2	–	–	11.1
Laos	0.4	.01	2.1	48.8	43.2	–	5.4
Malaysia	47.7	7.3	8.3	6.7	3.4	–	0.7
Pakistan	96.1	1.2	2.5	–	–	–	0.1
Palestine	73.5	–	8.6	–	–	12.3	7.4
Philippines	6.2	–	89.7	0.1	2.8	–	0.9
Russia	7.6	–	57.4	0.4	–	0.7	32.7
Saudi Arabia	93.7	1.1	3.7	0.3	0.3	–	0.6
Syria	89.3	–	7.8	–	–	–	0.2
Taiwan	0.4	–	6.3	20.9	50.7	–	4.4
Thailand	6.8	0.4	2.2	85.3	2.9	–	2.1
Turkey	97.2	–	0.6	0.1	–	–	2.1

Table 4.2 continued

	Muslims	Hindus	Christians	Buddhists	Tribal (Folk) Religionists	Jews	Non-religious, Atheists
United States	1.5	0.4	84.7	0.9	–	2.0	9.4
Vietnam(5)	0.7	–	8.3	49.5	9.5	–	20.5

(1) In Afghanistan, 1.5 % of the population are categorized as Zoroastrians.
(2) In India, 2.2% of the population are categorized as Sikhs.
(3) In Indonesia, 21.8% of the population are categorized as New-Religionists.
(4) In Japan, 2.1% of the population are categorized as Shintoists and 29.5% are categorized as New-Religionists.
(5) In Vietnam, 11.3% of the population are categorized as New-Religionists.
Source: World Christian Encyclopedia: A Comparative Study of Churches and Religions in the Modern World AD 1900–2000. David B. Barrett, ed. Oxford: Oxford University Press, 1982.

Table 4.3
Religious Adherents: Change Over Time in Selected Countries

	1900	1970	1990	1995	2000	2025 (Projected)
China						
Muslims	5.1	2.6	1.6	1.5	1.5	1.4
Christians	0.4	0.2	5.7	6.5	7.1	9.2
Buddhists	12.7	6.6	8.2	8.3	8.4	8.5
Tribal (Folk) Religionists	79.7	26.5	28.6	28.7	28.5	28.6
Nonreligious, Atheists	–	59.3	51.3	50.7	50.3	48.1
Egypt						
Muslims	81.1	81.6	84.1	84.2	84.4	84.9
Christians	18.6	18.0	15.5	15.4	15.1	14.3
Jews	0.3	–	–	–	–	
Nonreligious, Atheists	–	0.1	0.1	0.1	0.1	0.1
India						
Muslims	13.7	11.3	11.9	11.9	12.1	12.2
Hindus	80.0	78.1	75.2	75.0	74.5	72.9
Christians	1.7	4.2	5.7	5.8	6.2	7.4
Buddhists	0.1	0.7	0.7	0.7	0.7	0.7
Tribal (Folk) Religionists	2.9	3.5	3.5	3.4	3.0	
Nonreligious, Atheists	–	0.5	1.4	1.4	1.5	2.1
Iran						
Muslims	98.1	97.7	95.7	95.7	95.6	94.5
Christians	1.2	1.0	0.6	0.5	0.5	0.7
Jews	0.5	0.4	0.2	–	–	–
Nonreligious, Atheists	–	–	–	–	–	
Iraq						
Muslims	89.5	95.3	95.8	95.9	96.0	96.0
Christians	6.4	4.1	3.5	3.3	3.2	3.1
Jews	4.0	–	–	–	–	–
Nonreligious, Atheists	–	0.1	0.1	0.2	0.2	0.2
Israel						
Muslims	83.3	10.6	12.3	12.2	12.0	11.6
Christians	8.0	3.2	5.7	5.7	5.8	6.9
Jews	8.7	85.4	77.2	77.1	77.1	73.8
Nonreligious, Atheists	–	–	0.7	0.7	0.9	

Table 4.3 continued

	1900	1970	1990	1995	2000	2025 (Projected)
Japan						
Christians	1.0	3.0	3.5	3.6	3.6	4.1
Buddhists	79.6	62.0	55.5	55.4	55.2	51.2
Nonreligious, Atheists	–	10.5	12.8	12.9	11.1	16.1
New-Religionists	4.5	20.4	25.6	25.8	25.9	26.8
Shintoists	15.0	4.0	2.4	2.2	2.1	1.7
Jordan						
Muslims	94.2	95.2	94.0	93.9	93.5	91.5
Christians	5.8	3.6	3.9	4.0	4.1	5.3
Jews	–	–	–	–	–	
Nonreligious, Atheists	–	0.2	0.3	0.3	0.3	0.4
Pakistan						
Muslims	82.2	96.8	96.2	96.1	96.1	95.7
Hindus	14.0	1.4	1.2	1.2	1.2	1.2
Christians	0.4	1.8	2.4	2.5	2.5	2.8
Tribal (Folk) Religionists	0.5	0.1	–	–	–	
Nonreligious, Atheists	–	–	0.1	0.1	0.1	0.1
Russia						
Muslims	8.9	7.8	7.6	7.6	7.6	8.3
Christians	83.4	38.4	55.3	56.5	57.4	69.5
Buddhists	0.5	0.4	0.4	0.4	0.4	0.7
Jews	6.1	1.7	0.7	0.7	0.7	0.4
Nonreligious, Atheists	0.3	51.3	34.9	33.6	32.7	19.7
Syria						
Muslims	83.1	89.0	88.8	89.1	89.3	88.3
Christians	15.7	9.9	8.4	8.1	7.8	7.7
Jews	1.3	0.1	–	–	–	–
Nonreligious, Atheists	1.3	0.1	–	–	–	–
United States						
Muslims	–	0.4	1.4	1.4	1.5	1.8
Hindus	–	0.1	0.3	0.4	0.4	0.5
Christians	96.4	91.0	85.7	85.2	84.7	80.3
Buddhists	–	0.1	0.7	0.8	0.9	1.5
Tribal (Folk) Religionists	0.1	–	–	–	–	
Jews	2.0	3.2	2.2	2.1	2.0	1.9
Nonreligious, Atheists	1.3	4.9	8.7	9.1	12.8	

Source: *World Christian Encyclopedia: A Comparative Study of Churches and Religions in the Modern World AD 1900–2000.* David B. Barrett, ed. Oxford: Oxford University Press, 1982.

Quotations

The quotations that follow offer a window of sorts to the wide range of sentiment found in any discussion of religion and politics. No one person quoted here, however, necessarily speaks for any particular group as a whole. The Dalai Lama no more represents all Buddhists, for instance, than did Ayatollah Ruhollah Khomeini all Muslims.

The Catholic Church and Human Rights

International cooperation is needed today especially for those peoples who, besides facing so many other difficulties, likewise undergo pressures due to a rapid increase in population. There is an urgent need to explore, with the full and intense cooperation of all, and especially of the wealthier nations, ways whereby the human necessities of food and a suitable education can be furnished and shared with the entire human community.
—Promulgated by Pope Paul VI, Dec. 7, 1965

Society as a whole, acting through public and private institutions, has the moral responsibility to enhance human dignity and protect human rights. In addition to the clear responsibility of private institutions, government has an essential responsibility in this area. This does not mean that government has the primary or exclusive role, but it does have a positive moral responsibility in safeguarding human rights and ensuring that the minimum conditions of human dignity are met for all. In a democracy, government is a means by which we can act together to protect what is important to us and to promote our common values.
—A Pastoral Letter on Catholic Social Teaching and the U.S. Economy, Nov. 13, 1986

China and the Karmapa Lama

I hope you will study hard so that you can make a valuable contribution to the prosperity of Tibet when you grow up.
—President Jiang Zemin of China, speaking to the young eight-year-old Karmapa Lama in 1994 (six years later the Karmapa will flee China to India)

China and the Vatican

The majority of these people were executed for violation of Chinese laws during the invasion of China by imperialists and colonialists, or were killed for bullying Chinese people during the Opium War or the invasion by eight allied powers.
—Sun Yuxi, a spokesman for the Beijing government, referring the Vatican's plan to canonize 120 Catholics killed in China from 1648 to 1930, Sept. 2000

The Church in Latin America

From one country to another [in Latin America] one can find not only different but sometimes entirely opposed orientations: for instance, in Argentina, during the military dictatorship and its "dirty war" (thirty thousand killed or "disappeared") against "subversion," the Church condoned, by its obsequious silence, the policy of the regime; now it calls for a "pardon" of the torturers and killers of the Armed Forces, and mobilizes all its strength against the real dangers threatening the nation . . . divorce. Similarly, in Colombia, the Church remains committed body and soul to the oligarchic system, and legitimates in the name of religion the war against atheistic communism. On the other hand, in Brazil, the Church denounced, from 1970 onwards, the military regime, and during the last twenty-five years it has supported the workers' and peasants' struggle for better wages or agrarian reform.

—Michael Löwy, *The War of the Gods: Religion and Politics in Latin America* (1996)

Creation of a Jewish State

His Majesty's Government view with favour the establishment in Palestine of a national home for the Jewish people, . . . it being clearly understood that nothing shall be done which may prejudice the civil and religious rights of existing non-Jewish communities in Palestine, or the rights and political status enjoyed by Jews in any other country.

—Arthur James Balfour, quoting a declaration of His Majesty's Cabinet, Nov. 2, 1917

The Land of Israel was the birthplace of the Jewish people. Here their spiritual, religious and national identity was formed. Here they achieved independence and created a culture of national and universal significance. Here they wrote and gave the Bible to the world.

Exiles from Palestine, the Jewish people remained faithful to it in all the countries of their dispersion, never ceasing to pray and hope for their return. . . .

The State of Israel will be open to the immigration of Jews from all countries of their dispersion; . . . will be based on the precepts of liberty, justice and peace taught by the Hebrew Prophets; will uphold the full social and political equality of all

its citizens, without distinction of race, creed or sex; will guarantee full freedom of conscience, worship, education and culture; will safeguard the sanctity and inviolability of the shrines and Holy Places of all religions; and will dedicate itself to the principle of the Charter of the United Nations.
—Israeli Declaration of Independence, 1948

The Dalai Lama

Change only takes place through action. Frankly speaking, not through prayer or meditation, but through action.
—The Dalai Lama, speaking to the Parliament of the World's Religions in Cape Town, South Africa, Dec. 1999

Superficially, there is some religious freedom [in Tibet]. But there are restrictions on serious practice. The Chinese want religious people to be patriotic toward the Communist Party. The communists destroyed Tibetan Buddhism. A religious person should be faithful towards the destroyer of religion? How can that happen?
—The Dalai Lama, interview with *Newsweek,* March 2000

Oh, yes! I think the day of our return [to Tibet] with a certain degree of freedom will definitely come. I will definitely see that within my lifetime, I think.
—The Dalai Lama, interview with *Newsweek,* March 2000

The Failure of Liberal and Conservative Religion (United States)

In a bargain for power, some conservative religious leaders have aligned themselves with reactionary political elements, creating a particularly bizarre and frightening marriage of religion and politics. In the most materialistic culture in history, conservative religion produces a gospel of prosperity. In a society with an obscenely inequitable distribution of resources, conservative religion defends the wealthy. In the greatest military superpower in the world, conservative religion advocates extending American hegemony and consistently defends every U.S. military operation.

In an already divided and polarized society, the Religious Right has drawn even firmer boundaries. It has been a white religion, fueled the backlash against women's rights, and turned

gross caricatures of homosexuals into highly successful fund-raising techniques.
—Jim Wallis, 2000

Polarized religious leaders have behaved much like their political allies. The leaders of the Religious Right were the virtual chaplains of the White House during the Reagan and Bush years. The conservative presidents were the headline speakers at evangelical events, and the television preachers enjoyed unprecedented access to political power, along with honored places at Republican national conventions. With the Democratic victory in 1992, many conservative evangelicals treated the Clintons (especially Hillary) as the Antichrist.

At the same time, liberal Protestant leaders glowed in their newfound access to the corridors of power. Diatribes against the government were quickly toned down in favor of a much happier relationship on "the inside." Most religious leaders would rather be invited to testify before a Congressional committee or have breakfast in the White House than be arrested for protest outside on the street. With few notable exceptions, the involvement of both conservative and liberal religious leaders in politics has left the ground of a genuinely independent and prophetic political witness largely unexplored.
—Jim Wallis, 2000

Falun Gong

I believe Marxism can triumph over Falun Gong.
—President Jiang Zemin of China, Aug. 1999

We must be fully prepared, with powerful countermeasures, for the bitterness and complexity of the struggle against this evil force [Falun Gong]. . . . This is a major political issue that concerns the future of the country, the future of its people and the future of the great endeavor of reform and opening up and of socialist modernization.
—Editorial, *Beijing Daily,* Nov. 1999

They won't let us practice, they are trying to crush us. We're not against the government, we just want the government to have peaceful talks with our master, Li Hongzhi.
—Wang Xiaoping, a Falun Gong member from Beijing, Feb. 2000

Li Hongzhi's claim that he doesn't take part in politics and doesn't oppose the government is a cheap lie. . . . The result will only be to make people even more aware of the sinister political machinations of Li Hongzhi and his Falun Gong cult organization.
—Editorial, *Beijing Daily*, Jan. 2001

Louis Farrakhan

Until Jews apologize for their hand in that ugly slave trade; and until the Jewish rabbis and the Talmudic scholars that made up the Hamitic myth—that we were the children of Ham, doomed and cursed to be hewers of wood and drawers of water—apologize, then I have nothing to apologize for.
—Louis Farrakhan, Sept. 1996

A decree of death has been passed on America. The judgement of God has been rendered and she must be destroyed.
—Louis Farrakhan, New York, Aug. 1997

I believe that for the small numbers of Jewish people in the United States, they exercise a tremendous amount of influence on the affairs of government.
—Louis Farrakhan, Chicago, Feb. 1998

Hindus and Muslims

You will find that in the course of time, Hindus would cease to be Hindus and Muslims would cease to be Muslims, not in the religious sense because that is the personal faith of each individual, but in the political sense as citizens of the state.
—Mohammad Ali Jinnah, inaugural speech as the first governor general of Pakistan, 1947

Iran

How long do we have to be subjected to this trial run of democracy, which has turned into anarchy and puts the Islamic regime at risk. How long do we have to stand by idly watching, with extreme sadness, what is happening in the country?
—Excerpt, letter from leaders of Iran's Revolutionary Guard to President Mohammad Khatami, July 1999

The people of Iran accept religion, but they don't want a religious government.
—Dr. Parvis Varjovand, former Iranian minister of culture who now opposes the religious hard-liners, Feb. 2000

Our people voted for freedom to speak, freedom to assemble, freedom to criticize, all these are inalienable rights of the people. . . . Our people voted for Islam, which has a clear definition, not for those who wrongly see themselves as the embodiment of a pure Islam, those who excommunicate or kill their opponents. . . . Nobody has the right in the name of freedom to hurt our religion and our culture. And no one is allowed in the name of religion to harm the rights of the people.
—President Mohammad Khatami, speaking to an assembly of municipal council members, May, 2000

If a system creates peace in a society by using force, violence and intimidation, it has secured a temporary peace in a cemetery in which people are nothing more than animated corpses.
—President Mohammad Khatami, June 2000

If the enemies of Islam and the Islamic system take control of the press or infiltrate it, a big danger will threaten the security and faith of the people.
—Ayatollah Ali Khamenei, Supreme Leader, Iran, Aug. 2000

Khatami was elected because the country was like a time bomb, ready to explode. People voted for him because they expected more freedom. He delivers speeches for freedom and peace, but we don't think he's done anything. This time many university students are not going to participate in elections at all.
—An anonymous 21-year-old Iranian student, Dec. 2000

[President Mohammad] Khatami is insisting on democratic reforms where ballots determine the fate of the authorities, while hard-liners believe they are sacred and recognize votes only if they are in their favor. Khatami is worried about a widening in the gap between the people who want change and the establishment that resists it.
—Sadeq Zibakalam, Teheran University professor and political analyst, Feb. 2001

There are those . . . who accept no change. Their God is their narrow and dark concepts that fight all the people's demands in the name of religion.
—President Mohammad Khatami, Feb. 2001

Islam and Women

I broadly distinguish between two currents within contemporary Islamism on the subject of women. In those countries where women have been on the whole excluded from the domain of public life (such as Saudi Arabia), the Islamists project a thoroughly conservative position. In contrast, in those countries where women have been allowed a degree of participation in public life (such as Tunis or Sudan), the Islamists have produced what may be described as a "mixed discourse"—and hence they express on a surface level a degree of identification with the changes in the status of women while remaining at a deeper level committed to the traditional position of *shari'a*. (Hence, according to this position a woman can be a member of parliament and take part in formulating legislation but still remains a legal minor.)
—Muhammad Mahmoud, "Women and Islamism: The Case of Rashid al-Ghannushi of Tunisia," in Abdel Salam Sidahmed and Anoushiravan Ehteshami, eds., *Islamic Fundamentalism* (1996)

Islamic Fundamentalism

The defensive rigidity of neofundamentalism therefore demonstrates its inability to incorporate modernity. It has been a long time since Christianity was Islam's other. Even if there is a religious revival among Christians and Jews, it is in no way parallel to that of the fundamentalists. The culture that threatens Muslim society is neither Jewish nor Christian; it is secular, atheist, and ultimately empty; it has no values or strategies, but it is already here, in the cassette and the transistor, present in the most remote village.
—Olivier Roy, *The Failure of Political Islam* (1994)

I define *Islamic fundamentalism* or *Islamism* as a militant and antimodernist movement growing out of a belief that Islam is simultaneously a religion (Din), a way of life (Dunya), and a form of government (Dawla). This definition contains three elements. First, the Islamic fundamentalists have a holistic concept of Islam. They believe in the absolute indivisibility of the three famous D's. This characteristic marks the main difference between them and the liberal Muslims, who believe that at least a kind of separation between Islam and politics is possible and thus make an effort to conciliate Islam with modernity.

—Mehdi Mozaffari, "Islam in Algeria and Iran," in Abdel Salam Sidahmed and Anoushiravan Ehteshami, eds., *Islamic Fundamentalism* (1996)

Islamic Ideal

The ideal Islamic society is defined as *umma*, an egalitarian community of believers. The political concept that expresses *umma* for Islamists is thus *tawhid*, "oneness," the negation both of social classes and of national, ethnic, or tribal divisions. All differentiation is inherently a negation of *umma*. At the very worst, this leads to *fitna*, a rupture, separation, splitting of the community: this, no doubt, is the supreme political sin. Which is why Islamist thought denies whatever may result from divisions, first and foremost the division of religious schools . . . but also the division between countries, ethnic groups, tribes, classes, social categories, interest groups, and so on.

—Olivier Roy, *The Failure of Political Islam* (1994)

Islamic Politics, Law, and Society

The day Islam gave a new concept of values and standards to mankind and showed the way to learn these values and standards, it also provided it with a new concept of human relationships. Islam came to return man to his Sustainer and to make His guidance the only source from which values and standards are to be obtained, as He is the Provider and Originator. All relationships ought to be based through Him, as we came into being through His will and shall return to Him. Islam came to establish only one relationship which binds men together in the sight of God, and if this relationship is firmly established, then all other relationships based on blood or other considerations become eliminated.

—Sayyid Qutb, "A Muslim's Nationality and His Belief," c.1960

There is only one law which ought to be followed, and that is the Shari'ah from God; what is other than this is mere caprice.

—Sayyid Qutb, "A Muslim's Nationality and His Belief," c. 1960

The fundamental difference between Islamic government . . . and constitutional monarchies and republics . . . is this: whereas the representatives of the people or the monarch in such regimes engage in legislation, in Islam the legislative power and competence to establish laws belongs exclusively to God almighty. The Sacred Legislation of Islam is the sole legislative power. No one has the right to legislate and no law may be executed except the law of the Divine Legislator.
—Ayatollah Ruhollah Khomeini, 1981

If the ruler is unacquainted with the contents of the [Islamic] law, he is not fit to rule.
—Ayatollah Ruhollah Khomeini, 1981

Between the sacred family space (the *haram*), the mosque, and the institution of the state, viewed as a simple instrument of Islamization, there is no structure for the social space, except through traditional or business solidarities, which are obviously not open to the young unemployed generation. In short, what prevents Islamic society from producing totalitarianism (its respect for the family and lack of interest in the social sphere) also prevents it from producing any true social framework: it rejects any space for conviviality and sociability, if only by the strict implementation of the separation of the sexes and, particularly, of the confinement of women to the house. . . . This puritanism is profoundly modern and urban, in the sense that the most rigorous Muslim peasant society (such as the Afghan *mujahidin*, who are as fundamentalist as can be) knows what it means to enjoy laughter, humor, song, and poetry.
—Olivier Roy, *The Failure of Political Islam* (1994)

Islamists from Mawlana Sayyid Abul Ala Mawdudi to Sayyid Qutb (1906–1966) to the Ayatollah Khomeini (1900–1989) have also been animated by the same concerns. Unlike the modernists, the Islamists have not sought to interpret Islam in terms of dominant Western values—at least not explicitly. Rather, they have sought to assert Islam's domination, to interpret modernity according to Islamic values. Discussions of the Islamic state, Islamic economics, or the Islamization of knowledge all have this goal in mind. Both the modernist and Islamist interpretations as intellectual endeavors have failed. Islamism, however, has proved politically potent, whereas modernism has failed on that account as well.
—S.V.R. Nasr, "European Colonialism and the Emergence of Modern Muslim States," in *The Oxford History of Islam* (1999)

Those who say that I am not Islamic enough should re-read their Koran. Islam is about inclusion, tolerance, community.
—President Abdurrahman Wahid of Indonesia, Oct. 1999

In Islam, there is nothing such as appreciating the viewpoint of a person if it is against Islamic regulations.
—Sheik Muqbel bin Hadi al-Wadie, 2000

The whole of the globe belongs to Allah and the whole of [Allah's] law has to be executed on the globe.
—Major Ehsan ul-Haq, commander in the Muslim jihad in Kashmir, Feb. 2001

We want to send the message that only Islam has the capability of bringing peace and stability in the world. The West has failed.
—Mohammad Rahim Haqqani, speaking in Peshawar, Pakistan, April 2001

Israeli-Arab Conflict

The Temple Mount is the holiest place for the Jewish people—the remains of the temple are there. It is not only my right but my duty to go there. Before I went to the Temple Mount, I discussed it with the police and the security services. They said there would be no problem.
—Ariel Sharon, Israeli hard-liner whose visit to the Temple Mount ignites a furious protest, Oct. 2000

We will avenge [Binyamin Kahane's] death. They have to know and fear that for every hair on a Jew that is harmed, an Arab head may roll. If they understand and feel this, I'm sure we'll have quiet, because an Arab is like his donkey. Both understand only force.
—Tiran Pollack, family friend of assassinated Binyamin Kahane, Dec. 2000

Osama bin Laden

Right now, we still see Osama bin Laden as somebody who is continuously planning and plotting to kill Americans. We see no sign of his threat being diminished.
—Senior Clinton administration official, July 2000

We believe that the biggest thieves in the world and the terrorists are the Americans. The only way for us to fend off these assaults is to use similar means.
—Osama bin Laden, 2000

The American government is throwing away the lives of Americans in Saudi Arabia for the interests of the Jews. The Jews are a people who Allah cited in his holy book the Koran as those who attacked prophets with lies and killings, and attacked Mary and accused her of a great sin. They are a people who killed Allah's prophets—would they not kill, rape and steal from humans?
—Osama bin Laden, 2000

The Nation of Islam (U.S.)

From its inception, the Nation of Islam has promoted a black-nationalist outlook hostile to mainstream American culture and politics. "You are not American citizens," Elijah Muhammad, its longtime leader, told his followers. . . . Malcolm X, his most famous disciple, contrasted the pure evil of America with the pure good of Islam, saying that an American passport "signifies the exact opposite of what Islam stands for." Continuing in this spirit, the group's current leader, Louis Farrakhan, threatened some years ago to "lead an army of black men and women to Washington, D.C., and we will sit down with the president, whoever he may be, and will negotiate for a separate state or territory of our own." On a 1996 visit to the virulently anti-American regime in Teheran, Farrakhan declared that "God will destroy America at the hands of Muslims."
—Daniel Pipes, "In Muslim America: A Presence and a Challenge, " *National Review* (2000)

National Constitutions

Art IV: The Senators and Representatives . . ., and the Members of the several State Legislatures, and all executive and judicial Officers, both of the United States and of the several States, shall by Oath of Affirmation, to support this Constitution; but no religious Test shall ever be required as a Qualification to any Office or public Trust under the United States.
—United States, 1789

Congress shall make no law respecting an establishment of religion or prohibiting the free exercise thereof; or abridging the freedom of speech, or of the press; or the right of the people peaceably to assemble, and to petition the Government for a redress of grievances.
—First Amendment, U.S. Constitution, 1791

Article 25: Subject to public order, morality and health and to the other provisions of this part, all persons are equally entitled to freedom of conscience and the right freely to profess, practice and propagate religion.

Article 26: Subject to public order, . . . every religious denomination or any section thereof shall have the right

(a) to establish and maintain institutions for religious and charitable purposes;

(b) to manage its own affairs in matters of religion;

(c) to own and acquire movable and immovable property; and

(d) to administer such property in accordance with law.
—India, 1950

Article 1: The form of government of Iran is that of an Islamic Republic, endorsed by the people of Iran on the basis of their longstanding belief in the sovereignty of truth and Koranic justice. . . .

Article 12: The official religion of Iran is Islam and the Twelver Ja'Fari school, and this principle will remain eternally immutable. . . .

Article 13: Zoroastrian, Jewish, and Christian Iranians are the only recognized religious minorities, who, within the limits of the law, are free to perform their religious rites and ceremonies, and to act according to their own canon in matters of personal affairs and religious education.
—Iran, 1979

Article 36

(1) Citizens of the People's Republic of China enjoy freedom of religious belief.

(2) No state organ, public organization, or individual may compel citizens to believe in, or not to believe, in any religion; nor may they discriminate against citizens who believe in, or do not believe in, any religion.

(3) The state protects normal religious activities. No one may

make use of religion to engage in activities that disrupt public order, impair the health of citizens or interfere with the educational system of the state.

(4) Religious bodies and religious affairs are not subject to any foreign domination.

—People's Republic of China, 1982

Article 14

(1) The Russian Federation shall be a secular state. No religion may be instituted as state-sponsored or mandatory religion.

(2) Religious association shall be separated from the state, and shall be equal before the law.

Article 28: Everyone shall be guaranteed the right to freedom of conscience, to freedom of religious worship, including the right to profess, individually or jointly with others, any religion, or to profess no religion, to freely choose, possess and disseminate religious or other beliefs, and to act in conformity with them.

—Russia, 1993

National Destiny and Divine Guidance

We are not a perfect nation, but we are still a free nation because we have the blessings of God upon us. We must continue to follow in a path that will ensure that blessing. We must not forget that it is God Almighty who has made and preserved us as a nation.

—Jerry Falwell, *Listen, America!* (1980)

If you look at the cultural war that's going on, most of what those who disagree with us represent leads to death—abortion, euthanasia, promiscuity in heterosexuality, promiscuity in homosexuality, legalization of drugs. There are only two choices. It really is that clear. It's either God's way, or it is the way of social disintegration.

—James Dobson, *U.S. News & World Report*, May 4, 1998

We believe that after 2,000 years of Diaspora, God has brought back the people of the Bible to the land of the Bible. . . . We're sure that Jews cannot agree to give willingly one inch of the land God gives us.

—Ariyeh Lipo, a young Jewish settler protesting the return of occupied land to Arabs, Oct. 1999

I believe our nation was chosen by God and commissioned by history to be a model of justice and inclusion and diversity without division.
—Governor George W. Bush, speaking to the Simon Wiesenthal Center Museum for Tolerance, March 2000

Japan is a divine country with the emperor at its center, and we want the people of Japan to recognize this.
—Japanese Prime Minister Yoshiro Mori, May 2000

Legitimacy of our Islamic establishment is derived from God. It is divine legitimacy that makes people's support meaningful. This legitimacy will not wash away even if people stop supporting it.
—Hamad Reza Taraqi, a leader of Iran's Islamic Coalition Society, June 2001

Religious Freedom

Everyone has the right of freedom of thought, conscience and religion; this right includes freedom to change his religion or belief, and freedom, either alone or in community with others and in public or private, to manifest his religion or belief in teaching, practice, worship and observance.
—Universal Declaration of Human Rights, Art. 18, adopted by the U.N. General Assembly, Dec. 10, 1948

Religious freedom constitutes the very heart of human rights. Its inviolability is such that individuals must be recognized as having the right to change their religion if their conscience so demands.
—Pope John Paul II, speaking in New Delhi, Nov. 1999

Religious Nationalism

Religious nationalism is a fact of contemporary life. Whether the issue is building, restructuring or maintaining a nation, the process is, all over the world, deeply infused with religion. How else are we to understand Northern Ireland, Israel, Lebanon, the Sudan, Sri Lanka, or Iran? Or, more immediately, how else are we to understand former Eastern European satellites like Poland or Bulgaria, or the so-called "Soviet Nationalities," such as the Ukraine, Lithuania, or Azerbaijan and Armenia? Nor, for that matter, are the developed countries altogether exempt from the effects of religious nationalism. The influence of the Moral Majority and related movements on American public life during the 1980s left no doubt about that.

—David Little, in *Peacemaking: Moral and Policy Challenges for a New World* (1994)

Separation of Religion and State

We hold it for a fundamental and undeniable truth "that Religion or the duty which we owe to our Creator, and the manner of discharging it, can be directed only by reason and conviction, not by force or violence." The Religion then of every man must be left to the conviction and conscience of every man; and it is the right of every man to exercise it as these may dictate.

—James Madison, Memorial and Remonstrance against Religious Assessments, 1785

Well aware that Almighty God hath created the mind free; that all attempts to influence it by temporal punishments or burdens, or by civil incapacitations, tend only to beget habits of hypocrisy and meanness, and are a departure from the plan of the Holy Author of our religion, who being Lord both of body and mind, yet chose not to propagate it by coercion on either, as it was his almighty power to do. . . .

—Thomas Jefferson, The Virginia Act for Establishing Religious Freedom, 1786

Believing with you that religion is a matter which lies solely between man and his God, that he owes account to none other for his faith or his worship, that the legitimate powers of government reach actions only, and not opinions, I contemplate with sovereign reverence that act of the whole American people which declared that their legislature should "make no law respecting an establishment of religion, or prohibiting the free exercise thereof," thus building a wall of separation between Church and State.

—Thomas Jefferson, Letter to the Danbury Baptist Association, Connecticut, Jan. 1, 1802

The Taliban

We want to make quite clear that forcing social groups to wear distinctive clothing or identifying marks stigmatizes and isolates those groups and can never, never be justified.

—Richard Boucher, U.S. State Department, May 2001, referring to the Taliban policy regarding Hindus

The Taliban leadership harbors the world's most wanted terrorist: Osama bin Laden.
—Nancy Soderberg, Deputy U.S. Ambassador to the United Nations, Dec. 2000

We are not against culture, but we don't believe in these things. They are against Islam.
—Wakil Ahmed Muttawakil, Afghanistan foreign minister, on the destruction of Buddhist statues, March 2001

We do not understand why everyone is so worried. All we are breaking are stones.
—Mohammad Omar, Taliban leader of Afghanistan, on the destruction of treasured Buddhist statues, March 2001

Archbishop Desmond Tutu

Our freedom is here, we are about to touch it and there are people who are jealous, who say no, they don't want us to be free. Don't allow them to take away our prize. Don't allow it. Hold on to one another! Hold on to one another! Say, "We worship a God whom we know is a God who leads his people out of bondage into the promised land." That is the God we worship. We worship a God who will lead us out of the bondage of apartheid, the bondage of division, lead us into the promised land where black and white and all of us will be just one family, God's family.
—Archbishop Desmond Tutu, speech in Soweto, South Africa, 1990

The Vatican and India

Just as the first millennium saw the cross firmly planted in the soil of Europe, and the second in that of America and Africa, so may the third Christian millennium witness a great harvest of faith on this vast and vital [Indian] continent.
—Pope John Paul II, speaking in New Delhi, India, Nov. 1999

Jim Wallis on President Bush

I'm a Democrat. I didn't vote for George W. Bush, and did not agree with the way this election was finally decided. But I liked the new President's inaugural address. In fact, I thought it was great speech, both in tone and content. Sure, it was only a speech, all the pundits tell us how unimportant inaugural addresses are. Many of Bush's critics are already saying he didn't really mean the things he said or won't do anything about them.

I say let's give him a chance, and even help him turn his strong inaugural words into reality. I'm also a leader of two faith-based organizations, and I think the nation needs a little faith right now—the kind that really does bring people together to find some critically needed solutions.

—Jim Wallis, Jan. 2001

5

Directory of Organizations

This chapter provides a sampling of various religious groups that have become involved in political activity. Included is a wide variety of organizations from differing religious traditions and with varying objectives and strategies, from advocates of peace to active participants in violent conflict, from more fundamentalist groups to organizations having liberal reform as their main objective. Some organizations are primarily concerned with remaking society in the image of their conception of God's will for humankind, and they employ the institutions of government to achieve their objective; others focus on a more general understanding of human rights and wish to limit government intervention in the area of religious belief. Some groups are far more politically oriented, approaching the status of political parties (such as the Bharatiya Janata Party in India and the Jamaat-e-Islami Party in Pakistan), while others can more accurately be considered interest groups (for instance, the Religious Action Center and the Christian Coalition International in the United States), and still others focus on more general principles such as religious liberty, morality in government, and the ethics of decision making. Certain organizations have engaged in important political activity that has had significant impact on national and international politics and therefore are treated in greater detail. Where available, addresses, phone numbers, and Web site addresses are provided. Organizations in other countries, especially those that are actively engaged in conflict, do not have such information readily accessible.

Acton Institute for the Study of Religion and Liberty
161 Ottawa NW, Suite 301
Grand Rapids, MI 49503

(616) 454-3080
FAX: (616) 454-9454
http://acton.org
President: Robert A. Sirico

Named for Lord Acton, the Cambridge historian, the Institute was established to "promote a free and virtuous society characterized by individual liberty and sustained by religious principles." The organization works with seminarians, those in the ministry, educational institutions, businesses, and those in the ministry to promote an understanding of market principles, economic freedom, and personal moral responsibility. Business people are considered important contributors to the improvement of the condition of the poor. The Institute conducts seminars and publishes books, papers, and periodicals that focus on religion as a supporter of freedom within a community with limited government authority.

PUBLICATIONS: Various books and papers dealing with the relationship between religion, morality, and the free enterprise system.

As-Sunnah Foundation of America (ASFA)

607A W. Dana Street
Mountain View, CA 94040
(605) 968-7007
FAX: (415) 968-2526
http://www.sunnah.org
Founder: As-Sayyid Shaykh Muhammad Hisham Kabbani

The As-Sunnah Foundation of America, with offices in England, Germany, Pakistan, Indonesia, and Malaysia, calls for the formation of a Muslim *ummah,* or a unified Islamic community, composed of Muslims from varied backgrounds. The organization supports scholars to inform Muslims about the need for unity and community

PUBLICATIONS: *The Muslim Newsletter,* monthly; *Encyclopedia of Islamic Doctrine* and other books on Islamic doctrine.

Aum Shinrikyo

This Japanese religious cult gained notoriety in 1995 for the nerve-gas attack at five Tokyo subway stations in which twelve persons were killed and 5,000 injured. Founded in 1987 by Shoko Asahara, a legally blind former yoga teacher, Aum Shinrikyo

("Supreme Truth") involves an eclectic mix of religious doctrines. The cult is based on Buddhist beliefs with various influences from Eastern and Western mystic traditions, including the writings of Nostradamus, the sixteenth-century French astronomer and physician whose predictions of future events have been subject to various interpretations. Aum doctrine includes religious perspectives involving reincarnation and Tibetan beliefs about extrasensory perception and clairvoyance. In 1989 the Aum was granted religious status, which according to the Japanese Religious Incorporation law, virtually excluded the group from government investigation and left it free to pursue whatever enterprises it chose. With such recognition came tax exemption. In six years the organization's net worth grew from $4.3 million to more that $1 billion and its membership grew to an estimated 50,000 worldwide. The group has expressed anti-American as well as anti-Semitic sentiments. In 1990 Asahara and twenty-four other members of the group ran for seats in parliament, but received little electoral support. At this point the group most clearly turned to extralegal strategies. A major focus of the organization was a predicted Armageddon. In 1989 Asahara published a religious treatise on the subject, titled "The Destruction of the World." In 1993 he again made predictions of a coming Armageddon, and in a video message made shortly after the subway attack in March 1995 he explained the Aum's role in Armageddon while denying any role in the attack. Following the attack, several members of the Aum leadership were arrested and placed on trial. However, younger members of the group not implicated in the illegal activities maintained the organization. In 2000 it was discovered that M Group, a computer software contractor established by Aum Shinrykio, had since 1996 been providing computer software to major Japanese companies as well as the government's defense agency. Officials took defensive action to protect computer systems against possible sabotage.

Baptist Joint Committee on Public Affairs (BJCPA)
200 Maryland Avenue, NE
Washington, DC 20002
(202) 544-4226
FAX: (202) 544-2094
Executive Director: James M. Dunn

The BJCPA was formed in 1945 through the efforts of four Baptist conventions, which decided to maintain an office in Washington, D.C., in order to defend religious liberty. Since the organization's founding, the committee has grown to include eight conventions, including American Baptist Churches in the U.S.A., National Baptist Churches in the U.S.A., Progressive National Baptist Convention, Baptist Federation of Canada, National Baptist Convention U.S.A., Seventh-Day Baptist General Conference, Baptist General Conference, and North American Baptist Conference. In 1990 the Southern Baptist Convention, one of the founding groups, withdrew from the BJCPA and channeled its efforts for religious liberty through its own Christian Life Commission. The Joint Committee supports separation of church and state, opposing prayer in public schools, federal aid to parochial schools, and a constitutional amendment prohibiting abortions. The committee provides testimony before congressional committees and regulatory agencies and, in cooperation with other organizations, advocates policy positions in agreement with its basic goals.

PUBLICATIONS: *Report from the Capitol,* ten issues per year, and *Baptist News Service,* a daily report about Washington, D.C., politics.

Bharatiya Janata Party (BJP)
Bharatiya Janata Party (BJP), which in Hindi means Indian People's Party, has its roots in Rashtriya Swayamsevak Sangh (National Self-Service Organization), a movement begun in 1925 that was dedicated to orthodox Hindu religious practices and opposed Mohandas Gandhi. The BJP is a direct descendant of the Bharatiya Jana Sangh, a party begun in 1951 to oppose what was considered the evil effects of Western cultural imperialism. Renamed the BJP in 1980, the party objected to the Congress Party's support for a secular democracy. The BJP opposes separate civil laws for Muslims, backs India's nuclear weapons program, and supports limits on foreign investment in India. This religious party steadily gained strength in the 1980s and by 1989 controlled eighty-five seats in parliament. In the 1996 general elections the BJP became the largest party in parliament, holding 161 of 545 seats. After electoral victories in 1998 and 1999, the party succeeded in forming a government with Atal Bihari Vajpayee as prime minister. Along with softening his party's nationalist and anti-Muslim rhetoric, Vajpayee has called for free-market reforms, the elimination of the system of untouchability, and the guarantee of women's rights. However, he has continued India's movement toward becoming a nuclear power.

Buddhist Peace Fellowship (BPF)
P.O. Box 4650
Berkeley, CA 94704
(510) 655-6169
FAX: (510) 655-1369
http://www.bpf.org
Director: Alan Senauke

Founded in 1978, the BPF attempts to contribute to the analysis and solution of various social problems through the employment of the Buddhist teachings of wisdom and compassion. The organization supports nonviolent change, promotes the protection of human rights, works for economic justice and the elimination of poverty, advocates racial and gender equality, and calls for protecting the natural environment. Part of the Fellowship's activities is The Prison Project, a religious and educational ministry in the criminal justice system.

PUBLICATIONS: *Turning Wheel,* a quarterly journal.

Catholic League for Religious and Civil Rights (CLRCR)
1011 First Avenue
New York, NY 10022
(212) 371-3191
FAX: (212) 371-3394
President: William Donohue

Reverend Virgil Blum, S.J., established the Catholic League in 1973 and served as its president for several years. With approximately 17,000 members and chapters in ten states, the Catholic League strives to protect the religious freedoms guaranteed in the First Amendment. The organization has used litigation to defend the right of religious worship, the right to maintain religious beliefs without government intervention, and the rights of parents to determine the kind of education their children receive. Particularly, the organization provides information about Catholic schools.

PUBLICATIONS: *Catholic League Newsletter,* a monthly publication.

Center for Public Justice (CPJ)
2444 Solomons Island Road
Annapolis, MD 21401
(410) 571-6300
FAX: (410) 571-6365
http://cpjustice.org
Executive Director: James W. Skillen

Founded in 1969, the CPJ strives to further the rights of religious and ethnic groups in the United States and supports a proportional representation electoral system. Organization members believe that the work and life of Jesus Christ serve as a model for justice and that biblical revelation should guide just relations among people. The organization performs an education role on public policy issues, such as welfare, and the executive director has performed a lobbying role, testifying before congressional committees.

PUBLICATIONS: *Public Justice Report*, a quarterly magazine for policymakers and educators, and reports on public policy issues.

Center for Religious Freedom (CRF)
1319 18th Street NW
Washington, DC 20036
(202) 296-5101
FAX: (202) 296-5078
http://www.freedomhouse.org
Director: Nina Shea

The Center for Religious Freedom is a division of Freedom House, an organization established in 1941 by Eleanor Roosevelt and Wendell Wilkie to oppose Nazism and communism in Europe. The Center was established in 1986 to defend individuals and groups against religious persecution around the world. Presently the organization is leading an effort to assist Christians who are being persecuted anywhere in the world, publicizing alleged cases of mistreatment in the media and taking the issue before Congress, the U.S. State Department, and the president. The CRF initiates investigative missions and lobbies the U.S. government to act in support of religious freedom in such countries as China, Sudan, Pakistan, Saudi Arabia, and Egypt.

PUBLICATIONS: A bimonthly newsletter on anti-Christian persecution.

Center for the Study of Islam and Democracy (CSID)
P.O. Box 864
Burtonsville, MD 864
(202) 251-3036
http://www.islam-democracy.org
Executive Director: Radwan Masmoudi

The CSID was founded in 1999 to encourage the study of Islamic and democratic political thought. Holding that the topic has been widely misunderstood in the United States, members of the organization wish to clarify the nature of contemporary Islamic democratic thinking. Lectures on Islam and democracy are sponsored. The CSID focuses attention on the topics of individual freedom and civil rights.

PUBLICATIONS: Various lecture transcripts, summaries, and papers.

Center of Concern (COC)
3700 13th Street, NE
Washington, DC 20017
(202) 635-2757
FAX: (202) 832-9494
Executive Director: Rev. James E. Hug, S.J.

Three Jesuits established the Center of Concern in 1971 as a means of disseminating Catholic social teaching in the Catholic community and the general public. The organization focuses on the issues of peace, justice, and the environment, with an overriding commitment to the Catholic faith. More specifically, the Center has focused on education, women's issues, health care, the national debt, ecology, and Latin America, conducting research into these policy areas and developing papers that present the organization's policy recommendations.

PUBLICATIONS: *Center Focus,* a bimonthly newsletter, and various reports on issues that have been investigated.

Centre of Islamic and Middle Eastern Law (CIMEL)
47 Russell Square
London WC1B 4JP
England
http://www.soas.ac.uk/Centres/IslamicLaw
Chairman: H.H.J.Eugene Cotran

The CIMEL was founded in 1990 to promote the analysis of various systems of law in the Islamic and Middle Eastern world in order to contribute to legal stability and the rule of law. The Centre encourages interaction among Middle Eastern and Muslim lawyers, scholars, members of the business community, and government officials.

PUBLICATIONS: *The Yearbook of Islamic and Middle Eastern Law,* published semiannually by Kluwer publishers; series on Arab and Islamic laws.

Christian Coalition of America (CCA)
499 South Capitol Street, SW, Suite 615
Washington, DC 20003
(202) 479-6900
FAX: (202) 479-4260
http://christiancoalition.com
Executive Director: Randy Tate

The Christian Coalition of America, founded in 1989 by religious right leader Pat Robertson as the Christian Coalition, works to improve the alleged low moral standards in U.S. government. In 1999 the Christian Coalition was reorganized into two distinct organizations: the Christian Coalition of America, which is dedicated to voter education campaigns, and the Christian Coalition International, which acts as a political action committee to support candidates for public office who demonstrate high moral values and are willing to support the organization's policy agenda. The CCA opposes government funding of abortions, homosexuals in the military, legal recognition of homosexual marriages, and increased government spending and taxation. In an attempt to influence voting behavior and election outcomes, the organization has distributed congressional scorecards that provide candidates' positions on issues and the voting records of incumbents on issues important to the Coalition.

PUBLICATIONS: *Christian American,* a bimonthly newsletter.

Christic Institute (CI)
8773 Venice Boulevard
Los Angeles, CA 90034
(213) 287-1556
FAX: (213) 287-1559
Executive Director: Sara Nelson

The Christic Institute was established in 1980 by Jesuit priest William Davis and a group of Harvard Law graduates as a public interest law center designed to defend a liberal position on such causes as human rights, social justice, and personal freedom in the United States and abroad. Employing litigation as its major policy tool, the organization suffered a major defeat in 1988 when it lost a lawsuit against supporters of the Nicaraguan contras that the organization accused of being involved in illegal activities. The Institute was forced to pay court costs of over $1.5 million.

PUBLICATIONS: *Convergence,* a quarterly magazine; various reports.

Churches for Middle East Peace (CMEP)
110 Maryland Avenue, NE
Suite 108
Washington, DC 20002
(202) 546-8425
FAX: (202) 543-7532
Executive Director: Corrine Whitlach

Churches for a Middle East Peace was formed in 1984 by a coalition of religious organizations—including the American Baptist Churches in the U.S.A. American Friends Service Committee, Evangelical Lutheran Church in America, Presbyterian Church USA, United Church of Christ, and the Mennonite Central Committee—to encourage the U.S. government to pursue a policy of peace and justice for all people in the Middle East. The organization advocates peaceful resolution of conflicts in the region, limitations on arms sales, expansion of foreign aid, and recognition of the special status of Jerusalem. The CMEP supports both Israel's right to exist and the right of Palestinians to be granted self-determination. Acting as an interest group, members of the coalition lobby Congress and the diplomatic community.

PUBLICATIONS: *Middle East Advocacy: A Handbook.*

Council on American Islamic Relations (CAIR)
453 New Jersey Avenue
Washington, DC 20003-4034
(202) 488-8787
FAX: (202) 488-0833
http://www.cair-net.org
Executive Director: Nihad Awad

The CAIR was established to promote a more positive image of Islam and Muslims to the population of the United States. The organization strives to present an Islamic view of issues that concern the American people and public officials. In achieving its goals, the Council encourages increased political activity within the Muslim community in the United States and works with the mass media to form a more favorable image of Islam. It organizes conferences and seminars for those in the mass media, government, and the academic community to provide information about Islam.

PUBLICATIONS: *Faith In Action,* a quarterly newsletter; "Hajj and Ramadan Publicity Kits," for use by Muslim activists; "Actions Alerts," communications to local Muslim communities intended to initiate local response to public issues.

Ethics and Public Policy Center (EPPC)
1015 Fifteenth Street NW, #900
Washington, DC 20005
(202) 682-1200
FAX: (202) 408-0632
http://www.eppc.org
Vice President: Michael Cromartie

Established in 1976, the Ethics and Public Policy Center strives to elucidate and support the relationship between the Judeo-Christian tradition and the discussion of domestic and foreign policy issues, supporting research, publication, and conferences. The Center adheres to the "great Western ethical imperatives": respect for the dignity of the individual, individual freedom and responsibility, the maintenance of justice and the rule of law, and limited government. The organization states that it "openly and explicitly stands with religiously based moral values in addressing contemporary issues."

PUBLICATIONS: A quarterly *Newsletter* providing a summary of the Centers activities; *Conversations,* transcripts of seminars sponsored by the Center; books on various subjects of concern to the organization.

Evangelicals for Social Action (ESA)
10 Lancaster Avenue
Philadelphia, PA 19151
(215) 645-9390
FAX: (215) 649-3834
President: Ronald J. Sider

Established in 1978, Evangelicals for Social Action advocates the formation of public policy based on biblical principles and encourages churches and individual Christians to act in their local communities to bring about peace and social justice. ESA supports arms control, nuclear disarmament, stronger family ties, environmental protection, greater political influence for the poor, and expanded democracy and freedom. In the pursuit of the organization's goals, staff members maintain contact with officials in Congress and the White House, and provide information to its membership of approximately 2,000 and to Evangelicals generally.

PUBLICATIONS: *PRISM,* a monthly newsletter.

Falun Gong

In recent years this spiritual movement, also known as Falun DaFa, has gained worldwide prominence due in part to the efforts of the Chinese government to suppress its practice. Chinese Communist efforts at repression notwithstanding, estimates of the number of movement followers in China are as high as 70 million, with an additional 30 million worldwide. Li Hongzhi founded the movement in China in 1992. Although he left China in 1996, he still attempts to maintain his leadership position within that nation as well as throughout the world. Falun Gong follows the tradition of Xulian, which involves methods to cultivate body and mind in order maintain physical fitness and healing. Falun means "law wheel," Gong means "cultivation of energy and capabilities," and DaFa means "great law" or "universal principles." Although members of the movement deny being a religion, certain of its principles come from Daoism and Buddhism. The Chinese Communist regime, not willing to accept the existence of a group with independence from the official authority, outlawed the movement in July 1999, labeling it a threat.

Friends Committee on National Legislation (FCNL)
245 2nd Street, NE
Washington, DC 20002-5795
(202) 547-5795
FAX: (202) 547-6019
Executive Secretary: Joseph Volk

The FCNL was formed by the Quakers (Religious Society of Friends) in 1943 with the initial objective of supporting the rights of conscientious objectors during World War II. The organization, composed of an appointed committee of approximately 250 Friends, seeks to establish a society based on justice and equality and encourages government institutions and officials to be honest, thus creating a circumstance of high ethical standards. Among the Committee's present concerns are the protection of human rights, health care, refugees, United Nations activities, and treaty rights of Native Americans. The organization monitors the actions of the national government, lobbies members of Congress and federal officials, and encourages grassroots activities in pursuit of its goals.

PUBLICATIONS: *Action Report,* an occasional publication; *Washington Newsletter,* a monthly publication, and *Indian Report,* published three or four times per year.

Government of Tibet in Exile
Tibet House
1 Culworth Street
London NW8 7AF
England
0044-20-7722 5378
FAX: 0044-20-7722 0362
http://www.tibet.com

The Government of Tibet in Exile was established following a series of events beginning with the Chinese invasion of the country in 1950. For a time Tibet continued under the traditional rule of the Dalai Lama, but with actual control in the hands of a Chinese commission. The Chinese put down a 1959 revolt against their occupation, which began in part due to Tibetan concerns for the safety of the Dalai Lama. The Dalai Lama escaped to India, where he established an organization in exile. The government in exile monitors the conditions of the people of Tibet, fighting a public relations campaign against the Chinese occupation and attempting to maintain the legitimacy of the Dalai Lama's leadership among the nations of the world. For instance, the Dalai Lama met briefly with President George W. Bush in 2001.

Gush Emunim
The Gush Emunim, which means "the Bloc of the Faithful," is a fundamentalist religious group in Israel formed in 1974 that claims that Jews have a divine right to maintain settlements on the West Bank, the Gaza Strip, and the Golan Heights as legitimate parts of Israel. As a result of the June 1967 Six-Day War with its Arab neighbors, Israel had occupied additional territory that fundamentalist Jews claimed were a part of the biblical land of Israel. Although secular Israelis viewed the occupied territories as potential bargaining chips for future negotiation with hostile neighboring countries and supported Israeli settlements as a means of controlling the areas, religious elements in the population viewed the acquisitions as sanctioned by God. Gush Emunim, which became the most influential voice for those opposing any compromise, perceived the establishment of settlements as means of creating for Jews a more unified religious identity. Following Israeli agreements with Egypt in 1977 and with the Palestine Liberation Organization in 1993, Gush Emunim became a major opponent of Israeli laws and policies. The organization is not the most extreme Israeli religious faction, for, though the movement has equivocated over the question of the status of

non-Jewish residents in the occupied territories, other groups have supported the eviction of Arabs.

Hizbullah

This militant Islamic organization was established in Lebanon in 1982 with the assistance of Syria and the Shi'ite regime in Iran and has contributed to the intensity of the conflict in the Middle East. Islamic clerics head the group. The Iranian revolution provided the ideological basis for the organization, which has as its principal goal the formation of an Islamic republic headed by clerics. Sheikh Mohammed Hussein Fadlallah is the spiritual leader of the organization and serves as the primary *mujtahid* (interpreter of the law and formulator of rules and regulations). Hizbullah opposes alleged Western imperialism in the Middle East and attempts to eliminate the Western presence in Lebanon. The organization has continued the conflict, or jihad (holy war), with Israel, regarded as "the Little Satan." A stated goal of the organization is the total destruction of the state of Israel and the establishment of Islamic rule in Jerusalem. Hizbullah trains and maintains military forces in Lebanon, where its presence is especially strong in the Beqa'a valley, Beirut, and southern Lebanon.

Institute on Religion and Democracy (IRD)

1331 H Street, NW
Suite 900
Washington, DC 20005-4706
(202) 393-3200
FAX: (202) 638-4948
Executive Director: Kent R. Hill

Established in 1981 by a group of Protestant and Roman Catholic clergy and laity, the Institute on Religion and Democracy promotes democratic values within churches and in political institutions around the world. With a membership of some 1,200 clergy and lay persons, the IRD seeks to unite people of differing political positions, encourages democratic values in churches, and opposes the activities of U.S. churches to provide financial support to movements in other nations that are considered undemocratic.

PUBLICATIONS: *Religion and Democracy*, a monthly newsletter, and *Anglican Opinion*, a quarterly publication.

Institute on Religion and Public Policy (IRPP)
1011 15th Street NW, Suite 115
Washington, DC 20005
(202) 835-8760
FAX: (734) 423-6153
http://www/religionandpolicy.org
President: Joseph K. Grieboski

The Institute on Religion and Public Policy, an interreligious organization (including, but not limited to, Catholics, Protestants, Jews, and Muslims), holds the position that there is a positive role for religion, ethics, and morality in the formulation and implementation of public policy. The organization was founded to encourage interaction between religious, ethical, and moral thinking on the one hand and government, politics, and public policy on the other. The institute engages in inquiries about the relationship between religion and public policy at the local, state, national, and international levels. The organization promotes interaction between government policy makers and faith-based groups and charities. Among the issues of concern to the organization are international religious freedom, care for the elderly, conflict resolution, national security, and community renewal.

PUBLICATIONS: Various books and reports relevant to the concerns of the institute are available for purchase.

International Christian Concern (ICC)
2020 Pennsylvania Avenue NW #941
Washington, DC 20006
(301) 989-1708
FAX: (301) 989-1709
www.persecution.org
President: Steven L. Snyder

Founded in 1995, International Christian Concern is an interdenominational human rights organization working to protect the religious freedom of Christians around the world who are suffering persecution and discrimination. Recognizing that over half the world's population lives in countries where Christianity is discouraged, ICC assists through prayer and other means those Christians the organization believes are suffering persecution. The organization strives to increase public awareness of such persecution and to gain the support of the American population and government in improving the condition of Christians in other countries. ICC conducts research intended to

develop policies that will promote religious freedom as a fundamental human right.

PUBLICATIONS: *Concern,* a newsletter.

Islamic Jihad (IJ)

There are several organizations in various countries, such as
Egypt, Jordan, and Yemen, that have the name "Islamic Jihad,"
but the group often identified as the largest and most influential
is the Islamic Jihad movement in Palestine, which is led by Fathi
Shaqaqi and Abdul-Aziz Odeh. In 1988 Israel deported Shaqaqi
and Odeh from the Gaza Strip to Lebanon. Contributing to the
formation of the organization was the influence of the Egyptian
Jihad and the noted Egyptian Islamist Sayyid Qutb. Several of
Jihad's leaders, including Shaqaqi and Odeh, had been students
in Egypt when the organization was first established in that
country. Another influence on the formation of the Islamic Jihad
in Palestine was the success of the Islamic revolution in Iran. In
fact, the Islamic Jihad was established in Palestine in 1979, the
same year as the Iranian revolution. The Islamic Jihad emphasizes military resistance to Israeli occupation (jihad meaning
"holy war") rather than political activity. The organization dis-
tinguishes itself from the Palestine Liberation Organization, a
largely secular movement. For the Jihad, the cause of Palestinian
independence should be the primary focus of Islamism, first, because Palestine is a holy land for Muslims, second, because Palestine was the traditional focus of Western intervention into the
region, and, third, because the state of Israel is considered a
major threat to Palestinians.

Islamic Society of North America (ISNA)

P.O. Box 38
Plainfield, IN 46168
(317) 839-8157
FAX: (317) 839-1840
http://isna.net
Secretary General: Sayyid M. Syeed

The primary objective of the ISNA, an organization "committed
to the cause of Allah," is to further the wish of Muslims in North
America to continue an Islamic way of life. The Society promotes
various programs intended to apply the teachings of the Qur'an
and the Sunnah in the everyday lives of Muslims. The organization supports better schools, the establishment of community

centers, and the greater involvement of Muslim communities in the political process.

Jamaat-e-Islami
Mansoorah, Multan Road
Lahore 54570
Pakistan
92-042-5419520
FAX: 92-042-7832194
http://www.jamaat.org
President: Qazi Hussain Ahmad Ameer

Jamaat-e-Islami, an Islamic organization in Pakistan founded by Maulana Sayyid Abul Ala Mawdudi in the 1940s, acts largely as a political party, although it has refused to take part in recent elections. The group calls itself a "religio-political organization" that believes in the universality of Islam, referred to as "The Religion." Jamaat has criticized U.S. foreign policy and has expressed support for the activities of Islamic insurgent groups around the world. Reminiscent of political parties in the United States in the nineteenth and early twentieth centuries, Jamaat performs various social roles to assist people at the local level. For instance, the organization supports Mansoorah Hospital, which was established in 1982 with an initial objective of caring for those injured in the war in Afghanistan, but subsequently extended services to the local community. The organization supports the Islamic Research Academy, founded in 1963 to investigate the various difficulties facing the Muslim world, the codification of Islamic law, and the Islamic economic system. Other branches of the organization are educational institutions such as Markaz Ulum-al-Islamia (Center for Islamic Education) that focus on understanding of the Qur'an.

PUBLICATIONS: *Tarjuman-al-Qur'an* (Urdu monthly), available in the United States.

Muslim Brotherhood
The Muslim Brotherhood (al-Ikhwan) has branch organizations in over seventy countries. In 1928 Hasan al-Banna established the original organization in Egypt with the objective of establishing an Islamic society and state governed under Islamic law (*shari'a*), furthering the teachings of Islam, and advancing unity among Islamic societies worldwide. Becoming involved in intense political conflict, Banna was assassinated in 1949. Branches of the

organization had been formed in Palestine even before the founding of the Israeli state in 1948. It was the Muslim Brotherhood that was instrumental in the formation of Hamas, an organization dedicated to resisting the Israeli presence in Palestine. Although the Brotherhood is generally considered a moderate Islamist organization, the tactics employed by individual organizations tend to vary widely according to the political and social conditions that prevail in a particular country. In Jordan, the Brotherhood has had a close relationship with the monarchy, and King Hussein was able to cooperate with the movement, linking it to his political agenda. Thus, the Brotherhood has expressed its commitment to the regime and the monarchy as well as a program of democratization. In Syria, the Brotherhood has experienced significant conflict with the ruling regime. From 1977 to 1980 the organization repeatedly challenged the government, waging a campaign of sabotage and assassination, an effort that ended in defeat. In Sudan the National Islamic Front (NIF), a puritanical group intent on establishing the dominance of *shari'a*, grew out of the Brotherhood and gained power by a coup d'état in 1989. The Brotherhood supports more traditional social and economic arrangements and has consistently opposed socialist and communist movements. For instance, the Yemeni branch has strongly disapproved of the communist regime of South Yemen.

Nation of Islam (NOI)
Mosque Maryam
7351 Stony Island Avenue
Chicago, IL 60649
(773) 324-6000
FAX: (773) 324-6409
http://www.noi.org
Minister: Louis Farrakhan

The Nation of Islam, also known as the Black Muslims, was founded by W. D. Fard as the Lost-Found Nation of Islam. In the early 1930s Elijah Poole became a disciple of Fard, changing his name to Elijah Muhammad. When Fard disappeared in 1934 Elijah assumed leadership of the organization. The NOI combined Islamic beliefs with a philosophy of black separatism, emphasizing self-reliance and community solidarity and calling for the renunciation of extramarital sex, drugs, gambling, and dancing. The organization gained a reputation for its success in reforming drug addicts and criminals. In 1963 a split occurred in the organization between Elijah and Malcolm X, a popular minister in the group. In 1965 Malcolm, who had formed a separate organization, was assassinated by three members of the NOI. When Elijah died in 1975, his son, Wallace Muhammad, succeeded him as leader of the Black Muslims. Muhammad changed the organization's name to the World Community of Islam in the West and subsequently to Muslim American Society, while changing his own name to Warith Deen Mohammed. Under Mohammed's leadership, the organization de-emphasized black nationalism and admitted nonblack members. In 1978 Louis Farrakhan, dissatisfied with the direction the group was taking, left to form a new organization with the original name of Nation of Islam. The organization became controversial due to Farrakhan's strong attacks on white society and Jews. The NOI supported education, the maintenance of strong families, and less dependence on government welfare, and called for an end to black-on-black crime. In 1995 Farrakhan organized the Millioin Man March in Washington, D.C., calling the thousands of men in attendance to commit themselves to personal responsibility, family, and community. In 2000, following treatment for prostate cancer the year before, Farrakhan joined forces once more with Warith Deen Mohammed, moving the Nation of Islam closer to traditional Islamic beliefs and practices, such as the observance of Ramadan, the holy month of fasting. The NOI still calls for black separatism, advocating the formation of a black nation carved from territory within the United States.

Religious Action Center of Reform Judaism (RAC)
2027 Massachusetts Avenue, NW
Washington, DC 20036
(202) 387-2800
FAX: (202) 667-9070
http://www.rac.org
Director and Counsel: Rabbi David Saperstein

Created in the 1970s as a political arm of the Commission on Social Action and Reform Judaism, which itself is under the joint control of the Central Conference of American Rabbis and the Union of American Hebrew Congregations representing over 1.5 million Reform Jews in the United States, the Religious Action Center lobbies the U.S. Congress on various issues of concern to the membership and keeps its members informed about the status of legislative proposals. Among the issues on which the organization has advocated legislative action are policies relevant to the status of Israel, Jews in the former Soviet Union, economic justice and civil rights, religious liberty, and the maintenance of international peace. In the 2001 session of Congress, the RAC publicized its opposition to proposals that would provide federal aid to faith-based organizations performing social services.

Religious Network for Equality for Women (RNEW)
475 Riverside Drive
Room 812-A
New York, NY 10115
(212) 870-2995
FAX: (212) 870-2338
Coordinator: Zelle W. Andrews

Beginning in 1976 as the Religious Committee for the ERA, a coalition of forty-two religious organizations supporting passage of the Equal Rights Amendment, RNEW expanded its objectives beyond establishing legal rights for women to include broader issues of justice for women, such as economic concerns affecting working women, poor women, and older women. Composed of members from Catholic, Jewish, Mormon, and Protestant denominations, the coalition lobbies at the national level for legislation to guarantee civil rights and to bring about economic reform, and has campaigned for ratification of the United Nations Convention on the Elimination of Discrimination against Women. In addition, the coalition has supported passage of the Medical Leave Act and other health care legislation.

PUBLICATIONS: *RNEW Update,* issued three time per year.

Religious Taskforce on Central America (RTFCA)
1747 Connecticut Avenue, NW
Washington, DC 20009-1108
(202) 387-7625
Coordinators: Lee Miller and Margaret Swedish

Established in 1980 by Catholic religious leaders in order to monitor U.S. policies in El Salvador by gathering information from missionaries and other local sources of information, the group has expanded its concerns to the entire Central American region. The Taskforce supports those in the United States who are striving to bring peace and greater social justice to Central America, and serves as an advocate for the interests of the poor and those seeking to bring about social change in the region. Much of the work of the Taskforce focuses on U.S. foreign policy, encouraging an effective human rights policy, respect for the dignity and sovereignty of the region's poor, and increasing the involvement of churches in attaining justice for the people of Central America.

PUBLICATIONS: *Central America Report,* a bimonthly publication.

Southern Christian Leadership Conference (SCLC)
334 Auburn Avenue NE
Atlanta, GA 30312
(404) 522-1420
FAX: (404) 659-7390
Executive Director: Martin Luther King III

The SCLC was formed in 1957 by African American ministers, including Martin Luther King Jr., Ralph Abernathy, Joseph Lowery, and Fred Shuttlesworth, as an advocacy group to further social, political, and economic equality for blacks and other minority groups in the United States. The SCLC played a significant role in the early days of the civil rights movement, and its leader, Martin Luther King Jr., actively engaged in nonviolent demonstrations in the late 1950s and 1960s to force racial integration in southern states. Following King's assassination in 1968, Abernathy headed the group. The organization has traditionally employed nonviolent tactics of civil protest to further its goals and has initiated community development programs. Most of the organization's affiliates are churches and civil rights groups and the leadership is composed primarily of black Protestant ministers, although membership is not restricted to a particular religious or ethnic group.

PUBLICATIONS: *SCLC Magazine,* published five times annually.

Taliban
The Taliban, which means Islamic students, is an Islamic faction that gained control over approximately 90 percent of the territory of Afghanistan, imposing strict rules of religious, economic, and social conduct over the population. Following the withdrawal of the Soviet Union from Afghanistan in 1989 after a long struggle with groups of *mujahidin,* or holy warriors, who regarded themselves as participating in a jihad, or holy war, various factions began yet another bitter struggle for control of the country. In 1994 a group of young men led by Mullah Mohammed Omar, a combatant in the conflict against the Soviet Union, arose in Kandahar, Afghanistan's second-largest city. The group, calling itself the Taliban, began a campaign against lawlessness in the city,

driving out criminals and applying Islamic law. It banned such things as education and employment for women, nonreligious music, and photographs. The Taliban quickly spread its influence to other cities, calling for the surrender of weapons in the name of Allah. By 1998 the Taliban had extended its control over 90 percent of Afghan territory, including Kabul, and imposed its interpretation of appropriate behavior on Afghans. The remaining 10 percent of the territory, in the northeast, remained under the control of Ahmad Shah Masoud and his organization, the National Islamic United Front for the Salvation of Afghanistan, also known as the Northern Alliance. Masoud was assassinated at the same time as the September 11, 2001, attack against the United States. The Taliban-controlled government created a Department of Religion, which determined the punishments for various misdeeds. A man discovered without a beard would receive ten days in jail and a thief would have his right hand severed. The Taliban imposed strict limitations on the conduct of women, who were required to wear burqas, or shrouds, which completely covered their faces and bodies. Women could leave home only in the company of a male relative. If Talibs discovered a woman in public without the mandated covering, she would be severely beaten or lashed. The United Nations imposed trade sanctions against Afghanistan because the Taliban provided sanctuary for Osama bin Laden, the Saudi who was blamed for the 1998 bombings of the American embassies in Tanzania and Kenya. Following the terrorist attacks on the Pentagon in Washington, D.C., and the World Trade Center in New York, the United States launched a bombing campaign against the Taliban regime in an effort to bring bin Laden and his terrorist network to justice. The intensity of the bombing allowed the Northern Alliance and other factions to topple the Taliban regime.

Tibetan Buddhist Cultural Society, Inc. (TBCS)
P.O. Box 391037
Cambridge, MA 02139
(877) 324-9778
http://www.tbcsonline.org

The primary objective of the Tibetan Buddhist Cultural Society is to assist the public in the understanding and practice of Tibetan Buddhism. The Society is associated with Sera Je Monastic University in Southern India, and three monks from the university are in residence with the organization.

PUBLICATIONS: The TBCS offers various publications on Buddhism by such authors as the Dalai Lama and Geshe Ngwang Dhargyey.

Washington Office on Latin America (WOLA)
110 Maryland Avenue, NE
Washington, DC 20002
(202) 544-8045
FAX: 546-5288
Executive Director: Alexander Wilde

Established in 1974 by a group of religious and lay leaders, the WOLA works to mold a U.S. foreign policy toward Latin America that guarantees human rights, encourages democratic government, and establishes peaceful relations in the region. The organization tracks human rights practices, political activities, and U.S. policy in Latin America and the Caribbean and provides information to policy makers and the American public. Among the organization's sources of financial support are approximately thirty religious organizations. The WOLA sponsors conferences and seminars that offer a forum for discussion among scholars, public officials, and visitors from Latin American countries.

PUBLICATIONS: *Latin America Update,* a bimonthly newsletter, and occasional reports analyzing various issues.

Witness for Peace (WFP)
2201 P. Street, NW
Room 109
Washington, DC 20037
(202) 797-1160
FAX: (202) 797-1164
Executive Director: Leigh Carter

Beginning in 1983 as a temporary coalition of those opposed to U.S. policy in Central America, Witness for Peace has grown to approximately 40,000 individuals supporting a shift in U.S. foreign policy away from a dominant military emphasis toward assisting in the economic development of nations in Central America and around the world. WFP describes itself as an organization based in religious faith and the belief that if anyone remains in tyranny, no one can be free. In more recent years, the organization has shifted emphasis from Central America to the Middle East. The Board of Advisors includes representatives from such religious organizations as the African Methodist Episcopal Church, the National Council of the Churches of Christ in the United States, the American Friends Service Committee, and Church Women United.

PUBLICATIONS: *Witness for Peace Newsletter,* issued quarterly.

Women's Christian Temperance Union (WCTU)
1730 Chicago Avenue
Evanston, IL 60201
(708) 864-1396
President: Rachael B. Kelly

The WCTU was founded in 1874 to combat what were considered the evil effects of alcoholic beverages on the American family. Supported largely by mainstream Protestant churches, the WCTU contributed significant efforts to the ratification in 1919 of the Eighteenth Amendment to the U.S. Constitution, which established prohibition of alcoholic beverages in the nation. This policy came to an end with ratification in 1933 of the Twenty-first Amendment. The organization presently has chapters in over seventy countries and emphasizes a broader range of social issues including better treatment of women, improved schools for the disadvantaged, and the provision of day-care centers. To its original emphasis on alcohol it has added the adverse effects of narcotics and cigarettes.

PUBLICATIONS: *The Union Signal,* a monthly magazine; *The Legislative Update,* a monthly newsletter; *The Young Crusader,* a children's magazine.

6

Print Resources

Abdo, Geneive. *No God But God: Egypt and the Triumph of Islam*. New York: Oxford University Press, 2000.

Abdo proposes a model for converting a secular state into a social order based on Islamic principles. Rejecting what he considers Western stereotypes of Islam, the author argues that many Islamists in Egypt do not advocate the violent overthrow of the government and support the continuance of a modern society rather than a return to a more primitive time.

Abootalebi, Ali Reza. *Islam and Democracy: State-Society Relations in Developing Countries, 1980–1994*. Levittown, PA: Garland, 1999.

The author introduces into the political science investigation of democracy the influence in developing countries of the Islamic tradition in order to evaluate the possible future success of democratization in such nations.

Abrams, Elliott, ed. *The Influence of Faith: Religious Groups and U.S. Foreign Policy*. Lanham, MD: Rowman and Littlefield, 2001.

This collection of essays examines the role of religion in U.S. foreign policy and world politics. Authors focus on U.S. policy relating to the persecution of Christians and Jews in other countries and the role of faith-based organizations in the determination of U.S. humanitarian aid policy.

Adelkhah, Faribah. *Being Modern in Iran*. Irvington, NY: Columbia University Press, 2000.

Adelkhah investigates the Iranian political culture in the context of the Islamic regime that came to power after the fall of the shah in 1979. The author explores the meaning of modernity for what is often considered the paradigm of the Islamic state.

Afshar, Haleh. *Islam and Feminisms: An Iranian Case-Study.* New York: St. Martin's, 1999.

Afshar presents a case study of the status of women in the Islamic Republic of Iran. He focuses on the attempts by fundamentalist and more secularist women to come to a reconciliation, in the context of Islamic belief, for the pursuit of common objectives.

Ahmed, Akbar S. *Jinnah, Pakistan and Islamic Identity: The Search for Saladin.* New York: Routledge, 1997.

Ahmed examines the life of Mohammed Ali Jinnah, considered the architect of Pakistani statehood. Although Jinnah wished to establish a homeland for Muslims, the author claims that the Pakistani partisan was not an Islamic fundamentalist. Following an analysis of Indian-Pakistani history and Jinnah's role in it, Ahmed speculates about the future of Pakistan and Islam.

————. *Islam Today: A Short Introduction to the Muslim World.* New York: St. Martin's, 1999.

Ahmed discusses the origins and traditions of Islam, claiming that many Western perceptions of the Muslim world are based on misunderstandings. The author argues that Islam is not appropriately associated with such things as the subjection of women, intolerance of other religions, opposition to modernity, or draconian penalties for minor offenses.

Alexander, Amy, ed. *The Farrakhan Factor: African-American Writers on Leadership, Nationhood, and Minister Louis Farrakhan.* New York: Grove, 1998.

Sixteen essays by African Americans examine the life and the social, political, and cultural influence of Louis Farrakhan, leader of the Nation of Islam (Black Muslims). Individual essays comment on Farrakhan's impact in such areas as the mass media, community activism, ethnic identity, sexual politics, and the culture of black youth. The essays vary in their evaluation of Farrakhan, focusing on such questions as his rise to leadership and his media personality, the viability of the Black Muslim economic model, and the controversy Farrakhan has created in the organization he heads.

Alley, Robert S. *School Prayer: The Court, the Congress, and the First Amendment*. Amherst, NY: Prometheus, 1994.

Alley explores the historical background to the religion clauses in the First Amendment, examines court interpretations of these clauses, and investigates the debates among members of Congress over the First Amendment's significance to the question of prayer in the public schools.

Alley, Robert S., ed. *The Constitution and Religion: Leading Supreme Court Cases on Church and State*. Amherst, NY: Prometheus, 1999.

Alley includes the text of Supreme Court decisions involving the religion clauses of the First Amendment. Among the subjects of individual cases are public support for religious schools, religious practice in the public schools, and restrictions on the free exercise of religion.

Allitt, Patrick. *Catholic Intellectuals and Conservative Politics in America, 1950–1985*. Ithaca, NY: Cornell University Press, 1995.

Allitt narrates a history of conservative Catholic social and political thought during the cold war and competition from more liberal influences within the church. Beginning his analysis with the 1950s, when Francis Cardinal Spellman led a church characterized by a common religious tradition and fervent anticommunism, the author moves to the 1960s, when the liberal agenda of Pope John XXIII's Vatican II and the issues of Vietnam, feminism, birth control, and civil rights challenged the conservative consensus. Allitt examines the more recent work of four Catholic intellectuals: John Lukacs, Thomas Molnar, Garry Wills, and Michael Novak.

Appleby, R. Scott. *Religious Fundamentalisms and Global Conflicts*. New York: Foreign Policy Association, 1994.

In this brief overview, Appleby comments on Muslim, Hindu, and Christian fundamentalist movements around the world, focusing on their involvement in politics. The author notes that while fundamentalists claim to uphold orthodox beliefs, they willingly adopt new methods, employ new ideologies, and adopt innovative organizational structures in order to combat what they perceive as threats to tradition. Appleby notes that fundamentalists shrewdly observe the social, political, and economic shortcomings of their societies and make use of them in attracting adherents.

————. *The Ambivalence of the Sacred: Religion, Violence, and Reconciliation.* Lanham, MD: Rowman and Littlefield, 1998.

Appleby investigates the curious situation in which religious terrorists and religious peacemakers derive from the same traditions. The author identifies the common elements in the terrorist and the peacemaker and what causes each to respond differently to injustice. Appleby argues that a better understanding of religious extremism can play an important role in explaining conflict at the local, national, and international levels.

Arjomand, Said Amir, ed. *The Political Dimensions of Religion.* Albany: State University of New York Press, 1993.

The eleven essays contained in this volume examine the relationship between religion and politics, focusing on Jewish, Christian, and Muslim movements. The essays offer comparative analyses and case studies of the political implications of religious belief. The contributors are united in the conclusion that the acknowledgment of religious diversity should lead to an acceptance of pluralism.

Armstrong, Karen. *The Battle for God: Fundamentalism in Judaism, Christianity, and Islam.* New York: Knopf, 2000.

Armstrong investigates religious fundamentalism in three contexts: Protestant fundamentalism in the United States, Jewish fundamentalism in Israel, and Muslim fundamentalism in Egypt and Iran. Tracing the roots of fundamentalism to the sixteenth century, the author argues that this mode of religious belief arose as a reaction against modernity. Fundamentalism in its various forms is a particularly modern religious faith that depends for its existence on significant social, political, technological, and intellectual transition. Highly critical of fundamentalist religions, Armstrong claims that fundamentalist theologies are rooted in fear.

Audi, Robert, and Nicholas Wolterstorff. *Religion in the Public Square: The Place of Religious Convictions in Political Debate.* Lanham, MD: Rowman and Littlefield, 1996.

The authors debate the question of the role of religion in politics. Although Audi contends that people in a democracy must separate religious from secular elements in society, Wolterstorff argues that religious considerations must play a role in politics and are highly important to the survival of pluralist democracy.

Awde, Nicholas, ed. *Women in Islam: Anthology from the Qur'an and Hadith.* New York: St. Martin's, 1999.

The editor has collected references to women from Islam's holy scriptures in order to clarify the status of women within Islamic legal and social practice.

Barber, Benjamin. *Jihad vs. McWorld.* New York: Random House, 1996.

Barber analyzes the significant conflict between consumerist capitalism and religious and tribal fundamentalism. Although consumer capitalism is creating a uniform world market, eliminating social and economic barriers between nations, traditional religious beliefs and ethnic loyalties act as a force of disunity, splintering the political realm into ever smaller units. The author observes these opposing tendencies around the world, including Asia, the Middle East, Europe, and North America.

Barlow, Philip L. *Mormons and the Bible: The Place of the Latter-Day Saints in American Religion.* New York: Oxford University Press, 1991.

Barlow examines Mormon interpretation of scripture and investigates actual Mormon practice in light of that interpretation. The author places Mormon scriptural interpretation in the context of overall American religious and cultural life.

Barton, David. *Original Intent: The Courts, the Constitution, and Religion.* 2d ed. Aledo, TX: Wallbuilders, 1997.

Attempting to prove that the United States is a Christian nation, Barton presents evidence of the intentions of noted early Americans such as George Washington and Thomas Jefferson to promote Christianity. The author criticizes the U.S. Supreme Court and judicial activism, arguing that the Court has ignored the original intent of the constitutional framers who allegedly supported religion in public affairs, limitations on federal government powers, and states' rights.

de Bary, William Theodore, and Tu Weiming, eds. *Confucianism and Human Rights.* Irvington, NY: Columbia University Press, 1999.

The eighteen essays in this volume explore the compatibility of the Confucian tradition with the Western understanding of human rights. Authors investigate the claim for the existence of basic human values independent of cultural differences that are common to all societies.

Bayer, Richard C. *Capitalism and Christianity: The Possibility of Christian Personalism.* Washington, DC: Georgetown University Press, 1999.

Employing Catholic social thought and orthodox economic theory, Bayer argues that market systems can provide the foundation for accommodating the theory and operation of capitalism with Christianity. Limiting the role of the state in social affairs, the author describes what he calls a "share economy" in which worker solidarity is encouraged, economic efficiency is promoted, and employee participation in profit-sharing and decision making is increased.

Benedetto, Robert, Darrell L. Guder, and Donald K. McKim. *Historical Dictionary of the Reformed Churches.* Lanham, MD: Scarecrow, 1999.

The authors present entries on the various aspects of the Reformed tradition in Protestant Christianity, including its influence on theology, politics, and education. Entries treat the individuals who have taken part in this religious movement from the Reformation to the present, and provide an overview of theology from the Reformed perspective.

Berger, Peter L., and Jonathan Sacks, eds. *The Desecularization of the World: Resurgent Religion and World Politics.* Grand Rapids, MI: Eerdmans, 1999.

Seven social theorists examine several regions of the world and the dominant religions, including Roman Catholicism, Protestantism, Judaism, Buddhism, and Islam. The book's overall theme is that, contrary to the long-held assumption that religious belief has been in decline, modernization has in fact contributed to a resurgence of religion.

Berrigan, Philip. *Fighting the Lamb's War: Skirmishes with the American Empire: The Autobiography of Philip Berrigan.* Monroe, ME: Common Courage Press, 1996.

Berrigan traces the influences, including that of his mother and father and his own training for the priesthood, that led him and his brother Daniel to become radical Catholic resisters of American involvement in Vietnam. He describes the events of the Vietnam era, including the burning of draft cards at Catonsville, Maryland, the attempts to evade agents of the Federal Bureau of Investigation, and courtroom and prison experiences, as well as more recent antiwar activities and the continuing struggle for justice through the Ploughshares movement.

Billingsley, Andrew. *Deep River: The Black Church as Agent of Social Reform.* New York: Oxford University Press, 1999.

Billingsley argues that the black church holds a special position in the black community to bring about social change. The author notes that the general waning of organized religious institutions notwithstanding, churches maintain a large following in the black community, play an important service role in the community, and demonstrate a continuing energy to influence the social and political status of their members.

Bloom, Irene, J. Paul Martin, and Wayne L. Proudfoot, eds. *Religious Diversity and Human Rights.* Irvington, NY: Columbia University Press, 1996.

The theme of this collection of essays is how religiously diverse beliefs and practices conform to, and can conflict with, the human rights notion of moral universalism. The religions treated include Buddhism, Christianity, Confucianism, Hinduism, Islam, and Judaism.

Bluckert, Kjell. *The Church as Nation: A Study in Ecclesiology.* New York: Peter Lang, 2000.

Bluckert identifies common threads in the growth of national identity and nationally recognized churches in Europe during the twentieth century. The author focuses on the Swedish experience, describing the emphasis on national identity within the Lutheran state church during the first forty years of the twentieth century.

Boff, Leonardo, and Clodovis Boff. *Introducing Liberation Theology.* Trans. Paul Burns. Maryknoll, NY: Orbis, 1987.

Leonardo Boff, a Brazilian theologian, and his brother, Clodovis Boff, a Servite priest in Brazil, explain the basic features of liberation theology. The authors describe liberation theology as originating in the needs of the oppressed populations of South America rather than in academic institutions or the hierarchy Catholic Church.

Bokenkotter, Thomas. *Church and Revolution: The Quest for Social Justice in the Catholic Church.* New York: Doubleday, 1998.

Bokenkotter deals with the extremes of religious involvement in, or reaction to, political affairs, examining the history of the Catholic Church's response to political revolution and the church's evolving understanding of social justice. The author examines the lives of fifteen revolutionaries over the past 200 years, their political activities, and their influence on the church.

Borer, Tristan Anne. *Challenging the State: Churches as Political Actors in South Africa, 1980–1994.* Notre Dame, IN: University of Notre Dame Press, 1998.

Borer investigates the roles played by two religious organizations that participated in the South African antiapartheid movement, the South African Council of Churches and the Southern African Catholic Bishops' Conference. The author identifies the factors that led to these organizations becoming more politically active, moving from moderate political statements to active involvement in civil disobedience. Theoretically, Borer contends that increasing political repression and revised religious beliefs encouraging political action explain the direction of change, and the institutional context explains the degree of change.

Brasewell, George W. *Islam: Its Prophet, Peoples, Politics, and Power.* Nashville, TN: Broadman and Holman, 1996.

Brasewell presents an analysis of Islam from a Western Christian perspective. Along with an overview of its history and the social customs and traditions, the author examines Islam's significant influence in world affairs. Brasewell focuses on the place of Islam in North America.

Brassloff, Audrey. *Religion and Politics in Spain: The Spanish Church in Transition, 1962–96.* New York: St. Martin's, 1998.

Brassloff investigates the Spanish church following the death of dictator Francisco Franco, who ruled Spain from 1939 to 1975. Although the church attempted to respond to fundamental social change, accepting a democratic system, the institution found it difficult to accept many aspects of modernization. The author contends that the church's attempts to form political, social, and economic alliances with secular groups proved futile in a society that had become unresponsive to organized religion.

Brown, L. Carl. *Religion and the State: The Muslim Approach to Politics.* Irvington, NY: Columbia University Press, 2000.

Brown explores the commonly held belief that there is no separation between religion and politics in Islam. The author emphasizes both the continuities between premodern and modern Islamic political thought as well as contemporary breaks with tradition. In conducting his analysis, Brown compares contemporary Islam with Christianity during the Protestant Reformation.

Brown, Robert McAfee. *Gustavo Gutierrez: An Introduction to Liberation Theology.* Maryknoll, NY: Orbis, 1990.

Using the writings of Gustavo Gutierrez and drawing on conversations with this strong advocate of liberation theology, Brown presents the basic ideas of the movement that has molded a new understanding of social justice in Latin America. The author investigates the thoughts of those people upon whom Gutierrez established his theology and proceeds to describe the development of Gutierrez's thought. Brown clarifies the relationship between a commitment to bettering the condition of the poor and the foundation of liberation theology in scripture. A separate chapter deals with criticisms of Gutierrez's theology and his response.

———. *Liberation Theology: An Introductory Guide.* Louisville, KY: Westminster John Knox, 1993.

Brown provides an introduction to liberation theology as an active Christian social movement. The author associates this theology with scripture as well as with the Christian commission to work for social justice for all people.

Bstan-Dzin-Rgya-Mtsho, Fabien Ouaki, and Anne Benson. *Imagine All the People: A Conversation with the Dalai Lama on Money, Politics, and Life as It Could Be.* Somerville, MA: Wisdom Publications, 1999.

The Dalai Lama, in an interview, presents his views on several current issues, including abortion, protecting the environment, disarmament, economic well-being, and standards for ethical conduct.

Burdick, John, and W. E. Hewitt, eds. *The Church at the Grass-roots in Latin America: Perspectives on Thirty Years of Activism.* Westport, CT: Praeger, 2000.

Contributors to this edited volume focus on the grassroots level, offering accounts of progressive movements within the Catholic Church in such Latin American countries as Brazil, Ecuador, Chile, Guatemala, El Salvador, and Nicaragua. The authors focus on the church's influence on politics and political leadership and such issues as labor, race, gender, and landownership, noting that in more recent years the liberation movement within the church has lost considerable influence due to such factors as the decline of authoritarian governments and the rise in popularity of other religious organizations.

Burdick, Michael A. *For God and Fatherland: Religion and Politics in Argentina.* Albany: State University of New York Press, 1996.

Burdick investigates the controversial relationship between the Catholic Church and the state in Argentina. He provides an overview of the Catholic Church and its involvement in politics during the Juan Peron era. A section of the book deals with the church's role in the development of democratic politics.

Burke, Kevin F., S.J. *The Ground beneath the Cross: The Theology of Ignacio Ellacuria.* Baltimore, MD: Georgetown University Press, 2000.

Burke analyzes the liberation theology of Ignacio Ellacuria, a Jesuit philosopher-theologian, president of the University of Central America, and proponent of liberation theology who was killed by the Salvadoran military in 1989. Ellacuria is portrayed as attempting to discover the connection between the needs of a particular social circumstance and the demands of Christian revelation. "The ground beneath the cross" refers to a particular historical period in which a people suffer, as Jesus suffered crucifixion.

Bush, Perry. *Two Kingdoms, Two Loyalties: Mennonite Pacifism in Modern America.* Baltimore, MD: Johns Hopkins University Press, 1998.

Bush examines the historical development of the Mennonite movement in the United States from the 1920s to the 1970s. Although Mennonites traditionally attempted to separate themselves from the secular world as much as possible, considering politics of little note in their social lives but maintaining obedience to laws as long as religious principles were not violated, the group has been more willing in recent years to engage in secular society.

Bushart, Howard, John R. Craig, and Myra Barnes. *Soldiers of God: White Supremacists and Their Holy War for America.* New York: Pinnacle, 1999.

The authors interviewed members of militant groups such as the Aryan Brotherhood and the Ku Klux Klan to determine their views on race, religion, and government. The book details the Christian Identity doctrine; the alleged conspiracy called the Zionist Occupation Government; fears of evil attempts to rule a disarmed citizenry under a world government; claims that the Aryan race is the true chosen people of God; and the defense of certain violent acts as sanctioned by scripture.

Bushman, Claudia L., and Richard L. Bushman. *Mormons in America.* New York: Oxford University Press, 1998.

The authors trace the history of the Mormon Church from its beginnings in New York in the 1830s to the present. Among the topics covered include early leaders such as Joseph Smith and Brigham Young, the move west to Utah, Mormon beliefs and traditions, and its present position in U.S. society. The authors describe the numerous social, political, and legal struggles in which the Mormon community found itself engaged, including the controversy over plural marriage.

Butler, Jon, and Harry S. Stout, eds. *Religion in American History: A Reader.* New York: Oxford University Press, 1997.

The editors have collected various articles and other source materials on important issues, religious movements, group leaders, and changing perspectives in the history of American religion.

Byrnes, Timothy A. *Catholic Bishops in American Politics.* Princeton, NJ: Princeton University Press, 1993.

Byrnes focuses on the National Conference of Catholic Bishops and that organization's active participation in the antiabortion movement; involvement in such political issues as nuclear weapons and the U.S. economy; and attempts to influence the outcome of national election campaigns. The author attempts to explain the political activism of Catholic bishops not in terms of religious revival but as a result of secular political change.

Camp, Roderic Ai. *Crossing Swords: Politics and Religion in Mexico.* New York: Oxford University Press, 1997.

Among the topics that Camp covers are the internal workings of the church and recent changes, the 1992 reforms in the Mexican constitution that normalized church-state relations, the increasing willingness of bishops to criticize political corruption and human rights abuses, the views of clerics and politicians regarding the role of the church in politics, and attitudes of the population on the relationship between religion and politics.

Campbell, Margaret M. *Critical Theory and Liberation Theology: A Comparison of the Initial Work of Jurgen Habermas and Gustavo Gutierrez.* New York: Peter Lang, 1999.

Referring to the claimed failure of Christianity to develop an understanding of the connection between faith and the modern era, Campbell presents an overview of Gustavo Gutierrez's liberation theology, describing it as a critical treatment of Christianity that calls for Christian participation in public affairs. The author joins Gutierrez's liberation theology with Jurgen Habermas's attempt to discover a way in which the human striving for emancipation can enter the arena of reasoned political discourse.

Carmody, Denise Lardner, and John Tully Carmody. *Peace and Justice in the Scriptures of the World Religions.* New York: Paulist Press, 1988.

Religion has been portrayed as both an instigator of, and a means of resolving, conflict. The authors of this book focus on scriptural texts from the Hindu *Bhagavad-Gita,* the Buddhist *Dhammapada,* the Confucian *Analects,* the Daoist *Tao Te Ching,* the Jewish *Talmud,* and the Muslim *Qur'an,* which provide guidance for living in peace and justice. Although the texts emphasize the importance of developing personal spirituality, the authors comment that certain social structures are necessary for the spirituality recommended in the various religions to be effective in bringing about peace and justice.

Carter, Stephen L. *The Culture of Disbelief: How American Law and Politics Trivialize Religious Devotion.* New York: Anchor, 1994.

An African American Episcopalian, Carter examines the role of religion in the American political process, arguing that religious communities can fortify democracy, acting as vital intermediaries between citizens and government. However, in order to play this democratic role, the overall culture must accept the legitimacy of religious belief in political discourse. Carter discusses several religiously relevant issues currently under debate, including creationism versus evolution, prayer in the public schools, public funding of parochial schools, euthanasia, sex education, and abortion.

————. *The Dissent of the Governed: A Meditation on Law, Religion, and Loyalty.* Cambridge, MA: Harvard University Press, 1998.

Basing his discussion in the Declaration of Independence, Carter examines the receptiveness of the American political system to dissent. He focuses on those individuals and groups whose disagreement with government is based on moral and religious grounds. Among the instances of dissent that the author considers are pacifist objections to World War I, the civil rights movement of the 1960s, and present debates over such issues as abortion and public funding of private, religiously oriented schools. Critical of what he considers current liberalism's dismissal of religious dissent, the author contends that democracy should encourage discussion among citizens with diverse value orientations.

————. *God's Name in Vain: The Wrongs and Rights of Religion in Politics.* Boulder, CO: Basic Books, 2000.

Carter examines the role of religion in U.S. politics, indicating what he believes are areas of compatibility as well as conflict between the two realms. The author posits a relationship of benefit between religion and politics. Carter uses both historical and contemporary examples to illustrate how spiritual points of view affect debates on the nation's critical issues.

Chandhoke, Neera. *Beyond Secularism: The Rights of Religious Minorities.* New York: Oxford University Press, 2000.

Focusing on India, Chandhoke, a faculty member at the University of Delhi, investigates the concept of secularism and why it fails to deal adequately with the problems of society.

Choper, Jesse H. *Securing Religious Liberty: Principles for Judicial Interpretation of the Religion Clauses.* Chicago: University of Chicago Press, 1995.

Choper suggests ways of understanding and applying the First Amendment religion clauses in order to guarantee religious freedom without advantaging or disadvantaging any particular group or individual. The author's suggestions include maintaining a ban on vocal, but not silent, prayer in the public schools, taxing the property of religious institutions, and providing public funds for the nonreligious educational activities of parochial schools.

Choueiri, Youssef M. *Islamic Fundamentalism.* Boston: Twayne, 1990.

Choueiri describes Islamic fundamentalism as a contemporary product of the clash between the traditional ideology and values of the Muslim world and the Western influences of capitalism and socialism. Although Islam traditionally was an expansionist movement, the author observes that the fundamentalist hybrid is basically conservative and reactionary, attempting to exclude Western influences from the Muslim world. Subjects for investigation include Islamic revivalism, reformism, and radicalism, and the doctrine and methods of Islamic fundamentalism.

Cleary, Edward L., and Hannah Stewart-Gambino, eds. *Power, Politics, and Pentecostals in Latin America.* Boulder, CO: Westview, 1997.

This edited volume investigates the recent increase in membership in Latin American Protestant churches, the vast majority of which are Pentecostal. Some essays treat general themes related to the growth of the Pentecostal movement, while others focus on specific countries, attempting to explain the movement's growth, its effects on such cultural factors as gender relations, and its increased political influence.

Clifton, Thomas E., ed. *Central Thoughts on the Church in the 21st Century: Essays from the Faculty of Central Baptist Theological Seminary.* Macon, GA: Smyth and Helwys, 1998.

Clifton, president of the Central Baptist Theological Seminary, which is affiliated with the American Baptist Churches/USA and located in Kansas City, Missouri, presided over a meeting of theological educators who presented their speculations about the future of the Christian church in the twenty-first century. Each contributor comments on an aspect of the future of the church, including biblical studies, Christian education, theology, ethics, and spirituality.

Coffey, John. *Politics, Religion and the British Revolutions.* New York: Cambridge University Press, 1997.

This historical treatment of Scottish theologian Samuel Rutherford, his political and religious ideas, and the revolt of the Scottish Convenanters against Charles I in seventeenth-century England provides insight into the nature of contemporary religious-political conflicts.

Coffin, William Sloane, Jr. *Once to Every Man: A Memoir.* New York: Atheneum, 1977.

Coffin, Yale chaplain and vocal anti–Vietnam War activist during the 1960s and early 1970s, describes childhood and early adult experiences, including his work for the Central Intelligence Agency and participation in civil rights activities in the South, that molded his political views. He relates the successes and frustrations of his participation in the antiwar movement. In a concluding chapter, Coffin discusses his attempts to win support for amnesty for draft resisters and discusses his decision to step down as Yale chaplain.

Cohen, Asher, and Bernard Susser. *Israel and the Politics of Jewish Identity: The Secular-Religious Impasse.* Baltimore, MD: Johns Hopkins University Press, 2000.

The authors investigate the transformation in Israeli politics involving the breakdown of mutual agreements among groups and the increasing correspondence between religiosity and right-wing politics. Among the topics covered are the increased conflict between religious and secular Jews, the effects of immigration from the former Soviet Union, and increased concern for government reform.

Cohen, Naomi W. *Jews in Christian America: The Pursuit of Religious Equality.* New York: Oxford University Press, 1992.

Cohen focuses on the various ways in which the dominant Protestant religions in the United States have been favored. The author's ultimate objective is to suggest ways in which the ideal of religious equality may be made a reality.

Colaiaco, James A. *Martin Luther King, Jr.: Apostle of Militant Nonviolence.* New York: St. Martin's, 1993.

Colaiaco offers an overview of Martin Luther King, head of the Southern Christian Leadership Conference, and his nonviolent struggle to defeat segregation policies and to obtain civil rights for African Americans. One chapter provides an analysis of King's "Letter from the Birmingham Jail," a statement written in 1963 after the civil rights leader had been arrested in Birmingham, Alabama, for violating a state court injunction against protest demonstrations. The author calls the letter "one of the most significant documents in American history." In another chapter, Colaiaco deals with the apparent paradox that although King professed nonviolence, his strategies intentionally provoked violent responses.

Coogan, Michael D. *The Illustrated Guide to World Religions.* New York: Oxford University Press, 1998.

Coogan provides a good brief introduction to the major religions of the world. Each of seven chapters examines a religious tradition, detailing holidays and festivals, literature, spiritual founders, important dates, and language.

Cooper, John, Ron Nettler, and Muhammad Mahmoud, eds. *Islam and Modernity: Muslim Intellectuals Respond.* New York: Palgrave, 2000.

The contributors to this volume, who are contemporary modernist and liberal Muslim scholars, propose new understandings of Islam compatible with contemporary social and political conditions. Essays deal with the relationship between religion and politics and the assimilation of Western influences into traditionally Islamic societies.

Corbett, Michael, and Julia Mitchell Corbett. *Politics and Religion in the United States.* Levittown, PA: Garland, 1998.

Although the authors focus on more recent examples of interaction between politics and religion, they indicate how such events can be understood in the historical context of religious influences on political activity since the early colonial period. The authors have developed a Web site to be used along with the book so that the reader might be brought up-to-date on the topics discussed.

Courbage, Youssef, and Philippe Fargues. *Christians and Jews under Islam.* New York: St. Martin's, 1998.

The authors examine the past and present status of Christians and Jews in the Middle East and in Turkey, and identify the political and sociological variables that have influenced that status. They note that Christians and Jews were often able to survive and at times prosper, thus leading them to modify the common view that Islam is a radical religion devoid of tolerance.

Cowling, Maurice. *Religion and Public Doctrine in Modern England, Volume 3: Accommodations.* New York: Cambridge University Press, 2001.

Dealing with the role of religion in the public realm in contemporary England, Cowling examines three alternatives: latitudinarianism, which involves the promotion of free thought and behavior within religious belief; the Christian stance that latitudinarianism is too great a compromise; and the view that Christianity is outdated and irrelevant to contemporary social questions.

Craig, Robert H. *Religion and Radical Politics: An Alternative Christian Tradition in the United States.* Philadelphia, PA: Temple University Press, 1992.

Craig examines the historical convergence of radical politics and Christian faith among U.S. left-wing Christians, arguing that there is a unique tradition of Christian socialism in the United States. The author focuses much of the discussion on the lives and ideas of particular individuals within the Christian socialist tradition.

Craycraft, Kenneth R., Jr. *The American Myth of Religious Freedom.* Dallas, TX: Spence, 1999.

Craycraft argues that the intolerance of public religion he observes in contemporary America is a consequence rather than a violation of the nation's founding principles. Focusing on the Enlightenment influences on the First Amendment, the author claims that the notion of religious freedom has been used by the state to exile religion from U.S. public life.

Cronin, Kieran. *Rights and Christian Ethics.* New York: Cambridge University Press, 1993.

Providing concise descriptions of human rights theories, Cronin explores associations between religious understanding and secular philosophical analysis.

Crossette, Barbara. *So Close to Heaven: The Vanishing Buddhist Kingdoms of the Himalayas.* New York: Knopf, 1995.

Crossette portrays the Buddhist culture of Bhutan, a small country just north of India, where a traditional culture is being threatened by outside influences that have brought tourism and crime. Until the 1960s the Bhutanese were living largely in a medieval world where monks and lamas offered not only spiritual but also legal and medical assistance to the population. Although the rulers have attempted to minimize change, Crossette observes the gradual introduction of foreign influences.

Cunningham, Hilary. *God and Caesar at the Rio Grande: Sanctuary and the Politics of Religion.* Minneapolis: University of Minnesota Press, 1995.

Cunningham explores the Sanctuary Movement, which began in 1981 as a way for religiously motivated people to help those migrating to the United States from Central America. A church-state controversy developed when the movement helped Central Americans enter the United States illegally and provided them sanctuary in churches and synagogues. The author draws on documents acquired from investigations in Arizona, Mexico, and Guatemala, as well as interviews with Sanctuary workers.

Curtis, Susan. *A Consuming Faith: The Social Gospel and Modern American Culture.* Baltimore, MD: Johns Hopkins University Press, 1991.

Curtis describes the lives of fifteen Americans who were affected by the social gospel movement, which attempted to bring about the material as well as spiritual betterment of society. Those engaged in the social gospel movement experienced the ill effects of rapid social and economic change in the late nineteenth and early twentieth centuries, and the author argues that by attempting to deal with these changes, the leaders of the movement ultimately came to accept the developing consumer culture.

Dalacoura, Katerina. *Islam, Liberalism and Human Rights.* New York: St. Martin's, 1998.

Dalacoura explores what many consider the Western notion of human rights within the context of Muslim societies. The author confronts the common assumption that human rights is an inappropriate concept outside Western culture and examines the influence that Islamic beliefs have had on the understanding of such rights.

Daniels, Ted, ed. *A Doomsday Reader: Prophets, Predictors, and Hucksters of Salvation.* New York: New York University Press, 1999.

This edited volume is based on the theme of millennialism, a way of looking at the world that is based on the conviction that everything will soon reach a point of culmination. The book contains eleven writings, drawn primarily from the late twentieth century, including statements from the Branch Davidians, the Montana Freemen, and Heaven's Gate.

Darabi, Parvin, and Romin P. Thompson. *Rage against the Veil: The Courageous Life and Death of an Islamic Dissident.* Amherst, NY: Prometheus, 1999.

This account of the status of women in Iran portrays the severe limitations placed on the rights of women under fundamentalist Islamic rule. Of special note are marriage laws that permit planned marriages between very young girls and older men.

Davis, Joyce M. *Between Jihad and Salaam: Profiles in Islam.* New York: St. Martin's, 1997.

In preparing this book, Davis conducted interviews with seventeen Muslim thinkers and leaders who possess great moral authority among their followers. The individuals treated, who have significant influence on the contemporary Islamic thought, present varied opinions, from positive to highly critical, on relations with Western nations and the future of Islam in the Middle East.

Day, James M., and William S. Laufer, eds. *Crime, Values, and Religion.* Norwood, NJ: Ablex, 1987.

This volume of scholarly essays deals with various aspects of the interaction of religion with the criminal justice system. Essays deal with such topics as the influence of religion on traditional views of punishment, the development of religious commitment within the corrections environment, and the influences of contemporary religious movements, particularly conservative movements, on the political response to crime.

De Gruchy, John W. *Christianity and Democracy: A Theology for a Just World Order.* New York: Cambridge University Press, 1995.

De Gruchy investigates the role of Christianity in the historical development of democratic political systems. The author examines twentieth-century case studies, including Nazi Germany and South Africa, emphasizing the increased importance of churches in the struggle to form and maintain democratic governments. The conclusion is that democratic systems anticipate a theology of a just world order.

Dean, Kenneth. *Lord of the Three in One: The Spread of a Cult in Southeast China.* Princeton, NJ: Princeton University Press, 1998.

Dean presents an interesting account of the reemergence of a Chinese religious cult that continues to prosper despite efforts of the Chinese government to suppress it. Lin Zhao'en established the Three in One Teachings in the sixteenth century by combining Confucianism, Daoism, and Buddhist Chan philosophy. Especially appealing to rural Chinese popular culture, the cult involves healing rituals and spirit mediumism.

Deikman, Arthur J. *The Wrong Way Home: Uncovering the Patterns of Cult Behavior in American Society.* Boston: Beacon, 1990.

Deikman, a professional psychiatrist, begins his investigation of cults with a standard treatment of new religious movements. However, the author expands his analysis of cult behavior to include organizations to which many Americans are members. For instance, the corporation can elicit cultlike devotion through indoctrination, work schedules, hierarchical organization, and geographic relocation of families; and mainline churches can demonstrate cultic tendencies by idolizing leaders and discouraging independent thought. Deikman claims that the pervasiveness of cult behavior is a potential threat to democracy and freedom.

Dekker, Gerard, Donald A. Luidens, and Rodger R. Rice, eds. *Rethinking Secularization.* Lanham, MD: University Press of America, 1997.

Employing case studies from various countries around the world—including the Netherlands, South Africa, Australia, Canada, Japan, and the United States—the contributors to this volume indicate that, despite secularization at the national and denominational levels, active religious involvement continues at the personal level.

Dempsey, Carol J. *The Prophets: A Liberation-Critical Reading of the Old Testament.* Minneapolis, MN: Fortress, 2000.

Dempsey examines readings from the Hebrew Bible and Old Testament from the viewpoint of liberation theology and feminist criticism. The author examines power in the context of scripture, focusing on its ability to dominate, liberate, or encourage social consensus. Dempsey contends that the only way to engender stable peace is to follow the example of those Old Testament prophets who viewed power as something to be shared among God, human beings, and the natural world.

Dennis, Marie, Renny Golden, and Scott Wright. *Oscar Romero: Reflections on His Life and Writings.* Maryknoll, NY: Orbis, 2000.

This brief biography outlines the extraordinary life of Oscar Romero, Catholic archbishop of San Salvador. Originally a moderate conservative on good terms with the ruling elite, Romero experienced a religious conversion when he was sixty years old and joined the cause of the oppressed poor of El Salvador. He was ultimately assassinated.

Deol, Harnick. *Religion and Nationalism in India: The Case of the Punjab.* New York: Routledge, 2000.

In this volume in the Routledge Studies in the Modern History of Asia series, Deol investigates the reasons for the rise of Sikh militancy in India during the 1970s and 1980s, focusing on the increase in nationalist fervor among the Sikh community in the Punjab region of India.

Devi, Savitri. *Warning to the Hindus.* Columbia, MO: South Asia Books, 1993 (1939).

This book, originally published in 1939, argues for a change in Hinduism in order to ensure its preservation. The author calls for discarding the caste system, rejecting syncretism with other religious traditions—particularly Islam and Christianity—and accepting a greater role for women in preserving the Indian national consciousness.

Dillon, Martin. *God and the Gun: The Church and Irish Terrorism.* New York: Routledge, 1999.

Having conducted surveys with clergy, Dillon describes the history of the Catholic-Protestant conflict in Northern Ireland. The author examines the role of the clergy in the violence, including those Catholic priests and Protestant ministers who have attempted to moderate the violence, as well as those clerics, Protestant as well as Catholic, who have provided support for the terrorists on their respective sides of the conflict.

Dionne, E. J., Jr., and John J. DiIulio, Jr., eds. *What's God Got to Do with the American Experiment? Essays on Religion and Politics.* Washington, DC: Brookings Institution, 2000.

These essays examine the role of religion in contemporary public life. Among the topics treated are current religious belief and practice in the United States; religious, political, and moral values of the 1960s compared to those of the 1990s; religious responses to President Bill Clinton's impeachment proceedings; and the rise of faith-based social programs.

Dombrowski, Daniel A. *Christian Pacifism.* Philadelphia, PA: Temple University Press, 1991.

Dombrowski examines just war theorists from Thomas Aquinas to contemporary scholars, claiming that argument in favor of participation in so-called just wars ultimately cannot be reconciled with Christian belief. The author examines pacifist arguments and presents a defense of pacifism.

Dong, Paul, and Thomas Raffill. *The Allure of Falun Gong: Li Hongzhi and China's Most Dangerous Chi Gong Sect.* New York: Welcome Rain, 2001.

Dong, a chi gong master, and Raffill, a student of chi gong, examine Falun Gong, a controversial movement in China that teaches chi gong, the practice of relating mind, body, and spirit. The movement has gained the enmity of the Chinese leadership because adherents are unwilling to submit to the government's attempts to maintain control over all social and religious groups.

Douglas, R. Bruce, and Joshua Mitchell, eds. *A Nation under God? Essays on the Fate of Religion in American Public Life.* Lanham, MD: Rowman and Littlefield, 2000.

Contributors to this volume, who are political and legal theorists, examine the future of religion as an influence on public life in the United States. Although the authors view as a strength the American tradition of bringing religious faith to public affairs, they acknowledge the need for a revised public role for religion in light of altered social and political realities.

Doumato, Eleanor Abdella. *Getting God's Ear: Women, Islam, and Healing in Saudi Arabia and the Gulf.* New York: Columbia University Press, 2000.

Doumato examines the roles of women, particularly in the areas of religious worship, spiritual concerns, and medical practices, and how these roles developed in orthodox religious societies of the Arab world.

Dowty, Alan. *The Jewish State: A Century Later.* Berkeley: University of California Press, 1998.

Dowty elucidates the notion of a Jewish state, investigating the historical, cultural, religious, and ideological bases of the contemporary state of Israel. The author focuses on the strengths and weaknesses of Israel as a democracy.

Easwaran, Eknath. *Nonviolent Soldier of Islam: Badshah Khan, A Man to Match His Mountains.* 2d ed. New York: Publishers Group West, 2001.

Easwaran describes the activities of Badshah Khan, an Indian Muslim who subscribes to a nonviolent strategy in attempting to achieve political goals. Khan formed a nonviolent army of 100,000 men from the Pahans, a people living in the Northwest Territory of India.

Ehteshami, Anoushiravan. *After Khomeini: The Iranian Second Republic.* New York: Routledge, 1995.

Ehteshami examines the economic and political life of Iran as well as the position of the country in the Middle East and in world politics following the death of the Ayatollah Khomeini in 1989. The author investigates the critical problems faced by the Rafsanjani regime, which was faced with the responsibility of maintaining the government of clerics instituted by the ayatollah.

Eickelman, Dale F., and James P. Piscatori. *Muslim Politics.* Princeton, NJ: Princeton University Press, 1996.

Challenging the notion of Islam as monolithic, Eickelman and Piscatori examine the diversity of contemporary Islam from country to country. They investigate the unique political implications of Islam throughout the world, including such topics as the role of women in public life, the experience of modernization, and the protection of civil liberties.

Eisenach, Eldon J. *The Next Religious Establishment: National Identity and Political Theology in Post-Protestant America.* Lanham, MD: Rowman and Littlefield, 2000.

Arguing that the United States has been defined historically by a combination of cultural and religious structures that have provided legitimacy to the governing system and supported the national identity, Eisenach concludes that the United States cannot survive as a nation without common understandings of faith. Multicultural trends notwithstanding, the author believes that a new national identity and religious faith for the twenty-first century are emerging.

Ellwood, Robert S. *The Fifties Spiritual Marketplace: American Religion in a Decade of Conflict.* New Brunswick, NJ: Rutgers University Press, 1997.

Ellwood explores the major events of the 1950s in the United States, a time he claims is often mistakenly characterized as uniform in religious attitudes among Protestantism, Catholicism, and Judaism. In reality, religious leaders and many lay people were confronted with determining appropriate responses to such phenomena as communism and the rise of the cold war, a troubled younger generation, emerging racial politics, and nonconformist religious attitudes.

Entelis, John P., ed. *Islam, Democracy, and the State in North Africa.* Bloomington: Indiana University Press, 1997.

The authors of this volume deal with the popular movement, led largely by politicized Islamic groups, toward economic liberalization and political democratization in Algeria, Morocco, and Tunisia in the late 1980s. The authors describe the initial trends toward reform that authoritarian governments ultimately repressed.

Esposito, John L. *The Oxford Encyclopedia of the Modern Islamic World.* New York: Oxford University Press, 1995.

This four-volume set includes more than 750 entries focusing on the Islamic aspects of Muslim societies, including topics dealing with beliefs, institutions and movements, religious practices, politics, and culture and peoples in the Middle East as well as in Asia, Europe, and North America.

————. *The Islamic Threat: Myth or Reality?* 2d ed. New York: Oxford University Press, 1996.

Esposito examines the history of Islam and its relations with Western nations. The author focuses on Islamic politics in the nations of Iran, Libya, Lebanon, Egypt, Sudan, Tunisia, and Algeria. Contrary to the popular view that Islam is a monolithic force uniformly hostile to the West, Esposito emphasizes the diversity of the religious movement, which includes moderates as well as radicals. Among the issues currently facing Islam are the desirability of a pluralist society, human rights, and the social and political status of women and minorities.

————. *Islam: The Straight Path.* 3d ed. New York: Oxford University Press, 1998.

Esposito provides an overview of Islam, tracing the religion's historical development from its origin to the present and describing its influence on world history and politics. The author examines Muslim reactions to colonialism and modernization, which currently involves a highly active political agenda. The third edition contains a study of Islam in Pakistan and of the Muslim community in the United States, including a treatment of Malcolm X and Louis Farrakhan.

Esposito, John L., and John O. Voll. *Islam and Democracy: Religion, Identity and Conflict Resolution in the Muslim World.* New York: Oxford University Press, 1996.

Focusing on the six case studies of Algeria, Egypt, Iran, Malaysia, Pakistan, and Sudan, thus demonstrating the diversity within Muslim experience, the authors describe how governments and Islamic movements deal with the issues of democratization and the challenges of secular society. Esposito and Voll examine the beliefs and institutions relevant to each case.

Esposito, John L., ed. *Political Islam: Revolution, Radicalism, or Reform?* Boulder, CO: Lynne Rienner, 1997.

This volume includes paper presentations from a conference at the Center for Muslim-Christian Understanding at Georgetown University. The articles are organized into three sections: illegal opposition, Islam in the political process, and Islam in international relations. Discussing the experience of various regions and countries, including Algeria, Egypt, Pakistan, Sudan, Palestine, and Afghanistan, the authors attempt to distinguish radical Islam from Islam in general and reformist Islam in particular.

————. *The Oxford History of Islam.* New York: Oxford University Press, 2000.

This edited volume contains a wide range of information on Islam, including such topics as Islamic history, art and architecture, philosophy, science, medicine, and the contemporary status of the religion. The volume is worldwide in scope, treating Islam in the United States, Europe, Africa, Southeast and Central Asia, and China. More than 300 photographs are included in this 700-page book.

Esposito, John L., and Michael Watson, eds. *Religion and Global Order.* Cardiff, Wales: University of Wales Press, 2000.

These essays deal with such topics as religion's role in establishing international order and worldwide political stability, encouraging economic progress in developing countries, and safeguarding the environment. Other issues confronted are the religious challenge to the contemporary ideologies of socialism and liberalism and the spread of the consumerist values of Western nations.

Evans, Bette Novit. *Interpreting the Free Exercise of Religion: The Constitution and American Pluralism.* Chapel Hill: University of North Carolina Press, 1998.

Evans examines the free exercise clause of the U.S. Constitution's First Amendment within the context of U.S. religious experience and investigates major interpretations of religious freedom as applied to recent legal questions. The author concludes that the protection of religious freedom allows for alternative personal and social understandings within a pluralist political system.

Evans, M. Stanton. *The Theme Is Freedom: Religion, Politics, and the American Tradition.* Washington, DC: Regnery, 1996.

In challenging the doctrine of separation of church and state, Evans refers to the words of the nation's founders and the First Amendment to the Constitution in arguing that the basis of American liberties originates in Christian religious principles. The author contends that freedom and a religious tradition cannot exist independently of each other, and so contemporary liberalism represents a threat to both religion and freedom.

Evans, Malcolm. *Religious Liberty and International Law in Europe*. New York: Cambridge University Press, 1997.

Evans describes the incorporation of freedom of religious belief into the laws of various European countries, investigates the ways in which this guarantee is actually practiced, and focuses on disputed cases dealing with the exercise of this freedom that have gone before the Council of Europe. The author concludes with a discussion of the probable future direction religious liberty may take in international law.

Everett, William Johnson. *Religion, Federalism, and the Struggle for Public Life: Cases from Germany, India, and America*. New York: Oxford University Press, 1997.

Everett analyzes the interaction between religion and constitutionalism in three federal republics: Germany, India, and the United States. The author searches for ways to improve public life in a federal system by discovering religious sources for order and developing a possible religious framework for guiding that order. Alternatively, Everett searches for ways in which religious belief might subvert federal republican systems.

Fandy, Mamoun. *Saudi Arabia and the Politics of Dissent*. New York: St. Martin's, 1999.

Fandy examines the history of Islamic opposition in Saudi Arabia, particularly during the period of the Gulf War and thereafter. The author analyzes the recorded sermons of Islamic activists, noting their rhetorical styles and approach to political issues. Also included in the book are treatments of the Shi'a Reform Movement, the Committee for the Defense of Legitimate Rights, the Movement of Islamic Reform in Arabia, and Osama bin Laden.

Feigon, Lee. *Demystifying Tibet: Unlocking the Secrets of the Land of the Snows*. Chicago: Ivan R. Dee, 1996.

Feigon examines Tibetan culture, including the historical influences of the Dalai Lamas and the current importance of religion for the people. The author attempts to avoid common stereotypes of Tibet conveyed in popular literature and film. Feigon is highly critical of the Chinese intervention in Tibet that began in 1951, emphasizing the cultural antipathy that exists between the Chinese and the Tibetans.

Feldman, Stephen M., ed. *Law and Religion: A Critical Anthology*. New York: New York University Press, 2000.

This collection examines the cultural, ideological, sociological, and historical perspectives that have contributed to the development of public policy on law and religion in the United States. Individual essays treat such topics as religious freedom, fundamentalism, separation of church and state, religion and the public schools, and religious morality.

Findley, James F., Jr. *Church People in the Struggle: The National Council of Churches and the Black Freedom Movement, 1950–1970*. New York: Oxford University Press, 1993.

Findley details the ecumenical movement, primarily among Protestant churches, which took part in the civil rights movement. The author attempts to explain why churches were willing to come together at this particular time to advocate racial equality. Personal accounts of those participating in the movement are included.

Firestone, Reuven. *Jihad: The Origin of Holy War in Islam*. New York: Oxford University Press, 1999.

Firestone investigates the origins and traces the evolution of the notion of jihad, or Islamic holy war, which has played a crucial role in recent Middle Eastern politics. The author uses the Qur'an and early Islamic literary sources, concluding that the idea of jihad originated in the first generation of Muslims.

Fleet, Michael, and Brian H. Smith. *The Catholic Church and Democracy in Chile and Peru*. Notre Dame, IN: University of Notre Dame Press, 1997.

This book deals with important changes in the Catholic Church in Chile and Peru over the past thirty years. The church has shifted its attention from the wealthy elite to the poor, even though this change occurred in the face of opposition from the Vatican as well as local church organizations. The authors investigate future challenges to the church, including relationships with Rome, possible challenges from the political elite, challenges from Protestant movements for the loyalty of the population, and conflicts over such issues as abortion and the ordination of women.

Flood, Gavin. *An Introduction to Hinduism.* New York: Cambridge University Press, 1996.

Flood outlines the development of Hindu traditions from their beginnings to the present, treating Hinduism as a nationalistic, as well as a global, religion. The author focuses on such topics as the fundamental importance of Hindu ritual as opposed to doctrine; the Dravidian influences; and contemporary debates in the literature.

Formicola, Jo, and Hubert Morken, eds. *Everson Revisited: Religion, Education and Law at the Crossroads.* Lanham, MD: Rowman and Littlefield, 1997.

These essays explore the consequences and possible future implications of *Everson v. Board of Education* (1947), the controversial U.S. Supreme Court decision that attempted to maintain separation between religion and the public schools while allowing the use of public funds to transport students to parochial schools. The authors explore the impact of the decision on subsequent rulings dealing with such issues as school prayer, tuition tax credits, vouchers, and home schooling.

————. *Religious Leaders and Faith-Based Politics.* Lanham, MD: Rowman and Littlefield, 2001.

The contributors to this volume, basing their analyses on interviews with ten religious leaders including Bishop T. D. Jakes, Reverend Al Sharpton, Rabbi Daniel Lapin, and Reverend Benjamin Chavis-Mohammed, examine the interaction between religion and politics and its effect on public policy. They speculate about the extent of future religious involvement in American politics.

Forrester, Duncan B. *Christian Justice and Public Policy.* New York: Cambridge University Press, 1997.

Forrester examines secular theories of justice, providing a theological perspective to them. Although holding that Christian theology cannot provide a complete theory of justice, it nonetheless can clarify conventional notions of justice and contribute to the actual formation of just associations.

Fortin, Ernest L. *Human Rights, Virtue and the Common Good: Untimely Meditations on Religion and Politics.* Lanham, MD: Rowman and Littlefield, 1997.

Focusing on Roman Catholicism, Fortin discusses the problems Christianity faced during the twentieth century, including swift scientific advancement and resulting social and moral change. The author investigates the relationship between Christianity and the development of liberal democracy, the development of papal social policy, and the political involvement of the U.S. Catholic Church.

Fowler, Robert Booth, and Allen D. Hertzke. *Religion and Politics in America: Faith, Culture, and Strategic Choices.* Boulder, CO: Westview, 1995.

The authors cover the wide spectrum of religious groups and American politics, including Christian conservatives and their concerns for such issues as abortion, pornography, prayer in public schools, and the family, the Roman Catholic Church, liberal religious groups, African American churches, Jewish groups particularly prominent in advocating U.S. support for Israel, and a growing Islamic influence. Religious groups attempt to influence public decision making through campaign politics, lobbying, and the courts. Chapters deal with such topics as religion and political culture, women and religion, and the politics of unconventional religion. A final chapter presents various theories of religion, culture, and American politics.

Frady, Marshall. *Jesse: The Life and Pilgrimage of Jesse Jackson.* New York: Random House, 1996.

Frady portrays Jesse Jackson as the last remaining prominent personality from the height of the civil rights movement, who still expresses the evangelical political and social message of Dr. Martin Luther King Jr. Jackson is described as a religious and political leader whose strength lies in raising issues, not working for their resolution. The civil rights leader has worked to place the liberal political message within a biblical perspective.

Franklin, V.P. *Martin Luther King, Jr.* West Haven, CT: Park Lane, 1998

This brief biography examines the origins of the civil rights leader's aspiration to bring an end to segregation and racial discrimination in the United States. Franklin focuses on the impact of black churches and the black religious tradition on thought and actions. The author examines the influence of King's teachers at Crozer Theological Seminary, as well as the effect that the writings of Mahatma Gandhi and Karl Barth had on the future course taken by the civil rights leader.

Fraser, James W. *Between Church and State: Religion and Public Education in a Multicultural America.* New York: St. Martin's, 1999.

Fraser deals with the difficult theme of the place of religion in a multicultural society. The author describes the ways in which different generations of Americans have attempted to resolve questions arising from the principle of separation of church and state. Fraser advocates a willingness not only to accept toleration of differing beliefs, but also, in order to avoid communal separation and absolutist posturing, to engage in civil exchange on convictions and beliefs.

Friedman, Robert I. *Zealots for Zion: Inside Israel's West Bank Settlement Movement.* New Brunswick, NJ: Rutgers University Press, 1994.

Friedman, a journalist, reports on his visits to the West Bank, recounting the hostilities between Arabs and Jews. He examines the Israeli zealots who are intent on establishing Jewish settlements on Palestinian land in the Israeli occupied territories. The author also focuses on Jewish Americans who have supported these zealots with financial assistance.

Fuller, Graham E., and Rend Rahim Francke. *The Arab Shi'a: The Forgotten Muslims.* New York: St. Martin's, 2000.

Fuller and Francke examine the Arab Shi'a Islamic community that is in the majority in Iraq and Bahrain and constitutes the largest religious group in Lebanon. The authors discuss Shi'ite beliefs, community practices, major social and political concerns, and relations with the dominant Sunni sect.

Gallen, David, ed. *Malcolm X: As They Knew Him.* New York: Carroll and Graf, 1992.

Gallen divides this volume into three parts: (1) remembrances of twenty-five individuals who knew Malcolm X; (2) conversations with Malcolm, including a *Playboy* interview conducted by writer Alex Haley in 1963 and his last television interview before his assassination in 1965; and (3) six essays by writers such as James Baldwin, Robert Penn Warren, and Eldridge Cleaver, who discuss Malcolm's significance to the development of political consciousness and feelings of self-worth among African Americans.

Gardner, E. Clinton. *Justice and Christian Ethics*. New York: Cambridge University Press, 1995.

Gardner investigates the relationship between law and religion, devoting individual chapters to philosophical and religious traditions such as the classical tradition of virtue in the writings of Aristotle and Aquinas, biblical understandings of covenant and God's righteousness, and Puritanism that have contributed to the Western notion of justice. The author suggests a convenantal theory of justice that he argues will provide religious support for a renewed understanding and commitment to social justice.

Garrard-Burnett, Virginia, and David Stoll, eds. *Rethinking Protestantism in Latin America*. Philadelphia, PA: Temple University Press, 1993.

These essays describe the increased membership in Pentecostal and evangelical Protestant churches in Latin America, the corresponding decrease in adherence to Roman Catholicism, and the potential social and political consequences of this shift in loyalties to organized religion.

Gauchet, Mark. *The Disenchantment of the World: A Political History of Religion*. Princeton, NJ: Princeton University Press, 1997.

Gauchet presents a complex discussion of the origins and historical development of the world's major religions: Judaism, Christianity, Islam, Hinduism, and Buddhism. The author contends that the development of these religions involved, due to attempts to explain transcendence, an initial first step away from otherness and toward the ultimate victory of individualism and subjective inwardness.

Gaustad, Edwin S. *Church and State in America*. New York: Oxford University Press, 1998.

Gaustad presents a broad-brush treatment of the history of religious freedom in the United States, providing an initial basis for understanding contemporary political debates over the question of religious freedom.

Gerges, Fawaz A. *America and Political Islam: Clash of Cultures or Clash of Interests?* New York: Cambridge University Press, 1999.

Gerges offers an analysis of the interaction between the United States and the Islamic movements and regimes of the Middle

East, providing a critical look at the policies of the administrations of presidents Jimmy Carter, Ronald Reagan, George H. W. Bush, and Bill Clinton. The author examines U.S. policy toward such countries as Iran, Algeria, Egypt, and Turkey.

Gervais, Marty. *Seeds in the Wilderness: Profiles of World Religious Leaders*. Kingston, Ontario: Quarry, 1994.

Gervais profiles thirty-two religious leaders, several of whom are politically active. Examples include Rabbi Meir Kahane, founder of the Jewish Defense League; Archbishop Robert Eames, worker for peace in Northern Ireland; Gustavo Gutierrez, the Marxist priest of Peru and proponent of liberation theology; Domitilia de Chungara, known by many in Bolivia as "Joan of Arc," who has worked for better conditions for Bolivian tin miners; and Archbishop Desmond Tutu of South Africa, who worked in opposition to apartheid.

Geyer, Alan F. *Ideology in America: Challenges to Faith*. Louisville, KY: Westminster John Knox, 1997.

Geyer presents an overview of the evolving political and social conditions in the United States since the 1960s and the role of the religious right in that change. Criticizing the conservative view that government is the problem and business is the solution, the author suggests tactics for mainline religious organizations in meeting the challenge from the Christian right. He calls for a commitment to the poor and disadvantaged.

Gieling, Saskia. *Religion and War in Revolutionary Iran*. New York: St. Martin's, 1999.

Gieling investigates the religious justifications offered by Iran's Islamic clergy for the destructive eight-year war with Iraq. The author attempts to explain various policy decisions made by the Iranian government in terms of the theological rationalizations offered by clerical leaders.

Gietzen, Mark S. *Is It a Sin for a Christian to Be a Registered Democrat Voter in America Today?* Pittsburgh, PA: Dorrance Publishing Company, 2000

Reflecting observations about the political preferences of more conservative Christian groups that tend to support Republican candidates for public office, Gietzen raises questions in this brief book about a Christian's political party identification in the context of the abortion issue.

Gifford, Paul. *Christianity and Politics in Doe's Liberia.* New York: Cambridge University Press, 1993.

Gifford investigates the corrupt regime of Samuel K. Doe, who ruled Liberia from 1980 to 1990, and the role that Christianity played in maintaining Doe in power. The author claims that supporters of Doe, allegedly including U.S. interests, used the Christian beliefs of Liberians to encourage a quiescence, thus extending Doe's hold on power.

Gilesnan, Michael. *Recognizing Islam: Religion and Society in the Middle East.* Rev. ed. New York: Palgrave, 2000.

Gilesnan examines the social and political variations found in Islam, from the feudal aristocracy of northern Lebanon to the lower-class Sufi brotherhoods of Egypt and the middle-class Muslims of Algeria and Morocco.

Gill, Anthony. *Rendering unto Caesar: The Catholic Church and the State in Latin America.* Chicago: University of Chicago Press, 1998.

Gill investigates the political relationship between the Catholic Church and authoritarian regimes in Latin American countries, attempting to explain why some churches cooperate with such regimes and others oppose them. The author suggests that in countries where the Catholic Church has no strong competitor, it tends to ally itself with the authoritarian regime, while in countries where the church experiences significant competition from Protestant churches, there is a greater willingness to stand against a regime that is following policies harmful to the poor.

Ginsberg, Benjamin. *The Fatal Embrace: Jews and the State.* Chicago: University of Chicago Press, 1993.

Ginsberg examines the uneasy relationship between Jews and the political system, focusing first on Europe and the Middle East, but dealing primarily with the United States from the Civil War to the 1990s. The author argues that although Jews constitute just 3 percent of the U.S. population, they compose far greater percentages of journalists, publishers, the leadership of interest groups, and government officials. Therefore, Ginsberg contends, this religious/ethnic group has been subject to attacks from those on the left as well as the right of U.S. politics. Especially noteworthy has been the hostility between Jews and African Americans.

Gleave, Robert, and Eugenia Kermeli, eds. *Islamic Law: Theory and Practice.* New York: Palgrave, 2001.

These essays deal with the theory and practice of Islamic law in both Sunni and Shi'a formulations and in various societies. Among the topics covered are Islamic legal theory, the classical development of Islamic law, the status of religious minorities under the law, and recent developments in legal thinking.

Glenn, Charles L. *The Ambiguous Embrace: Government and Faith-Based Schools and Social Agencies.* Princeton, NJ: Princeton University Press, 2000.

Glenn argues that since "faith-based" schools and social agencies have been effective in assisting those in need, this constitutes a good reason for exploring the possibility of greater government collaboration with such private groups. The author contends that this cooperation can occur within the First Amendment's separation of church and state requirement, maintaining the independence of religiously based institutions. U.S. society can benefit from the strong commitment that such institutions have to service.

Goldberg, Steven. *Seduced by Science: How American Religion Has Lost Its Way.* New York: New York University Press, 2000.

Concerned with the role of religion in the contemporary public realm, Goldberg investigates the tendency of American religious leaders to speak in scientific terms on contemporary issues such as gene patenting. The author argues that attempts by religious spokespersons to validate their positions empirically leads to the trivialization of religion at the expense of the important ingredients of faith and humility.

Goodwin, Jan. *Price of Honor: Muslim Women Lift the Veil of Silence on the Islamic World.* New York: Penguin, 1995.

Investigating the expansion of fundamentalist Islam, Goodwin presents the results of interviews with Muslim women in ten countries. The book provides the female response to fundamentalist Islamic policies toward women.

Gorenberg, Gershom. *The End of Days: Fundamentalism and the Struggle for the Temple Mount.* New York: Free Press, 2000.

Gorenberg, an Israeli journalist, reports on and criticizes the objective, supported by leaders of fundamentalist movements in the United States, to construct a new Jewish temple on Temple Mount in Jerusalem. This site, which Jews, Muslims, and Christians alike consider sacred, is one of the world's more highly contested pieces of real estate.

Gorring, Timothy. *God's Just Vengeance: Crime, Violence and the Rhetoric of Salvation*. New York: Cambridge University Press, 1996.

Gorring examines the relationship between Christian theology, related specifically to understandings of atonement, and penal strategies. The author contends that a theology of atonement contributed to the development of a perspective that favors punishment as a response to crime.

Graham, Stephen A. *The Totalitarian Kingdom of God: The Political Philosophy of E. Stanley Jones.* Lanham, MD: University Press of America, 1998.

Graham recounts the life of E. Stanley Jones, a Christian missionary and evangelist who interpreted the Gospel in terms of social, economic, and political as well as personal salvation. During the 1930s and 1940s Jones strongly opposed Nazism and fascism along with communism. Graham notes that Jones's involvement in politics brought him into close contact with Indian leaders Gandhi and Nehru, and led to his influence on the political and religious ideas of Martin Luther King Jr.

Graham, Stephen A., and Marcia W. Graham. *First the Kingdom: A Call to the Conservative Pentecostal/Charismatics and the Liberal Social Justice Advocates for Repentance and Reunification.* Lanham, MD: University Press of America, 1994.

The authors outline the division in the Christian church between conservative Pentecostal charismatics and supporters of liberal social justice, calling for repentance from the charismatics for neglecting the political and social aspects of Christianity and from the liberals for ignoring what is considered the power and authority of the Holy Spirit.

Grasso, Kenneth L., Gerard V. Bradley, and Robert P. Hunt, eds. *Catholicism, Liberalism, and Communitarianism: The Catholic Intellectual Tradition and the Moral Foundations of Democracy.* Lanham, MD: Rowman and Littlefield, 1995.

The essays in this volume attempt to provide an understanding of the Catholic tradition in social thought, explicate that tradition in the context of human rights thinking, and suggest how Catholic social thought can contribute to those contemporary issues central to the American political debate. Individual essays deal with such topics as the common good as the goal of social life, the communal nature of human beings, and religious freedom and democracy.

Graybill, Lyn S. *Religion and Resistance Politics in South Africa.* Westport, CT: Praeger, 1995.

Graybill investigates the role of religious faith in the black nationalist movement in South Africa before the end of white rule. The author discusses the leaders (Albert Lutuli, Robert Sobukwe, Stephen Biko, and Desmond Tutu), the African nationalist organizations (the African National Congress, the Pan-Africanist Congress, the Black Consciousness Movement, and the United Democratic Front), and the influence of Christian beliefs and perspectives on each.

Graziano, Frank. *The Millennial New World.* New York: Oxford University Press, 1999.

Graziano focuses his study of millennial movements on Latin America, investigating its various origins and subsequent influence on social, religious, political, and revolutionary movements.

Green, John Clifford, Clyde Wilcox, and Mark J. Rozell, eds. *Prayers in the Precincts: The Christian Right in the 1998 Elections.* Washington, DC: Georgetown University Press, 2000.

Contributors provide analyses of the political activities of the religious right during the 1998 campaign in fourteen states, including South Carolina, Texas, California, Florida, Michigan, Minnesota, Illinois, and New York. The editors provide an overview of contributors' findings in individual states.

Gross, Rita M. *Feminism and Religion: An Introduction.* Boston: Beacon, 1996.

Gross focuses on feminism as a social movement, examining its effects on the religious thought, leadership, and institutions of the world's major religions, including Christianity, Judaism, Buddhism, Islam, and Hinduism, as well as new religious movements.

Guinness, Os. *The Great Experiment: Faith and Freedom in America.* Colorado Springs, CO: NavPress, 2001.

Guinness, senior fellow of the Trinity Forum in McLean, Virginia, discusses the importance of religious belief and practice to the maintenance of the United States as a free society and investigates what he considers major challenges to the political and social health of the country in the twenty-first century.

Gunton, Colin E., ed. *The Cambridge Companion to Christian Doctrine.* New York: Cambridge University Press, 1997.

These essays, written by theologians in North America and Great Britain, place Christian doctrine in its historical and cultural settings and outline its major themes. The authors present summaries of recent writings in Christian thought.

Gushee, David P., ed. *Christians and Politics beyond the Culture Wars: An Agenda for Engagement.* Grand Rapids, MI: Baker Book House, 2000.

Christian thinkers and social scientists, writing from differing theological perspectives, investigate the role of Christian belief and practice in the American political process. The essays are divided into two sections. In the first, authors focus on theoretical and historical topics, and in the second, contemporary moral and social issues are investigated and possible solutions are offered.

Gustafson, Carrie, and Peter Juviler, eds. *Religion and Human Rights: Competing Claims?* Armonk, NY: M. E. Sharpe, 1998.

The six essays and accompanying rejoinders included in this volume investigate possible influences of religion on human rights. The authors treat such topics as environmental rights, the place of women's rights in India, Iran, and Orthodox Judaism, the protection of rights in criminal justice systems, and the call for democratization in the Catholic Church in Latin America.

Guth, James L., John C. Green, Corwin E. Smidt, Lyman A. Kellstedt, and Margaret M. Poloma. *The Bully Pulpit: The Politics of Protestant Clergy.* Lawrence: University of Kansas Press, 1998.

The authors investigate the political role of Protestant clergy, providing empirical evidence of the differences between conservative and liberal theologians. Among the topics covered are the social theologies of Protestant clergy, the group's partisanship and voting behavior, attitudes about political involvement, and the perspectives on the American political system. The authors note that younger and more politically active clergy are replacing the older and politically inactive clergy in more conservative churches.

Gvosdev, Nikolas K. *Emperors and Elections: Reconciling the Orthodox Tradition with Modern Politics.* Huntington, NY: Nova Science, 2000.

Investigating the historical relationship between Orthodox Christianity and imperial rule, Gvosdev suggests that the Orthodox Christian faith has contemporary relevance to the stability of political regimes. The author claims that Orthodoxy can flourish in modern democracy and that Orthodox concepts such as the dignity of the individual and the value of community have a contribution to make to modern political thought.

Haddad, Yvonne Yazbeck. *Islamic Values in the United States.* New York: Oxford University Press, 1988.

Haddad focuses on the establishment of Islam in the United States, investigating the Islamic practices and the problems faced by the community, including the major social and political issues faced by American Muslims.

Haddad, Yvonne Yazbeck. *The Muslims of America.* New York: Oxford University Press, 1991.

This collection of essays by Haddad treats a variety of subjects, including the history, organization, and social, religious, and political thought and activity of the Muslim community in the United States. The author describes the unique challenges that have faced American Muslims who have enjoyed the freedom to experiment with differing religious practices, while at the same time suffering the consequences of sectarian division. One essay analyzes the effects of U.S. foreign policy in the Middle East on Arab Muslims in the United States.

Haddad, Yvonne Yazbeck, and John L. Esposito, eds. *Islam, Gender, and Social Change.* New York: Oxford University Press, 1997.

These essays trace the consequences for women of the religious revival of Islam around the world. This revival has included greater importance attributed to religious practice as well as the formation of Islamic institutions and movements. The essays evaluate the influence of Islam on gender issues in Iran, Egypt, Jordan, Pakistan, Oman, Bahrain, the Philippines, and Kuwait.

Haddad, Yvonne Yazbeck, and Jane Idleman Smith, eds. *Muslim Communities in North America.* Albany: State University of New York Press, 1994.

The essays in this volume treat the varied aspects of Islamic life in North America, including acculturation, ethnicity, orthodoxy, and the changing roles of women. Essays analyze the growing Islamic community among African Americans. Authors discuss the challenges faced by American Muslims, including prejudice and racism, pressure from Muslims in other countries, the use of traditional dress, and educational needs. Individual essays describe Muslim communities in various cities, including Los Angeles, California; Seattle, Washington; Rochester, New York; and Montreal, Canada.

Hadley, Michael L., ed. *The Spiritual Roots of Restorative Justice.* Albany: State University of New York Press, 2001.

Scholars from several disciplines explore approaches to the practice of criminal justice in a wide variety of religious traditions, including aboriginal spirituality, Buddhism, Hinduism, Islam, Judaism, and Sikhism.

Haleem, Harfiyah Abdel, Oliver Ramsbotham, Saba Risaluddin, and Brian Wicker, eds. *The Crescent and the Cross: Muslim and Christian Approaches to War and Peace.* New York: St. Martin's, 1998.

The articles herein examine the often intersecting histories of Muslim and Christian methods of developing the laws of warfare, which each religion bases on scripture. Authors explain the ways in which the laws of war still apply to violent conflict and how they relate to contemporary principles of international law.

Haleem, Muhammed Abdel. *Understanding the Qur'an: Themes and Styles.* New York: Palgrave, 2001.

Focusing on the basic tenets of Islam, which are important to understanding the social and political influences of the religion, Haleem investigates the major themes of the Qur'an. The author examines the construction of Islam's holy book, including the historical development of chapters and verses.

Hallaq, Wael B. *A History of Islamic Legal Theories.* New York: Cambridge University Press, 1997.

Hallaq outlines the evolutionary history of Islamic legal theory from its origins until modern times and identifies recent reforms. The author explicates legal concepts found in the Qur'an.

Halliday, Fred. *Islam and the Myth of Confrontation: Religion and Politics in the Middle East.* New York: I. B. Tauris, 1996.

Examining the perceived hostility between the West and Muslim nations, especially since the end of the cold war, Halliday attributes such tensions to those in the West who have replaced the communist threat with Islam, and those in Islamic countries who focus on differences with the West in order to establish their positions of power.

———. *Nation and Religion in the Middle East.* Boulder, CO: Lynne Rienner, 2000.

This book includes eleven essays by Halliday, each of which deals with some aspect of the interrelationships of religion and politics in the Middle East. Topics include the evolution of nationalism in Yemen and case studies of Saudi Arabia, Turkey, and Iran.

Hamdi, Mohamed Elhachmi. *The Making of an Islamic Political Leader: Conversations with Hasan Al-Turabi.* Boulder, CO: Westview, 1999.

Hasan al-Turabi, leader of the National Islamic Front, the Islamist party, which gained power in Sudan in 1989, was interviewed by Hamdi on three occasions over a period of a decade. Turabi discusses the growth of the Islamic political movement, the various conflicts that arose within the organization, and his position on various issues, including human rights, international relations, and the place of women within the movement.

Haney, Eleanor Humes. *The Great Commandment: A Theology of Resistance and Transformation.* Cleveland, OH: Pilgrim Press, 1998.

Focusing on the notion of oppression, Haney urges religious communities to confront instances of the phenomenon they either witness or are themselves engaged in perpetuating. She calls for economic, racial, and sexual justice, asking Christians to become more inclusive within the church as well as the larger society.

Hansen, Holger Bernt, and Michael Twaddle, eds. *Religion and Politics in East Africa: The Period since Independence*. Athens: Ohio University Press, 1995.

These essays analyze the increased importance of religious activities in protesting against postcolonial governments in East Africa. Among the topics covered are the rising influence of Islam, Christian involvement in the politics of Uganda, Christian and Muslim competition in Kenyan politics, and the complex combination of differing cultures in the interaction of religion and politics.

Hansen, Thomas Blom. *The Saffron Wave: Democracy and Hindu Nationalism in Modern India*. Princeton, NJ: Princeton University Press, 1999.

Concerned with the development of nationalist and religious movements in newly democratic countries, Hansen analyzes the popularity of the Hindu nationalist movement and the Bharatiya Janata Party in India. Associating the movement with conservative populism, the author notes that it appeals not only to the Indian middle class, but also to poor groups attracted by expressions of majoritarianism and nationalism.

Harper, Sharon, ed. *The Lab, the Temple, and the Market: Reflections at the Intersection of Science, Religion, and Development*. Bloomfield, CT: Bloomfield, 2000.

These essays examine the interaction of religious belief and economic development in differing cultures. Among the religions treated are Hinduism, Christianity, Islam, and the Baha'i faith. The authors suggest ways in which religious belief can be a potential motivator in scientific work.

Harris, Fredrick C. *Something Within: Religion in African-American Political Activism*. New York: Oxford University Press, 1999.

Focusing on explaining the political activism of African Americans, Harris examines the influence of religious belief and organized religion on the political behavior of African Americans. Through the use of such tools as historical investigation and survey research, the author portrays the contribution the church has made to democratic politics by encouraging political participation in the African American community.

Harris, Ian, ed. *Buddhism and Politics in Twentieth-Century Asia.* London: Continuum International Publishing Corporation, 2001.

The authors explore the nature of the interaction between Buddhist religious belief and politics in ten Asian countries. Investigating the ways in which Buddhist individuals and organizations have responded to such influences as westernization, nationalization, capitalism, socialism, and ethnic conflict, the essays focus on such issues as political divisions within monasteries and Buddhist social and political activism.

Hart, Stephen. *What Does the Lord Require? How American Christians Think about Economic Justice.* Piscataway, NJ: Rutgers University Press, 1996.

Basing his analysis on in-depth interviews with forty-seven church members, Hart investigates the relationship between Christians' religious beliefs and economic issues. The author concludes that the beliefs of many American Christians provide them with a perspective conducive to the pursuit of greater equality and economic justice as well as government intervention to achieve these objectives.

Hartman, David. *Israelis and the Jewish Tradition: An Ancient People Debating Its Future.* New Haven, CT: Yale University Press, 2000.

Hartman deals with the issues that have divided Israel's secular Jewish community from the religious Zionists and led to a polarization between religious and secular worldviews. Committed to religious pluralism, the author confronts the concerns of both groups and offers an understanding of Jewishness that involves different groups taking part in Jewish traditions.

Hatch, Nathan O. *The Democratization of American Christianity.* New Haven, CT: Yale University Press, 1989.

Hatch describes the development of a uniquely American brand of Christianity during the fifty years following the American Revolution. Examining five separate traditions—the Christian movement, the Methodists, the Baptists, black churches, and the Mormons—the author traces the emergence of a democratized Christianity in which the average American became a more active participant in religious affairs. These movements emphasized equality and individuality, focusing on each person's ability to interpret the Bible and take part in organizing congregations.

Haynes, Jeff, ed. *Religion, Globalization and Political Culture in the Third World.* New York: St. Martin's, 1999.

This work on the relationship between religion and politics contains treatments of such topics as the development of fundamentalist Islamic organizations in the Middle East and other Muslim countries, the political effects of the rise of Protestant evangelical groups in Latin America at the expense of the Catholic Church, the conflict between Hindu nationalist groups, and the political activity of Buddhists in Southeast Asia.

Hefner, Robert W. *Civil Islam.* Princeton, NJ: Princeton University Press, 2000.

Hefner presents a history of the interaction between Islam and democracy in Indonesia. He focuses on the Islamic reform movement, which assisted in the 1998 overthrow of Suharto's government and the establishment of a democratic system. In 1999 a moderate Muslim leader, Abdurrahman Wahid, was elected president. From this case study, Hefner concludes that there is no necessary inconsistency between Islam and democracy.

Hefner, Robert W., and Patricia Hovwatich, eds. *Islam in an Era of Nation-States: Politics and Religious Renewal in Muslim Southeast Asia.* Honolulu: University of Hawaii Press, 1997.

The essays in this volume are divided into three parts: descriptions of the relations between Southeast Asian governments and Islamic political organizations, analyses of the grassroots activities of reformist and resurgent Islamic movements, and explorations of the influence of reformist Islamic efforts on the attitudes of people at the grassroots level.

Heineman, Kenneth J. *God Is a Conservative: Religion, Politics, and Morality in Contemporary America.* New York: New York University Press, 1998.

Providing an overview of the interaction between religion and politics in the United States during the last three decades, Heineman considers whether the focus on morality in politics has led the nation toward a solution to its pressing problems, or represents a distraction from the real issues facing the country.

Hekmat, Anwar. *Women and the Koran: The Status of Women in Islam.* Amherst, NY: Prometheus, 1997.

Hekmat describes the severe social controls placed on the lives of women in Muslim countries, including Iran, Iraq, the United Arab Emirates, and Pakistan. Noting that Muhammad married a nine-year-old girl, the author observes that the Islamic religion has continued to sanction marriage between young girls and older men.

Hessel, Dieter T., and Rosemary Radford Ruether, eds. *Christianity and Ecology: Seeking the Well-Being of Earth and Humans.* Cambridge, MA: Harvard University Press, 2000.

The essays contained in this volume claim that Christian theology requires a reorientation toward a greater ecological consciousness. The authors explore themes within the Christian worldview that have contributed to ecological neglect and abuse and offer suggestions for greater social responsibility.

Hibri, Azizah, Jean Bethke Elshtain, and Charles C. Haynes. *Religion in American Public Life: Living with Our Deepest Differences.* New York: W. W. Norton, 2001.

This report of a meeting of the American Assembly focuses on the role of religion in U.S. public life and bridging the gap between the pubic realm and religion. Among the topics of discussion are religion's role in education, social services, and the mass media.

Hobbs, Ayaneda D., Avaneda D. Hobbs, and Demond Wilson. *From the Garden of Eden to America.* Forestville, MD: CAP Publishing, 1997.

The authors offer an historical and biblical investigation of religion among blacks and the development of black churches. Emphasis is placed on the social and psychological influences of race on religious organization. In addition, the book focuses on the importance of leadership in the development of black churches.

Hopkins, Dwight N. *Introducing Black Theology of Liberation.* Maryknoll, NY: Orbis, 1999.

Hopkins investigates the history of black theology from its origins in Africa and through its development in the United States. The author describes the role of black theologians during the political and racial disharmony of the 1960s and 1970s, from which emerged a clearer understanding of what it means to be black and Christian. Hopkins includes a discussion of women who criticized and confronted the sexist notions held by black male theologians.

Hoveyda, Fereydoun. *The Broken Crescent: The "Threat" of Militant Islamic Fundamentalism.* Westport, CT: Praeger, 1998.

Hoveyda examines the historical background to the rise of militant Islamic fundamentalism. The author attributes the stagnation in Muslim science and technology to the prevalence of fundamentalism beginning in the twelfth century. Hoveyda speculates that had it not been for the triumph of the fundamentalists, the industrial revolution could have occurred in the Muslim world.

Huang, Yong. *Religious Goodness and Political Rightness: Beyond the Liberal-Communitarian Debate.* Harrisburg, PA: Trinity Press International, 2001.

Huang analyzes the differing approaches of liberal and communitarian thinkers to the ideas of "the good" and "the right." He criticizes liberals as well as communitarians: the former for failing to recognize that politics cannot be neutral with regard to religious belief, and the latter for failing to recognize the dangers of establishing a single religion. Huang proposes a middle option that accepts the role of religious belief (hence recognizing the importance of religiously derived notions of the good) but within a religiously pluralistic society.

Hunt, Arnold D., Robert B. Crotty, and Marie T. Crotty. *Ethics of World Religions.* San Diego, CA: Greenhaven, 1991.

The authors examine the basic beliefs and ethical positions of Judaism, Christianity, Islam, Hinduism, Buddhism, Confucianism, and the Australian aboriginal religions. They focus on significant moral and social challenges (including dangers to the environment and the changing roles of women) facing those adhering to these religious traditions.

Hunter, Shireen T. *The Future of Islam and the West: Clash of Civilizations or Peaceful Coexistence?* Westport, CT: Praeger; with the Center for Strategic and International Studies, Washington, DC, 1998.

Hunter argues that Islamic civilization is not as monolithic as often assumed, referring to internal conflicts among Muslims. The author contends that Islam is not necessarily incompatible with democracy and rejects the idea that Islam will inevitably come into conflict with Western civilization, noting that many social, economic, and political conditions are responsible for the increased radical nature of Islam in some situations.

Hutson, James H., ed. *Religion and the New Republic: Faith in the Founding of America*. Lanham, MD: Rowman and Littlefield, 1999.

The authors of this collection of essays investigate the role of religion in the founding of the United States, and provide insight into the contemporary controversy over the relationship between church and state.

Ikeda, Daisaku. *For the Sake of Peace*. Chicago: Middleway Press, 2001.

Ikeda proposes methods of attaining worldwide peace, founded largely on Buddhist understandings of compassion and respect for human life. He bases his proposals on the teachings of Nichiren, a thirteenth-century Japanese Buddhist teacher, but also refers to such noted individuals through history as Plato, Aristotle, Leo Tolstoy, and Mohandas Gandhi. Ikeda's discussion of peace includes such topics as economics, the environment, disarmament, and religious belief.

Ireland, Rowan. *Kingdoms Come: Religion and Politics in Brazil*. Pittsburgh: University of Pittsburgh Press, 1992.

Ireland investigates the three major religious traditions in Brazil —Catholicism, Protestant Pentecostalism, and Afro-Brazilian spiritism—and their contrasting responses to the political realm. The author observes that adherents of each religion demonstrate distinctive attitudes toward political organization. Ireland finds within each religious tradition different perspectives on such structures as military authoritarianism and local political bosses.

Ivers, Gregg. *To Build a Wall: American Jews and the Separation of Church and State*. Charlottesville: University Press of Virginia, 1995.

Ivers examines the development of the American Jewish Committee, the American Jewish Congress, and the Anti-Defamation

League of B'nai B'rith (ADL) from social service agencies to interest groups influential in American public policy making particularly through the use of litigation to protect religious freedom. In his analysis, the author employs materials from each organization's archives, interviews with members, and amicus curiae briefs in establishment clause court cases. Ivers observes differing approaches to litigation among the three groups that he attributes to the ethnic, economic, and religious variations of their membership.

Jaber, Hala. *Hezbollah.* Irvington, NY: Columbia University Press, 1997.

Jaber, a journalist, gained access to the leadership of Hezbollah, a militant group working to bring about the Islamic revolution. The author reveals the history, ideology, culture, and tactics of this radical Islamic movement.

Janz, Danis R. *World Christianity and Marxism.* New York: Oxford University Press, 1998.

Janz recounts the confrontation between Christianity and Marxism in the twentieth century, noting the strong challenge Marxism posed for organized religion. The author begins with Karl Marx's attack on Christianity, the basis for all future Marxist confrontations with religion, and investigates Christian responses to Marxist thought from the midnineteenth century to the beginning of the cold war. Janz concludes that Christianity's rejection of Marxism was not completely successful.

Jawad, Haifaa A. *The Rights of Women in Islam: An Authentic Approach.* New York: St. Martin's, 1998.

Although the claim has been made that Islam freed Muslim women by providing them with the rights of citizenship, Jawad observes that in many places in the Muslim world, women have suffered from cultural and political subjugation. The author contrasts the actual treatment of women with what scripture in fact decrees.

Jelen, Ted. *To Serve God and Mammon: Church-State Relations in American Politics.* Boulder, CO: Westview, 2000.

Jelen analyzes the role of religion in the democratic political process, presenting an historical overview of church-state relations in the United States. The author discusses the conflict over church-state relations on various political levels, including local, state, and national government arenas. Jelen notes a shift in church-state debates from the First Amendment's establishment clause to questions of free exercise of religion.

Johnson, Curtis D. *Redeeming America: Evangelicals and the Road to Civil War.* Chicago: Ivan R. Dee, 1993.

Johnson examines the influences of evangelical Protestantism on American culture prior to the Civil War and analyzes the evangelical attitudes toward Roman Catholics and nonbelievers as well as the conflicts over theological ideas among evangelicals, including differing social classes and African Americans. The author focuses on the alteration of beliefs about slavery among evangelicals leading up to the Civil War.

Juergensmeyer, Mark. *Terror in the Mind of God: The Global Rise of Religious Violence.* Berkeley: University of California Press, 2000.

In an attempt to explain the relationship between religion and violence, Juergensmeyer describes the rise of religious terrorism, focusing on such topics as Hamas suicide bombers, antiabortion groups, and violence-prone Buddhist sectarians. The author bases his analysis on interviews that he conducted with several religious terrorists, many of whom were already imprisoned for their violent acts. Juergensmeyer associates religiously motivated violence with deeply held beliefs about good, evil, and eternal life that lead to the conviction that the forces of good must battle the perceived forces of evil.

Kamali, Mohammad Hashim. *Principles of Islamic Jurisprudence.* New York: Palgrave, 1999.

Kamali discusses the basic theory of Islamic law and jurisprudence as well as the derivation of religious laws from the Qur'an. Awareness of Islamic understandings of law has become increasingly important as Muslim countries have shifted toward reintroducing Islamic law.

Kang, Wi Jo. *Christ and Caesar in Modern Korea: A History of Christianity and Politics.* Albany: State University of New York Press, 1997.

Kang describes the history of Korean Christianity, focusing on the political activism of some South Korean Christians and their involvement in political reform. The author explores the possibility of unification between North and South Korea through religious cooperation.

Katzenstein, Mary Fainsod. *Faithful and Fearless: Moving Feminist Protest inside the Church and Military.* Princeton, NJ: Princeton University Press, 1998.

Katzenstein argues that the protests of the 1960s have not ceased, but have instead moved within particular institutions such as the military and the church. The author examines protests against various forms of discrimination and demands for change that women have made in the United States military and the Roman Catholic Church. In her treatment of the church, Katzenstein interviewed lay activists and nuns, discovering that women are loyal to the church at the same time that they are attempting to reshape the institution to grant them a larger role.

Kaza, Stephanie, and Kenneth Kraft, eds. *Dharma Rain: Sources of Buddhist Environmentalism.* Boston: Shambhala, 2000.

The essays in this volume investigate the increasing social activism of Buddhists who are concerned about harmful effects of unlimited consumerism on the environment. Case studies are presented of Thailand, where nearly 70 percent of the forests have been destroyed, and Tibet, where the Communist regime has allowed the destruction of wildlife. The essays propose that a Buddhist perspective can assist in dealing with the world's ecological crisis.

Khare, R.S. *Perspectives on Islamic Law, Justice, and Society.* Lanham, MD: Rowman and Littlefield, 1999.

Khare discusses various aspects of Islamic law, justice, and social tradition, ultimately focusing on interrelated legal, historical, and pragmatic issues involving Islamic law in such countries as Algeria, Morocco, and South Africa.

Khawaja, Mahboob A. *Muslims and the West: Quest for "Change" and Conflict Resolution.* Lanham, MD: University Press of America, 2000.

Khawaja calls for a reexamination of the meaning of Islamic fundamentalism. The author investigates the concept of change in Western and Islamic societies and discusses the difficulty involved in finding common ground between them.

Klaiber, Jeffrey. *The Church, Dictatorships, and Democracy in Latin America.* Maryknoll, NY: Orbis, 1998.

Klaiber investigates the history of the Catholic Church in Latin America from the colonial period to the present, focusing particularly on Peru, Mexico, Nicaragua, and Guatemala, and treating such topics as human rights and the development of democracy. Other countries examined are Brazil, Chile, Argentina, Bolivia, El Salvador, Paraguay, and Uruguay.

Kohut, Andrew, John C. Green, Scott Keeter, and Robert C. Toth. *The Diminishing Divide: Religion's Changing Role in American Politics.* Washington, DC: Brookings Institution, 2000.

The authors investigate the influence religion has had on American political attitudes and behavior. They argue that, despite the principle of separation of church and state, there has never been a strict division between the two spheres and that religion will continue to play a role in shaping American political life into the twenty-first century.

Konvitz, Milton Ridvas. *Torah and Constitution: Essays in American Jewish Thought.* Syracuse, NY: Syracuse University Press, 1998.

These thirteen essays cover such topics as the Greek foundations of the American Constitution, the connection between the Torah and the American governing document, the importance of law both in the American tradition as well as in Judaism, the covenants of the first European settlers compared to the covenant between the early Jews and the God of Israel, and the Jewish struggle for equality in the United States.

Kraybill, Donald B. *The Puzzles of Amish Life.* Intercourse, PA: Good Books, 1990.

Kraybill takes a brief look at the Amish sect, which has been at the center of important judicial decisions dealing with freedom of religion. The author answers eighteen questions about the Amish community, which rejects much of the scientific and technological advancement in modern society. The Amish try to remain separated from contemporary society, including politics and government. Kraybill notes that although some Amish vote, as a group they avoid public office, refuse to serve in the military, and decline to participate in government programs such as Social Security and subsidized agriculture.

Kraybill, Donald B., ed. *The Amish and the State*. Baltimore, MD: Johns Hopkins University Press, 1993.

Beginning in the early eighteenth century, the Amish came to North America expecting to obtain religious freedom. However, periodically they found themselves in conflict with government and the larger society. These essays examine these conflicts in the United States and Canada, including those over military service and conscription, Social Security and taxes, education, health care, land use, and regulation of slow-moving (horse-drawn) vehicles. In a concluding essay, William Ball analyzes the contribution the Amish have made to the preservation of religious liberty in the United States.

Kulczycki, Andrzej. *The Abortion Debate in the World Arena*. New York: Routledge, 1999.

Kulczycki conducted interviews with many government officials and church leaders and engaged in research in Kenya, Mexico, and Poland in order to determine how cultural history, women's movements, and the Catholic Church have affected abortion policies in those countries.

Kurzman, Charles. *Liberal Islam*. New York: Oxford University Press, 1998.

Kurzman provides a more balanced view of Islam, claiming that "Liberal Islam" is alive and well. The author presents the writings of thirty-two Muslims who offer more liberal positions on such issues as the separation of church and state, the place of democracy, the role of women in Islamic society, the rights of minorities, civil liberties, and the prospects for progress.

Lawler, Peter Augustine, and Dale McConkey, eds. *Faith, Reason, and Political Life Today*. Lanham, MD: Lexington Books, 2001.

This collection of essentially philosophical essays examines the importance of Christianity as well as classical thought for the modern age. Individual essays focus on such classical and contemporary thinkers as Aristotle, Augustine, Aquinas, Alexis de Tocqueville, Alexander Solzhenitsyn, Flannery O'Connor, and Walker Percy. Contributors treat such subjects as the relationship between reason and revelation, classical philosophy and Christianity, repentance and self-limitation, and philosophy and politics.

Lawrence, Bruce B. *Shattering the Myth: Islam beyond Violence.* Princeton, NJ: Princeton University Press, 1998.

Lawrence challenges what he considers the myths and biases created by Western journalists who portray Islam as a violent, monolithic religion whose adherents frequently engage in armed struggle with nonbelievers. The author views Islam as a multiethnic, worldwide religion whose adherents are influenced by basic religious principles and ethics as much as by contemporary political circumstances. Lawrence advises against stereotyping the role of women or attitudes toward democracy in Muslin societies.

Leege, David C., and Lyman A. Kellstedt. *Rediscovering the Religious Factor in American Politics.* Armonk, NY: M. E. Sharpe, 1993.

Leege and Kellstedt examine several aspects of the relationship between religious institutions and American politics, including the general significance of religion to politics, the relevance of religion to group membership, the conception of religion in terms of public and private practices, the effects of religious belief on perceptions of the world, and the possible effects of religious affiliation on political attitudes and voting behavior.

Lehmann, David. *Democracy and Development in Latin America: Economics, Politics and Religion in the Postwar Period.* Philadelphia, PA: Temple University Press, 1990.

Lehmann places a discussion of Latin American liberation theology in the wider context of social, economic, and political thought and the recent history of popular social movements. Economic, political, and religious reform merge in an emphasis on democratic development at the grassroots level that will contribute to the reestablishment of civil societies and states on the verge of disintegration. The author concentrates his investigation on Argentina, Brazil, and Chile.

Levenson, Claude B. *The Dalai Lama: A Biography.* New York: Oxford University Press, 1999.

Levenson recounts the story of how a child from a Tibetan peasant family became the fourteenth reincarnation of the Dalai Lama, or the Buddha of Infinite Compassion. More broadly, the author examines the Tibetan civilization based on a complex Buddhist tradition.

Levine, David H. *Religion and Political Conflict in Latin America*. Chapel Hill: University of North Carolina Press, 2001.

Levine focuses on changes in the Roman Catholic Church in Latin America since 1968. Investigating the popular calls at the grassroots level for social change, the author suggests those relationships with the local level that the Catholic Church should develop in order to regain its status in the societies of Latin America.

Levinsohn, Florence Hamlish. *Looking for Farrakhan*. Chicago: Ivan R. Dee, 1997.

Levinsohn presents a biographical portrait of Louis Farrakhan, leader of the Nation of Islam, also called the Black Muslims. The author places Farrakhan's leadership in historical context, exploring Marcus Garvey's nineteenth-century back-to-Africa movement and other precursors to Farrakhan's emphasis on racial pride as the foundation of his leadership. Levinsohn analyzes the common belief that the Black Muslim leader is revered among African Americans but generally disdained among whites.

Levinson, David. *Religion: A Cross-Cultural Dictionary*. New York: Oxford University Press, 1997.

Levinson chronicles the history of religion from its claimed beginnings in primitive spiritualism thousands of years ago. The author provides information on sixteen current religions, discussing each one's origins, philosophy, dogma, and practices. Other entries deal with similarities as well as differences among religious practices in differing cultures.

Li Hongzhi. *China Falun Gong*. Rev. ed. New York: Universe, 2000.

Li Hongzhi, the founder of the Falun Gong movement in China in the late 1990s, which became known worldwide due to the Chinese government's attempts to discourage adherents, introduces the training regimen involved in Falun Gong. Among the topics covered are the mind-body relationship, the origins of illness and the process of healing, and the nature of religious practice. The objective is to live a life of "truthfulness, compassion, and forbearance."

Lia, Brynjar, and Jamal Al-Banna. *The Society of the Muslim Brothers in Egypt: The Rise of an Islamic Mass Movement 1928–1942*. Chicago: Garnet/Ithaca, 1998.

The authors describe the swift rise of the Muslim Brotherhood, originally founded in 1928 by Hasan al-Banna, an Egyptian primary school teacher. They examine the social, economic, and cultural conditions, as well as organizational characteristics —including internal structure, strategies for action, and methods of recruiting members—that contributed to the movement's success.

Lischer, Richard. *The Preacher King: Martin Luther King, Jr. and the Word that Moved America.* New York: Oxford University Press, 1995.

Lischer employs a wide variety of sources, including King's unpublished sermons and speeches, recordings, and interviews to provide an accurate portrayal of the African American religious leader and his role in the civil rights movement in the United States.

Litvak, Meir. *Shi'i Scholars of Nineteenth-Century Iraq.* New York: Cambridge University Press, 1998.

Litvak investigates the social and political conditions of the shrine cities of Najaf and Karbala in nineteenth-century Iraq and follows the historical development of Islamic Shi'ite leadership. The book not only provides historical information about Shi'ism but also offers insights into the religious sect's social and political importance in the contemporary Middle East.

Long, Carolyn N. *Religious Freedom and Indian Rights: The Case of* **Oregon v. Smith.** Lawrence: University Press of Kansas, 2000.

The First Amendment protection of free exercise of religion has been open to controversy and ultimately court interpretation. Long recounts the case of two Native Americans, Alfred Smith and Galen Black, who lost their jobs as drug rehabilitation counselors because they participated in a religious ceremony of the Native American Church in which peyote, a controlled substance, was used. When Oregon denied unemployment benefits to the two men, they brought suit against the state, claiming infringement of religious freedom. The U.S. Supreme Court ultimately ruled against the two men, arguing that statutes indirectly restricting free exercise of religion do not violate the First Amendment. Long's treatment of the case is based on interviews with Smith, his lawyers, judges, public officials, and interest group representatives.

Lopez, Donald S. *Prisoners of Shangri-La: Tibetan Buddhism and the West.* Chicago: University of Chicago Press, 1998.

Lopez claims that Western writers have misinterpreted Tibetan Buddhism by attempting to understand aspects of the Buddhist religion and Tibetan culture in terms of their own psychological and professional needs. Taken out of context, Tibetan culture and religion become platitudes for Western writers. In order to win sympathy in the West for independence from China, Tibetans tend to support these misinterpretations, which, according to Lopez, actually impairs the nation's struggle for autonomy by weakening its cultural uniqueness.

Lowy, Michael. *The War of Gods: Religion and Politics in Latin America.* New York: Verso, 1996.

Employing a cultural perspective, Lowy investigates the relationship between religion, politics, and economic and social issues in Latin America. Focusing on Brazil and Central America, the author describes the social struggles that gave rise to liberation theology, including the Nicaraguan revolution, the rise of Jean Bertrand Aristide, a Roman Catholic priest, as president of Haiti, and the development of the Workers' Party in Brazil.

Lugo, Luis E., ed. *Religion, Public Life, and the American Polity.* Knoxville: University of Tennessee Press, 1994.

These ten essays deal with various topics related to religion and U.S. public life, including current opposing views on church-state relations; reappraisals of the positions of early Americans, such as James Madison and Thomas Jefferson, on the separation of church and state; the relationship between religion and law, particularly as presented in First Amendment court cases; and more general analyses of the influence that religion and U.S. liberal culture have had on each other.

Mackey, James P. *Power and Christian Ethics.* New York: Cambridge University Press, 1994

Mackey deals with such topics as the morality of ethics and apparent amorality of power, the humanizing of power and investing it with moral purposes, the Christian's role in the humanization of power, and Christians' attempts to deal with concrete instances of power in the civil and ecclesiastical realms.

Maddox, Graham. *Religion and the Rise of Democracy.* New York: Routledge, 1996.

In this extensive study, Maddox examines the role that religion has played in the development of democracy from the ancient Israeli tribes to the present.

Magesa, Laurenti. *African Religion: The Moral Traditions of Abundant Life.* Maryknoll, NY: Orbis, 1997.

Magesa explores the indigenous religions of Africa, focusing on the religious practices of various tribes. The author attempts to make the case that African religion represents one of the world's religions.

Magida, Arthur J. *Prophet of Rage: A Life of Louis Farrakhan and His Nation.* New York: Basic Books, 1996.

Magida, a Jew, examines the Nation of Islam leader Louis Farrakhan in the context of what the author considers the anti-Semitism of the organization's members. The author focuses on the attraction that Farrakhan has for African Americans who have suffered discrimination and deprivation. Magida, who was granted interviews with Farrakhan, doubts whether the religious leader can provide any answers to the plight of the people for whom he claims to speak.

Mahmood, Cynthia Keppley. *Fighting for Faith and Nation: Dialogues with Sikh Militants.* Philadelphia: University of Pennsylvania Press, 1996.

Mahmood discusses human rights abuses suffered by the Sikhs at the hands of India, using interviews with Sikh militants. The author explains the philosophical tradition of martyrdom and the meaning of death as presented in the Sikh faith. Although perspectives on the world may differ greatly, Mahmood attempts to discover avenues for practical solutions to such deep-rooted conflicts.

Maley, William, ed. *Fundamentalism Reborn? Afghanistan and the Taliban.* New York: New York University Press, 1998.

This collection of scholarly articles written by Afghan specialists explores what is considered the most important Islamic movement of the 1990s. Articles deal with the rise of the Taliban to power; outside economic and political influences on the Taliban; the Taliban's relationships with international aid organizations; the Taliban's policies toward women; and the organization's prospects for continuing success and as a future model for Islam.

Malik, Iftikhar H. *Islam, Nationalism and the West: Issues of Identity in Pakistan.* New York: St. Martin's, 1999.

Malik emphasizes the correspondence as well as conflict between Islam and the West. The author analyzes such events as the Salman Rushdie incident, the Iranian revolution, civil war in Afghanistan, and the diplomatic strategies of Western nations.

Manis, Andrew Michael. *A Fire You Can't Put Out: The Civil Rights Life of Birmingham's Reverend Fred Shuttlesworth.* Tuscaloosa: University of Alabama Press, 1999.

Manis provides an account of Reverend Fred Shuttlesworth and his leadership in the civil rights movement in Birmingham, Alabama, in the 1950s. Shuttlesworth's concern for social justice was closely related to his duties as pastor of a local church. The author describes the personal and professional costs that the civil rights advocate faced, including the 1956 bombing of his home and the disapproval of more cautious and conservative religious leaders in the community.

Marlow, Louise. *Hierarchy and Egalitarianism in Islamic Thought.* New York: Cambridge University Press, 1997.

Marlow analyzes Arab and Persian literature, concluding that although Islam's original orientation was egalitarian, the social manifestations of egalitarianism were seriously weakened due to Islam's political success.

Marsden, George M. *The Soul of the American University: From Protestant Establishment to Established Nonbelief.* New York: Oxford University Press, 1994.

Marsden analyzes and critiques the era when the Protestant establishment dominated much of higher education in the United States, from the founding of Harvard in the 1630s to the 1960s. The author recounts the secularization of such institutions, including the accommodation of such movements as feminism and multiculturalism, and recommends that traditional religious viewpoints should be granted a place once more in the academy.

———. *The Outrageous Idea of Christian Scholarship.* New York: Oxford University Press, 1997.

Marsden argues that religious belief, just as race and gender, can serve as a legitimate consideration in noting the relevant influences on a scholar's perspective. The author argues that higher education in the United States should be receptive to expressions of faith and should acknowledge the significance of religious belief in intellectual inquiry. To the extent that the educational establishment influences the larger society, Marsden's recommendation has potential social and political significance.

Marsden, Peter. *The Taliban: War, Religion and the New Order in Afghanistan*. New York: Zed Books, 1998.

After the Taliban takeover of Afghanistan in 1996, Islamic law was severely imposed on the population, including removing women from workplaces and ending education for girls until an Islamic school system could be established. Marsden traces Taliban ideology to the Sunni Wahhabi movement in the 1700s, provides an analysis of views within the contemporary movement, and describes its strained relations with international relief organizations.

Marsh, Charles. *God's Long Summer: Stories of Faith and Civil Rights*. Princeton, NJ: Princeton University Press, 1997.

Arguing that the civil rights movement should be understood in religious terms, Marsh provides an account of the freedom marches in the American South during summer 1964. The book includes personal accounts of the activities of civil rights leaders, offering evidence of the major role played by religious conviction in a political struggle.

Martin, David. *Does Christianity Cause War?* New York: Oxford University Press, 1997.

Martin provides a more complex answer to the question posed in the title, shunning what he considers the overly simplistic beliefs that religion either incites war or that religion promotes peace. The author examines case studies from Great Britain, the United States, Latin America, and Rumania to present an approach that includes such sociological variables as national and ethnic identity.

Marty, Martin E. *Politics, Religion, and the Common Good*. San Francisco: Jossey-Bass, 2000.

Marty investigates the role of religion in contemporary American politics. Although the author cautions that "public religion" can lead to dangers, including extremism and religious violence, he notes that churches, denominations, and wider religious organizations can encourage political participation and provide a public voice for those who have religious beliefs.

Matinuddin, Kamal. *The Taliban Phenomenon: Afghanistan 1994–1997.* New York: Oxford University Press, 1999.

Matinuddin investigates the origin and objectives of the Islamic Taliban movement in Afghanistan. The author analyzes the possible reasons for the Taliban's success and speculates on the religious regime's effects on its neighbors, including Pakistan.

Mayer, Ann Elizabeth. *Islam and Human Rights: Tradition and Politics.* 3d ed. Boulder, CO: Westview, 1998.

Mayer investigates the political objectives of conservative Islamic groups that allegedly oppose democracy and human rights in the name of Islamic law. The author contends that certain Islamic pronouncements on human rights jeopardize the recognition of human rights within international law. Mayer does not portray a monolithic Islamic position on human rights, observing progress toward protection of such rights in some Islamic countries.

Mazur, Eric Michael. *The Americanization of Religious Minorities: Confronting the Constitutional Order.* Baltimore, MD: Johns Hopkins University Press, 1999.

Investigating the sometimes incompatible demands of church and state, Mazur recounts the experiences of Jehovah's Witnesses, Mormons, and Native Americans. The author discusses instances in which religious minorities attempted to maintain their religious practices in a larger political order that was at times hostile to their beliefs.

McClory, Robert. *Power and the Papacy: The People and Politics Behind the Doctrine of Infallibility.* Chicago: Triumph Books, 1997.

McClory outlines the historical evolution and present meaning of papal infallibility and analyzes disputes over this doctrine, which establishes the Roman Catholic pope as the supreme authority within the church hierarchy and over Catholics worldwide.

McKean, Kise. *Divine Enterprise: Gurus and the Hindu Nationalist Movement.* Chicago: University of Chicago, 1996.

McKean analyzes the relationship between religious leaders, politics, and business interests in India, tracing the origins of the Hindu nationalist movement. The author discusses the ways in which gurus advocate Hindu nationalism through the use of religious symbolism, illustrates the use of Hindu images in the market economy, and explains the close relationship of religious groups with political parties.

Melling, Philip. *Fundamentalism in America: Millennialism, Identity and Militant Religion.* Chicago: Fitzroy Dearborn Publishers, 2000.

In this examination of the religious right in the United States, Melling describes how a combination of scriptural interpretation and political beliefs led to strong opposition to President Bill Clinton's administration. The author investigates the writings of such Christian figures as Pat Robertson and Hal Lindsey and their response to the evolution of the world system and the role the United States is playing in rapidly changing conditions.

Menashri, David. *Post-Revolutionary Politics in Iran.* London: Frank Cass Publishers, 2001.

Menashri explores the various tensions that have developed in Iran's Islamic government between dedication to revolutionary Islamic ideology and the pull toward pragmatic responses to the imperatives of actual governing. The author examines the complex relationship between domestic conditions and Iran's foreign policy.

Mendelsohn, Ezra. *On Modern Jewish Politics.* New York: Oxford University Press, 1993.

Investigating such widely varying areas as literature, art, and music, Mendelsohn explores the nature of contemporary Jewish political involvement.

Menendez, Albert J. *Church and State in Canada.* Amherst, NY: Prometheus, 1996.

Menendez provides an overview of the relationship between religion and politics in Canada, focusing on such topics as abortion rights, Sunday closing laws, the religious rights of employees, divorce, and religious observance in public education. A final chapter compares the Canadian experience with the United States.

Mernissi, Fatima. *The Veil and the Male Elite: A Feminist Interpretation of Women's Rights in Islam.* Trans. Mary Jo Lakeland. Boulder, CO: Perseus, 1992.

This book examines the place of women in Islam, focusing on the origins of the religion and Muhammad's claimed intention to create a society free of slavery and sexual discrimination. The author argues that the male elite within Islam that is concerned about maintaining its political and economic status, rather than the injunctions of Islam, is responsible for denying equal rights to women.

Messaoudi, Khalida, with Elisabeth Schemla. *Unbowed: An Algerian Woman Confronts Islamic Fundamentalism.* Trans. Anne C. Vila. Philadelphia: University of Pennsylvania Press, 1998.

Messaoudi reveals her own experience as leader of feminist and democratic movements in Algeria and as an opponent to Islamic fundamentalism. Sentenced to death in 1993 by the Islamic Salvation Front, Messaoudi went into hiding in Algeria, continuing her struggle for emancipation for women and freedom from religious extremism. She calls for women's right to become engaged in a profession and earn a living, marry and divorce as they wish, and be seen in public without a veil.

Milton-Edwards, Beverly. *Islamic Politics in Palestine.* New York: St. Martin's, 1999.

Milton-Edwards investigates the identity and characteristics of the Palestinian Islamists who are associated with attempts to upset the Palestinian-Israeli peace process. Using interviews with Palestinian and Jordanian Islamists and other primary sources as well as historical records, the author discusses what motivates the Palestinian Islamists and how they became a powerful influence in the Middle East.

Mische, Patricia M., and Melissa Merkling, eds. *Toward a Global Civilization? The Contribution of Religions.* New York: Peter Lang, 2001.

The twenty-one contributors to this volume, drawn from the world's major religions, explain the contributions their respective religious traditions can make to the development of a global perspective that respects cultural and religious diversity. The authors are concerned with the application of such a perspective to the establishment of an international governing system.

Mishal, Shaul, and Avraham Sela. *The Palestinian Hamas: Vision, Violence, and Coexistence.* Irvington, NY: Columbia University Press, 2000.

Through an examination of the activities of the Hamas (Islamic Resistance Movement), the authors, who are Israeli scholars, attempt to show that the organization is basically a social and political movement that offers community services and engages in political bargaining. They portray the organization as facing difficult choices between the call for all-out warfare in support of the Islamic cause (jihad) and more limited options for violence.

Moin, Baqer. *Khomeini: Life of the Ayatollah.* New York: St. Martin's, 2000.

Moin, a British Broadcasting Company journalist, offers a highly detailed history of the Ayatollah Khomeini and his rise to power in Iran. Although Khomeini was born into a clerical family and received a traditional religious education, the author contends that the ayatollah's participation in politics was a thoroughly modern phenomenon. Moin traces Khomeini's opposition to Shah Mohammad Reza's attempts to westernize and secularize Iran and focuses on the crucial factors that led to the shah's fall from power. The ayatollah demonstrated great skill in consolidating his political influence while eliminating competing groups. Although the influence of Khomeini's institutional reforms and devotion to his memory remain strong more than ten years after his death, Moin perceives signs of significant change in Iranian society and politics based on the Western liberal tradition.

Moldovan, Russel. *Martin Luther King, Jr.: An Oral History of His Religious Witness and His Life.* New York: Cambridge University Press, 1999.

Moldovan examines the influence of Martin Luther King's religious convictions and rhetorical style on those who heard him preach in Selma and Birmingham, Alabama, and in Chicago, Illinois, during the civil rights era. The author places King's oratory within the context of racial discrimination, which he calls "America's social and cultural nightmare."

Monshipouri, Mahmood. *Islamism, Secularism, and Human Rights in the Middle East.* Boulder, CO: Lynne Rienner, 1998.

Monshipouri investigates the political histories of three countries—Turkey, Iran, and Pakistan—in order to evaluate the role of

Islam in discouraging the acceptance of human rights among its followers. The author concludes that Muslims should distinguish between Western political and economic influence and assent to principles of human rights.

Monsma, Stephen V. *When Sacred and Secular Mix: Religious Nonprofit Organizations and Public Money.* Lanham, MD: Rowman and Littlefield, 2000.

Monsma bases his analysis of public support for religiously based nonprofit organizations on a survey of approximately 800 faith-based groups. The First Amendment principle of separation of church and state notwithstanding, hundreds of millions of dollars flow from government to religious organizations for what are considered socially useful purposes.

Monsma, Stephen V., and J. Christopher Soper. *The Challenge of Pluralism: Church and State in Five Democracies.* Lanham, MD: Rowman and Littlefield, 1997.

Monsma and Soper illuminate church-state relations in the United States by presenting a cross-national analysis of such relations in five countries. The authors pay close attention to the similarities across national boundaries as well as the uniqueness of each country.

Morcillo, Aurora G. *True Catholic Womanhood: Gender Ideology in Franco's Spain.* DeKalb: Northern Illinois University Press, 2000.

Morcillo investigates the status of women during Francisco Franco's rule in Spain, contrasting the official promotion of economic development and the simultaneous attempt to maintain the traditional Catholic expectation that women remain passive and outside the public realm.

Moses, Greg. *Revolution of Conscience: Martin Luther King, Jr., and the Philosophy of Nonviolence.* New York: Guilford, 1997.

Moses traces the intellectual development of the understanding that Martin Luther King Jr., religious leader and civil rights advocate, had of the notion of nonviolent resistance, focusing on the philosophical linkages of King's activism in American politics with earlier African American thinkers.

Mott, Stephen Charles. *A Christian Perspective on Political Thought.* New York: Oxford University Press, 1993.

Mott combines a Christian theological viewpoint with analyses of contemporary political thought. The author's objective is to demonstrate the practical value of a Christian democratic approach to public policy.

Moussalli, Ahmad. *Historical Dictionary of Islamic Fundamentalist Movements in the Arab World, Iran, and Turkey.* Lanham, MD: Scarecrow, 1999.

This extensive reference work provides information on a wide variety of topics, including the basic doctrines, ideologies, leaders, groups, and movements of Islamic fundamentalism. The author offers information about the origins and activities of Islamic fundamentalists as well as the principles on which such activities are based.

Moyser, George, ed. *Politics and Religion in the Modern World.* New York: Routledge, 1991.

Recognizing that religion is intimately involved in many contemporary political questions, Moyser, a political scientist, searches for reasons why religion and politics have proven such a volatile force in various parts of the world.

Mudimbe, V. Y. *Tales of Faith: Religion as Political Performance in Central Africa.* Somerset, NJ: Athlone Press, 1997.

Mudimbe, professor of comparative literature and the classics at Stanford University, investigates the tensions between the Christian communities and others in Africa and the attempts to find common philosophical agreement.

Murphy, Larry G. *Down by the Riverside: Readings in African American Religion.* New York: New York University Press, 2000.

Murphy investigates the development of African American religion and theology in the United States from the era of slavery to the present. Moving beyond Protestant Christian movements, the author examines a wide variety of religious expression, including Black Judaism, African American Catholicism, Islam, black religious nationalism, and black feminist theology.

Naraghi, Ehsan. *From Palace to Prison: Inside the Iranian Revolution.* Trans. Nilou Mobasser. Chicago: Ivan R. Dee, 1993.

Naraghi, a sociologist in Iran before the Islamic revolution of 1979, presents a personal account of Iran's transformation from a monarchy to an Islamic state. In 1978 the author was summoned by Mohammad Reza, the Shah of Iran, who asked for the scholar's counsel regarding the increasing tension within the country. Following the revolution and the Ayatollah Ruhollah Khomeini's rise to power, Naraghi spent nearly three years in prison before his release and exile in France.

Nardin, Terry, ed. *The Ethics of War and Peace: Religious and Secular Perspectives.* Princeton, NJ: Princeton University Press, 1998.

The essays contained in this edited volume explore attitudes found in religious and secular ethical traditions regarding war and its conduct. Jewish, Islamic, and Christian perspectives are presented, covering such topics as the possible justifications for involvement in warfare, the limitations that each religious tradition observes in the conduct of hostilities, and under what extreme circumstances such limitations might be set aside.

Nasr, Seyyed Vali Reza. *Mawdudi and the Making of Islamic Revivalism.* New York: Oxford University Press, 1996.

Nasr recounts the political influence of Islamic leader Mawdudi, who attempted to interpret Islam as a response to European colonization. The author provides an understanding of the historical background to contemporary Islamic religious and political movements.

Nesbitt, Paula, ed. *Religion and Social Policy.* Lanham, MD: Rowman and Littlefield, 2001.

Although the general assumption has been that religion in industrialized countries has become a private matter while questions of social justice are considered a public realm that is necessarily secular, the authors of these essays investigate the role that religious values play at various levels of governing, from the local to the international sphere, in influencing those who make, and those who are affected by, policies. The authors make explicit the religious positions of national governments and international nongovernmental organizations on such issues as gender roles, economic inequality, and religious tolerance.

Nichols, David. *God and Government in an "Age of Reason."* New York: Routledge, 1995.

Nichols argues that much of the language about deity has a political focus, as in biblical references to God as ruler, lord, king, and judge. The author observes that the ways in which a society perceives God closely interacts with its conception of authority, a crucial concept in politics.

Nielsen, Jorgen. *Christian-Muslim Frontier: Chaos, Clash, or Dialogue?* New York: St. Martin's, 1998.

Nielsen investigates popular beliefs about the conflict of beliefs between the contemporary world of Islam and Christianity, contending that much of the discussion about this issue has been uninformed and inspired by the mass media. There has been a more serious attempt by scholars to identify a threat from Muslim fundamentalism that is considered a replacement for the now-defunct competition between free enterprise and communism. Nielsen evaluates these claims of an antagonistic confrontation between two major world religions and cultures.

Nisan, Mordechai. *Identity and Civilization: Essays on Judaism, Christianity, and Islam.* Lanham, MD: University Press of America, 1999.

Nisan examines Judaism, Christianity, and Islam as political rivals in the conflict between Israel and the Arab states. The author investigates the role of religion and culture in the political conflicts in the Middle East in order to clarify what might contribute to a lasting peace in the region.

Nonneman, Gerd, Tim Niblock, and Bogdan Szajkowski, eds. *Muslim Communities in the New Europe.* Chicago: Garnet/ Ithaca, 1998.

These essays survey Muslim communities in Europe. The first part deals with Eastern Europe and the second with Western Europe. The essays on Eastern Europe focus on such countries as Bosnia, Bulgaria, Albania, and Greece, determining how the Muslim communities were created and how they interact with the non-Muslim population. The essays on Western Europe, including treatments of such countries as Belgium, France, Germany, the Netherlands, Sweden, and Spain, discuss the arrival of Muslim immigrants and their formation of identifiable communities rather than assimilation into the existing culture, as the host populations expected.

Novak, David. *Covenantal Rights: A Study in Jewish Political Theory.* Princeton, NJ: Princeton University Press, 2000.

Attempting to introduce the Jewish political tradition into contemporary political and legal discussions, Novak offers a theory of rights based on a scriptural presentation of the covenant between God and the Jewish people. This enterprise contrasts with liberal and conservative understandings of rights and duties and provides insights into Jewish political thought.

O'Donovan, Oliver. *The Desire of the Nations: Rediscovering the Roots of Political Theology.* New York: Cambridge University Press, 1996.

O'Donovan argues for a revised Christian political thought that is informed by the Western Christendom tradition. The author combines biblical interpretation, a historical narrative of the Western political and theological tradition, and a discussion of contemporary views of the subject.

Olson, Laura R. *Filled with Spirit and Power: Protestant Clergy in Politics.* Albany: State University of New York Press, 2000.

Focusing her study on Milwaukee, Wisconsin, Olson examines the various roles urban Protestant clergy play in the political realm. She concludes that the level of political involvement is determined not only by religious affiliation, but also by the socioeconomic status of the neighborhoods in which their churches are located. Those pastors serving in economically disadvantaged inner-city neighborhoods tend to devote the most time to political activity.

Olson, Laura R., and Ted G. Jelen. *The Religious Dimension of Political Behavior: A Critical Analysis and Annotated Bibliography.* Westport, CT: Greenwood, 1998.

Olson and Jelen review research conducted in recent years on religion and political behavior in the United States. This research has proliferated as a result of the significant increase in religiously related political activity since the 1980s. The literature reviewed includes a treatment of the various ways in which religious groups attempt to influence political behavior, depending on the political circumstances.

Opposing Viewpoints Series. *Islam.* San Diego, CA: Greenhaven, 2001.

This edited volume contains essays presenting opposing views on such topics as the conflicting values of Islam and the West, the status of women under Islam, the contemporary role of terrorism in Islam, and United States policies toward Islamic nations.

Orfield, Gary, and Holly J. Lebowitz, eds. *Religion, Race, and Justice in a Changing America*. Washington, DC: Brookings Institution, 2000.

The essays in this volume investigate the ways in which various American religions and their leaders and adherents perceive their role in advancing civil rights.

Palm, Daniel C., ed. *On Faith and Free Government*. Lanham, MD: Rowman and Littlefield, 1997.

Palm has included in this work five essays by scholars who discuss the way in which the founders of the United States construed the relationship between church and state. The authors then suggest how present political institutions might be made to reflect the founders' principles. Included are statements by the founders expressing their views of the role of religion in American politics.

Pals, Daniel L. *Seven Theories of Religion*. New York: Oxford University Press, 1996.

Pals makes a more basic contribution to a recognition of the significant role that religion plays in politics by presenting various attempts that noted scholars and philosophers have made to explain and understand religious belief. Among them are James Frazer, author of *The Golden Bough,* who claimed that contemporary religion has roots in primitive custom and belief; Sigmund Freud, who argued that religion is similar to neurosis, characterized by irrational thought and action; Mircea Eliade, who contended that an adequate understanding of religious behavior and ideas must be achieved from the perspective of the believer; and E. E. Evans-Pritchard and Clifford Geertz, whose empirical research emphasized the ideas, attitudes, and purposes that give rise to religious belief.

Parsons, Susan Frank. *Feminism and Christian Ethics*. New York: Cambridge University Press, 1996.

Parsons presents the varied strands of moral thinking within contemporary feminism. By providing an overview and analysis of the major components within feminist ethics from a Christian perspective, the author lays the groundwork for further investigation in the area.

Pattnayak, Satya R., ed. *Organized Religion in the Political Transformation of Latin America.* Lanham, MD: University Press of America, 1995.

This examination of religion and politics in Latin America focuses on religious innovation in differing national settings. Covering the Catholic Church as well as Protestant denominations, the essays note that religious change that emphasizes community organization, mobilization, and education has a greater chance of gaining legitimacy among the population.

Pegram, Thomas R. *Battling Demon Rum: The Struggle for a Dry America, 1800–1933.* Chicago: Ivan R. Dee, 1998.

Pegram describes the struggle of the temperance movement, largely influenced by religious organizations, to regulate the consumption of alcohol in the United States. The movement employed both moral persuasion as well as legal coercion in the attempt to limit the negative social effects of alcohol. The ultimate failure of the temperance movement to control alcohol consumption is an example of the difficulties faced by any religious or social movement attempting to bring about moral change through political action.

Pellegrino, Edmund D., and Alan I. Faden, eds. *Jewish and Catholic Bioethics: An Ecumenical Dialogue.* Washington, DC: Georgetown University Press, 1999.

The editors offer a dialogue between Jewish and Christian scholars on the difficult issues of health care and medical ethics. Primarily Orthodox scholars provide the Jewish position, while Catholic thinkers offer responses. The contributors deal with such issues as the provision of health care, euthanasia, abortion, technologically supported reproduction, and genetic screening.

Perry, Bruce. *Malcolm: The Life of a Man Who Changed Black America.* Barrytown, NY: Station Hill, 1991.

This biography of Malcolm X traces the African American leader's rise from a life marred by racial discrimination and participation in criminal activity to self-pride and independence. Malcolm used his own liberating experience to work for the political liberation of African Americans. In preparing this volume, Perry conducted interviews with more than 400 people who knew Malcolm X and examined school, prison, and Federal Bureau of Investigation records.

Perry, Michael J. *Love and Power: The Role of Religion and Morality in American Politics.* New York: Oxford University Press, 1991.

Perry investigates the appropriate relationship between religious morality and the public realm in a pluralistic society. He suggests the notion of a universally accepted basis for politics in which commitments to the human good can play a positive role in political debate.

———. *Religion in Politics: Constitutional and Moral Perspectives.* New York: Oxford University Press, 1999.

Perry investigates the proper role of religion in American politics, given that the United States is so religiously pluralistic. There have been two crucial debates over the place of religion in politics: the constitutional question of the role of religion in public life, and the debate over the moral function of religion in politics. Perry concludes that because of the tendency of religiously oriented moral injunctions to prohibit some sorts of human actions, the role of religion in politics should be peripheral.

Peterson, Anna L. *Martyrdom and the Politics of Religion: Progressive Catholicism in El Salvador's Civil War.* Albany: State University of New York Press, 1997.

This book investigates the role of religious organizations in formulating political ideology and mobilizing a community against repression. Focusing on political violence in El Salvador in the 1970s and 1980s, Peterson describes the ways in which Catholic activists provided a justification for resisting the violence and destruction that occurred.

Pirzada, Sayyid A. S. *The Politics of the Jamiat-i-Ulema-i-Islam: Pakistan, 1971–1977.* New York: Oxford University Press, 2000.

Pirzada examines the ulema claim that they support an Islamic governing system based on rule by a caliphate, which involves secular-religious leaders. The author compares the success of the Pakistani religious parties with socialist and centrist parties.

Plant, Raymond. *Politics, Theology, and History.* New York: Cambridge University Press, 2000.

In this theoretical work, Plant, professor of politics at Southampton University in England, questions the moral basis of liberal societies and the role of religious belief in discussions of public policy in pluralistic societies. Plant focuses on issues of primary concern to Christians.

Polkinghorne, John. *Belief in God in an Age of Science*. New Haven, CT: Yale University Press, 1998.

This book makes a contribution to the investigation of the sometimes contentious interaction of religion and science in the modern world.

Poya, Maryam. *Women, Work, and Islamism: Ideology and Resistance in Iran*. New York: Zed Books, 1999.

In this examination of Islamism in everyday life, Poya explores the influence of the combination of politics, economics, and religious traditions and practices on women in Iran. The author presents a historical overview of Iran, provides an introduction to Islam, and analyzes the role of women in the Islamic state.

Prendergast, William B. *The Catholic Voter in American Politics: The Passing of the Democratic Monolith*. Baltimore, MD: Georgetown University Press, 1999.

Religious affiliation can often be associated with voting preferences in a democracy. Prendergast traces the voting behavior of Catholics in American elections from the 1840s to the 1990s, noting that while Catholics traditionally have been supporters of the Democratic Party, more recently they have tended to switch their voting loyalties to the Republican Party. The author identifies possible reasons for this shift, including socioeconomic advancement among Catholics, the decline of Catholic-Protestant animosity, and the salience of new issues such as abortion.

Raboteau, Albert J. *A Fire in the Bones: Reflections on African-American Religious History*. Boston: Beacon, 1995.

Focusing on the wide variety of African American religious experiences, including Baptist revivals, the African Methodist Episcopal Church, and black Catholics, Raboteau discusses the ways in which religious faith structured the struggle for social justice in the United States.

Rahnema, Ali, ed. *Pioneers of Islamic Revival*. Atlantic Highlands, NJ: Zed Books, 1994.

By examining major Islamic intellectual leaders of the nineteenth and twentieth centuries and their reaction against Western influences in Muslim nations, the essays in this book provide an introduction to the various elements in Islamic social thought. The authors describe the contributions made to a revolutionary Islamic perspective by Sayyid Jamal al-Din al-Afghani, Muhammad Abduh, Ayatollah Khomeini, Maulana Sayyid Abul Ala Mawdudi, Hasan al-Banna, Sayyid Qutb, Musa al-Sadr, Ali Shariati, and Muhammad Baqer As-Sadr.

————. *An Islamic Utopian: A Political Biography of Ali Shariati.* New York: Palgrave, 2000.

Focusing on the life of Ali Shariati, an individual who played a major role in the Iranian revolution, Rahnema analyzes the influence that political Islam has had on popular movements in the Middle East. The author examines the Iranian political, social, and cultural influences on Shariati.

Rashid, Ahmed. *Taliban: Militant Islam, Oil, and Fundamentalism in Central Asia.* New Haven, CT: Yale University Press, 2000.

Rashid investigates the Taliban, the radical Islamic organization that gained power in Afghanistan. The author traces the Taliban's rise to power, its influence on Afghanistan and the rest of central Asia, the organization's impact on oil and gas company policy, and the changing attitudes of Americans toward this extremist religious organization.

Ravitch, Frank S. *School Prayer and Discrimination: The Civil Rights of Religious Minorities and Dissenters.* Boston: Northeastern University Press, 2001.

Ravitch alleges that public school religious observances are harmful, citing examples of intimidation, harassment, and physical violence, and proposes an approach to protecting the rights of minorities and dissenters that employs civil rights principles and antidiscrimination laws. The author presents a draft statute intended to provide further protection against such discrimination.

Ravitzky, Aviezer. *Messianism, Zionism, and Jewish Religious Radicalism.* Trans. Michael Swirsky and Jonathan Chipinan. Chicago: University of Chicago Press, 1996.

Ravitsky examines the Orthodox Jewish tradition and its relationship to Zionism, which vacillates between complete rejection and complete acceptance. In the contemporary nation of Israel, the author describes such groups as the Haredim, which strongly oppose Zionism, and the Gush Emunim, which support Israel as a divinely established state.

Reader, Ian. *Religion in Contemporary Japan.* Honolulu: University of Hawaii Press, 1991.

Reader offers a solid foundation for understanding the influence of religion on contemporary Japanese society. The author investigates instances of Japanese participation in religious events, the role of religious belief and practice in the social system, and the varieties of religious belief. Of particular interest is the author's discussion of attempts to maintain the relevance of religion in a society that has undergone significant modernization.

———. *Religious Violence in Contemporary Japan: The Case of Aum Shinrikyo.* Honolulu: University of Hawaii Press, 2000.

Employing interviews with members and former members of Aum Shinrikyo, Reader investigates the Japanese religious group's turn to violence when it attacked the Tokyo subway system with poison gas. The author discusses the leader's personality and teachings, the group's millennialist beliefs, and its growing separation from Japanese society. Reader compares Aum Shinrikyo with other religious and political groups that ultimately resorted to violence.

Reese, Thomas J. *Inside the Vatican: The Politics and Organization of the Catholic Church.* Cambridge, MA: Harvard University Press, 1998.

Reese, a Jesuit priest trained in political science, describes the politics and organization of the Roman Catholic bureaucracy and its central administrative and governing procedures, focusing on the work of the Vatican, the difficulties the organization faces, and its internal culture. Reese interviewed several cardinals, bishops, and priests, as well a lay people who work in the Vatican. He provides suggestions for reforming the organization.

Reid, Daniel G., Robert D. Linder, and Bruce L. Shelley, eds. *Dictionary of Christianity in America.* Downers Grove, IL: Inter-Varsity, 1990.

This volume contains entries treating various subjects, including individuals, institutions, denominations, events, and ideas, which have contributed to molding religious belief and traditions in North America.

Rejwan, Nissim. *The Many Faces of Islam: Perspectives on a Resurgent Civilization.* Gainesville: University Press of Florida, 2000.

In this introduction to contemporary Islam, Rejwan provides several perspectives on Islamic culture and religious practice. He includes samples of writing of Muslim and non-Muslim scholars. Among the topics covered are the varieties of Islam, the impact of modernity, the fundamentalist revival, and Western misunderstandings of Islam.

Riccards, Michael P. *Vicars of Christ: Popes, Power, and Politics in the Modern World.* New York: Crossroad/Herder and Herder, 1998.

Riccards examines the papacy from the fall of the papal states to John Paul II. The author analyzes the political and social, as well as religious, significance of the contemporary papacy.

Robinson, Francis, ed. *The Cambridge Illustrated History of the Islamic World.* New York: Cambridge University Press, 1996.

Emphasizing the interaction between Islam and the West, the authors confront the complexities of Muslim culture. Among the topics covered are the role of religious and political fundamentalism, the importance of commerce, literacy and learning, Islamic art, the historical influences of immigration and conquests, and the origins of current conflicts in the Middle East, Bosnia, and the Persian Gulf.

Roded, Ruth, ed. *Women in Islam and the Middle East.* New York: St. Martin's, 1999.

Roded has gathered materials from various Islamic sources from early times to the present in order to clarify the role of women in Islam and Middle Eastern society. The entries deal with various aspects of women's lives in the Middle East, including political, cultural, and legal considerations.

Ro'i, Yaacov. *Islam and the Soviet Union: From the Second World War to Gorbachev.* Lanham, MD: Rowman and Littlefield, 2000.

Basing his analysis on official archives made available after the fall of the Soviet Union, Ro'i presents a historical study of Islam under postwar Soviet rule. The author focuses on the survival of Islam in the context of a political regime hostile to religious belief.

Romero, Oscar A. *The Violence of Love.* Farmington, PA: Plough Publishing House, 1998.

James R. Brockman compiled these sermons of Oscar Romero, the archbishop of San Salvador who was assassinated in 1980. Late in life Romero decided to devote his life to bettering the conditions of the poor. In these sermons, Romero drew from Bible readings to formulate a call for social justice and an end to poverty.

Rosander, Eva Evers, and David Westerlund, eds. *African Islam and Islam in Africa: Encounters between Sufis and Islamists.* Athens: Ohio University Press, 1997.

This collection of essays examines the political implications of the interaction between African Sufism and reformist Islam. The authors focus on the varying perspectives evident in Islamic thought as well as the relationship between Islam and politics.

Rosenblum, Nancy L., ed. *Obligations of Citizenship and Demands of Faith.* Princeton, NJ: Princeton University Press, 2000.

These essays argue for greater interaction between religion and the contemporary workings of public life in a democracy. The authors contend that a greater role for religion is compatible with the liberal notion of a pluralist society in which various religious traditions participate.

Rowland, Christopher, ed. *The Cambridge Companion to Liberation Theology.* New York: Cambridge University Press, 1999.

These essays introduce liberation theology, commenting on its basic characteristics and expression in various parts of the world, including Korea and India. Edward Antonio's essay describes black theology as a part of the liberation movement. In an epilogue, Rowland contends that liberation as a grassroots movement continues even though academic interest appears to have declined in recent years.

Roy, Olivier. *The Failure of Political Islam.* Cambridge, MA: Harvard University Press, 1994.

The failure that Roy speaks of involves the attempt to create a universal Islamic state, which the author considers highly unlikely because of divisions within Islam, particularly conflicts between the Sunni and Shi'a sects and ethnic variations. The author examines various contemporary Islamic movements that have attempted to challenge the West as well as various regimes in the Middle East that they judge unfaithful to Islam and the Qur'an.

Rudolph, Susanne Hoeber, and James Piscatori, eds. *Transnational Religion and Fading States.* Boulder, CO: Westview, 1997.

Under the general theme that state sovereignty is weakening, these essays investigate the ways in which religious movements, by crossing state boundaries, contribute to the development of a truly transnational civil society. Religion is viewed as an important element in filling the vacuum left by the decline of ideologically motivated movements.

Ruthven, Malise. *Islam: A Very Short Introduction.* New York: Oxford University Press, 1998.

Ruthven deals with several questions about the nature of Islam. He investigates the notion of jihad, or holy war; the divisions within Islam (the Shi'is, Sunnis, and Wahhabis); and the importance of *shari'a* (sacred law) to Islamic life. The author focuses on the problems presently facing Islam and its relationship to the contemporary world, including the role of women and their ability to achieve equality within the Islamic tradition.

Sachedina, Abdulaziz Abdulhussein. *The Just Ruler in Shi'ite Islam: The Comprehensive Authority of the Jurist in Imamite Jurisprudence.* New York: Oxford University Press, 1988.

Sachedina examines classical and modern legal works in order to clarify the orthodox view of authority and its relevance to the religious leadership of the imam, the secular ruler, and the judicial expert.

Saha, Santosh C., and Thomas K. Carr, eds. *Religious Fundamentalism in Developing Countries.* Westport, CT: Greenwood, 2001.

The contributors to this volume examine the influences of fundamentalist religious beliefs on the social and political developments of countries such as Bangladesh, Egypt, India, Pakistan, and the Philippines. Emphasis is placed on the complex interaction between fundamentalism and political motivations.

Sahliyeh, Emile, ed. *Religious Resurgence and Politics in the Contemporary World.* Albany: State University of New York Press, 1990.

The authors of this group of essays investigate the rise since 1970 of politically oriented religious groups in such areas of the world as the United States, Central America, South Africa, the Philippines, India, and the Middle East. In contrast to the assumption that modernization would lead to increased secularization, the authors note that religious revivalism and fundamentalism appear to be the result of modernization efforts.

Saktanber, Ayse. *Living Islam: Women, Politics and Religion in Turkey.* New York: St. Martin's, 2000.

Saktanber investigated traditional families in a suburb of Ankara, focusing on women living outside modern society. Rather than examining the influence of Islamic belief on the status of women, the author is concerned with the role women play in creating viable Islamic traditions in a larger secular society.

Sanasarian, Eliz. *Religious Minorities in Iran.* New York: Cambridge University Press, 2000.

Sanasarian investigates the political relationship between religious minorities and the Iranian state in the years immediately following the establishment of the Islamic regime in Teheran. The author focuses on the history of the non-Muslim groups and how they have responded to government policies regarding religious minorities.

Sands, Kathleen M., ed. *God Forbid: Religion and Sex in American Public Life.* New York: Oxford University Press, 2000.

The thirteen essays in this volume respond to the religious reaction to issues of sexuality and reproductive rights that arose in the United States during the last two decades of the twentieth century. The authors explore the conflicts between and within American religious groups that have arisen over these issues. Topics include the pro-choice stance within Christian history, support by many religious groups for gay rights, and questioning of the patriarchal family structure within some religious communities.

Saroush, Abdolkarim. *Reason, Freedom, and Democracy in Islam.* Ed. Mahmoud Sadri and Ahmad Sadri. New York: Oxford University Press, 1999.

Saroush, considered a major moderate Muslim thinker, presents his beliefs on such issues as the freedom and ability of the average Muslim believer to interpret the Qur'an, the role of change in religious belief, the importance of freedom of belief, and the potential harmony between Islam and democracy.

Sato, Tsugitaka. *Islamic Urbanism in Human History: Political Power and Social Networks.* Irvington, NY: Columbia University Press, 1998.

The essays in this volume examine the connection between political power and social organization in medieval and modern Islamic history. Treatment is given to the social, religious, and administrative arrangements that were involved in the formation of the modern state.

Schechter, Danny. *Falun Gong's Challenge to China: Spiritual Practice or "Evil Cult"?* New York: Akashic Books, 2000.

Schechter examines the Falun Gong in China, attempting to provide an in-depth treatment of the spiritual movement that elicited a strong negative reaction from the Chinese government and a worldwide response in the mass media.

Schlabach, Theron F., and Richard T. Hughes, eds. *Proclaim Peace: Christian Pacifism from Unexpected Quarters.* Champaign: University of Illinois Press, 1997.

The essays in this volume explore pacifist beliefs in churches not usually noted for pacifism. Among the topics treated are antimilitaristic currents in Mormonism, liberal Protestant opposition to military buildup prior to World War II, and pacifist sentiments in the Catholic Worker movement.

Schultz, Jeffrey D., John G. West Jr., and Iain MacLean, eds., *Encyclopedia of Religion in American Politics.* Phoenix, AZ: Oryx, 1999.

The volume offers a comprehensive look at topics dealing with religion and politics in the United States, including biographies, major events, legal decisions, and organizations. The authors discuss the positions that religious groups have taken historically on such issues as freedom of worship, prohibition, the gold standard, women's suffrage, and civil rights. In contemporary politics, religious groups have taken stands on such questions as abortion, capital punishment, sex education, racism, prayer in the public schools, and family values generally.

Schulze, Reinhard. *A Modern History of the Islamic World.* New York: New York University Press, 2000.

Schulze, a professor of Islamic studies at the University of Berne, examines Islam as the significant cultural influence in such countries as Bosnia, Morocco, Indonesia, and Somalia. The author's historical treatment deals with the effects of colonialism on Muslim attitudes toward the West and focuses on the skirmish between Islamic culture and contemporary civil society.

Segers, Mary, ed. *Piety, Politics, and Pluralism: Religion, the Courts, and the 2000 Election.* Lanham, MD: Rowman and Littlefield, 2000.

Contributors to this edited volume investigate the compatibility between liberal democracy and the rights of believers. Events of the 2000 presidential campaign are used as examples of the interaction between religion and politics in American society.

Segers, Mary, and Ted G. Jelen. *A Wall of Separation? Debating the Public Role of Religion.* Lanham, MD: Rowman and Littlefield, 1998.

Segers and Jelen examine the long-standing question of the relationship between church and state, and the involvement of religion in politics in contemporary liberal democratic society.

Sernet, Milton C. *Bound for the Promised Land: African American Religion and the Great Migration.* Durham, NC: Duke University Press, 1997.

Sernet examines the religious and cultural effects of the migration of African Americans from the South to the North following World War I. As African Americans brought their religious beliefs and institutions with them, they began to look upon their churches as sites for more than the narrow religious practices of praying and preaching.

Shahak, Israel, and Norton Mezvinsky. *Jewish Fundamentalism in Israel.* Herndon, VA: Stylus Publishing, 1999.

The authors describe the various fundamentalist religious groups in Israel including Haredim, Shas, and Gush Emunim, elaborate on the distinctions among them, and discuss their influence on contemporary Israeli politics. These groups not only take an uncompromising position toward the Palestinians, but also disagree strongly among themselves and with the more mainline political organizations.

Shain, B.A. *The Myth of American Individualism: The Protestant Origins of American Political Thought.* Princeton, NJ: Princeton University Press, 1994.

Shain examines the basic political understandings of Americans during the nation's founding, employing various public documents, including Revolutionary-era sermons. Unlike the contemporary popular understanding that Americans of the eighteenth century possessed an individualistic conception of such concepts as liberty and the public good, Shain argues that the founding period of the nation was characterized by a reformed Protestant communalism.

Sharkansky, Ira. *Israel and Its Bible; A Political Analysis.* Levittown, PA: Garland, 1996.

Sharkansky, a professor at Hebrew University in Jerusalem, offers an interpretation of the legal and political system presented in the Old Testament and discusses the relevance of the Hebrew Bible to the contemporary governing system of Israel. The author examines such topics as the politics of compiling the Hebrew Bible, the geopolitics of the Bible, and literary devices of the Bible.

———. *Ambiguity, Coping, and Governance: Israeli Experiences in Politics, Religion, and Policymaking.* Westport, CT: Praeger, 1999.

Focusing on the interaction of religion and politics as well as specific issues in the Arab-Israeli conflict, Sharkansky observes the use of ambiguity and other methods of coping with, but not directly resolving, social, cultural, and political difficulties in Israel. The author concludes that such coping methods have their virtues when dealing with extremely difficult issues.

Sharma, Arvind, ed. *Hinduism and Secularisation: After Ayodhya.* New York: St. Martin's, 2001.

Nine academics investigate the significance for the relations between the Hindu and Muslim communities of the destruction of the Babri Mosque at Ayodhya in India in December 1992.

Sharot, Stephen. *A Comparative Sociology of World Religions:*

Virtuosi, Priests, and Popular Religion. New York: New York University Press, 2001.

This study in the comparative sociology of religion presents an analysis of the differences and similarities between religious leaders and lay people in various religious traditions around the world. Sharot discusses the ways in which the elite-mass relationships within religious structures coincide with the social and political context of the larger society and how that context influences the character of social interaction within the religious realm.

Sheffer, Martin S. *God Versus Caesar: Belief, Worship, and Proselytizing under the First Amendment.* Albany: State University of New York Press, 1999.

Sheffer examines the development of the free exercise of religion as protected in the First Amendment to the U.S. Constitution. He focuses on the divide between the guarantee of free exercise and the right of government to protect the health, welfare, safety, and morals of its citizens. The author discusses such examples as court cases involving conscientious objection to military service, which highlight possible legal inconsistencies that may have implications for the guarantee of freedom.

Sidahmed, Abdel Salam, and Anoushiravan Ehteshami, eds. *Islamic Fundamentalism.* Boulder, CO: Westview, 1996.

This edited work contains fourteen essays dealing with the rise of fundamentalist Islam and its destabilizing influence on many Arab states. Fundamentalists have been engaged in struggles for power with the more traditional rulers of these states. Part one includes essays dealing with the theoretical underpinnings of Islamist movements and attitudes toward international relations, and the second part contains case studies of Islamist movements in specific countries, including Algeria, Jordan, post-Khomeini Iran, Palestine, Sudan, Syria, and Yemen.

Siebers, Tobin, ed. *Religion and the Authority of the Past: Authority and Religious Aspects.* Ann Arbor: University of Michigan Press, 1993.

Examining basic religious doctrines, including those of Islam, Hinduism, and Roman Catholicism, these essays discuss the ways in which those in power influence religious doctrine, interpretation, behavior, and expression. A major theme treats the importance of authority in religion and culture and the effects of the past on religious authority.

Simone, T. Abdou Maliqalim. *In Whose Image? Political Islam and Urban Practices in Sudan.* Chicago: University of Chicago Press, 1994.

Simone, a Muslim scholar who was engaged as a consultant by the Islamic fundamentalist Shari'a Movement in Sudan to improve relations between Muslims and non-Muslims in Khartoum, describes the use of Islam as a means for political change. Although maintaining confidence in the productive application of Islam to politics, the author disapproves of Islamic radicalism that can have highly disruptive economic and cultural consequences.

Smart, Ninian. *The World's Religions.* New York: Cambridge University Press, 1995.

Smart, a scholar of comparative religion, provides an introduction to the world's major religions. The author touches on their beginnings, historical development, major characteristics, and rituals and practices. Smart places the religions in cultural context, noting their position in the contemporary world. The book is organized regionally and contains many photographs and illustrations.

Smidt, Corwin E., ed. *In God We Trust? Religion and American Political Life.* Grand Rapids, MI: Baker Book House, 2001.

This book explores the relationship between religion and politics in the United States. Individual chapters supplement the topics usually included in political science textbooks, such as public opinion, public institutions such as Congress, and American political culture.

Smith, Christian, ed. *Disruptive Religion: The Force of Faith in Social Movement Activism.* New York: Routledge, 1996.

These essays investigate the role that religion has played in social and political movements in various parts of the world. Individual essays focus on commitment to political causes that religious faith can initiate such as the black churches and the civil rights movement in the United States, the Islamic insurgency during the Iranian revolution in 1978–1979, the religious mobilization in the Solidarity movement in Poland, and the role of church leadership in the South African antiapartheid movement from 1983 to 1990.

Smith, Oran P. *The Rise of Baptist Republicanism.* New York: New York University Press, 1997.

Smith, who contends that the Southern Baptist Convention closely reflects southern culture and politics, presents the results of a quantitative study focusing on southern white Baptists and concludes that in the last half century Southern Baptists have become politically and theologically more militant. Much of recent national political leadership, including conservatives such as Newt Gingrich, Strom Thurmond, and Trent Lott and liberals such as Bill Clinton, Al Gore, and Richard Gephardt, are Southern Baptists.

Song, Robert. *Christianity and Liberal Society.* New York: Oxford University Press, 1997.

Song deals with the attempts by three twentieth-century theologians—Reinhold Niebuhr, George Grant, and Jacques Maritain—to develop a correspondence between liberal political thought and Christian theology.

Soper, J. Christopher. *Evangelical Christianity in the United States and Great Britain: Religious Beliefs, Political Changes.* New York: New York University Press, 1994.

Soper concentrates on movements of the late nineteenth and early twentieth centuries that promoted prohibition as well as contemporary efforts to ban abortion, using them as case studies of evangelical political behavior in the United States and Great Britain. Among the explanations that the author introduces for the greater success of evangelicals in the United States are that nation's more decentralized governmental structure and much weaker political party system.

Soroush, Abdolkarim. *Reason, Freedom, and Democracy in Islam: The Essential Writings of Abdolkarim Soroush.* Ed. Mahmoud Sadri and Ahmad Sadri. New York: Oxford University Press, 2000.

The editors present a collection of essays by Soroush, a major moderate Muslim revisionist theorist. Soroush deals with such topics as the compatibility of Islam with democracy, the inescapability of religious change, and the ability of the Muslim believer to interpret the Qur'an.

Sprinzak, Ehud. *Brother against Brother: Violence and Extremism in Israeli Politics from Altalena to the Rabin Assassination.* New York: Free Press, 1999.

Sprinzak focuses on the troubling extremist violence within Israeli society, including the 1994 Hebron massacre, in which a Jewish doctor used a machine gun to kill twenty-nine Muslims who were at prayer, and the 1995 assassination of Prime Minister Yitzhak Rabin by an Orthodox Jewish student. The author examines other instances of extremist violence in Israel's relatively brief history.

Starrett, Gregory. *Putting Islam to Work: Education, Politics, and Religious Transformation in Egypt.* Berkeley: University of California Press, 1998.

Starrett explores the Egyptian government's program of providing religious education to students in order to counter Islamist political opposition and establish support for the regime's economic, political, and social policies. The author notes that, ironically, the educational techniques geared to increase political stability instead contributed to Islamization of the public realm and challenges to traditional religious and political authority.

Steigenga, Timothy J. *The Politics of the Spirit: The Political Implications of Pentecostalized Religion in Costa Rica and Guatemala.* Lanham, MD: Lexington Books, 2001.

Steigenga examines the political implications of the spread of evangelical Protestantism in Central America. Confronting conflicting claims that the spread of evangelical Christian belief hampers, as well as contributes to, the growth of democracy, the author presents a comparative analysis of Costa Rica, with a democratic system, and Guatemala, governed by an undemocratic regime, concluding that the relationship between religion and politics is complex, with the character of the political culture also affecting religious observance.

Stevens-Arroyo, Anthony M., and Ana Diaz-Stevens. *Recognizing the Latino Resurgence in U.S. Religion.* New York: HarperCollins, 1997.

The authors recount the efforts since 1967 of Latinos in the United States to remedy a long history of nonrecognition in the larger society. Latinos worked to establish their ethnic identity, employing religion as a primary fountainhead for social identity.

Stewart, Omer C. *Peyote Religion: A History*. Norman: University of Oklahoma Press, 1993.

Stewart provides a historical overview of the use of peyote, a hallucinatory drug, in Native American religious ceremonies. The use of peyote in religious ceremonies has raised legal questions regarding freedom of religion when they involve actions that are prohibited by law.

Stiltner, Brian. *Religion and the Common Good: Catholic Contributions to Building Community in a Liberal Society*. Lanham, MD: Rowman and Littlefield, 1999.

Stiltner contends that twentieth-century Catholic thought provides a theory of the common good that bridges the gap between liberal and communitarian conceptions of the common good. The author claims Catholic theory can combine the liberal emphasis on individual rights and social tolerance with the communitarian concern for a shared history and the preservation of valued social practices.

Stout, Harry S., and D. G. Hart. *New Directions in American Religious History*. New York: Oxford University Press, 1998.

Stout and Hart appraise the condition of the historiography of American religious history. The authors focus on the literature of the last few decades dealing with the social history of American religious groups.

Stump, Roger W. *Boundaries of Faith: Geographical Perspectives on Religious Fundamentalism*. Lanham, MD: Rowman and Littlefield, 2000.

Stump investigates the social and cultural influences of fundamentalist religious movements in differing regions of the world and explores the geographical characteristics that foster the formation of such movements.

Sullivan-Gonzalez, Douglass. *Piety, Power, and Politics: Religion and Nation Formation in Guatemala, 1821–1871*. Pittsburgh, PA: University of Pittsburgh Press, 1998.

Sullivan-Gonzalez investigates the influence of the Guatemalan Catholic Church on the development of a sense of national identity in Guatemala during the period 1821–1871. The author highlights the interaction of religious belief, popular political involvement, and military leadership to forge an alliance among various ethnic groups and classes to protect the Guatemalan nation.

Swatos, William H., Jr., and Daniel V. A. Olson, eds. *The Secularization Debate*. Lanham, MD: Rowman and Littlefield, 2000.

The thesis regarding the increasing secularization of Western society has come under challenge since the 1980s. The authors of these essays investigate the major issues regarding secularization and its relevance to the social and political realms.

Taiz, Lillian. *Hallelujah Lads and Lasses: Remaking the Salvation Army in America, 1880–1930*. Chapel Hill: University of North Carolina Press, 2001.

Taiz examines the migration of the Salvation Army religious movement from Great Britain in 1879, its early appeal to young working-class men and women, the development of a democratic ethos among the members, and the ultimate shift in emphasis toward ministering to the needs of the masses that was accompanied by the development of a more centralized organizational structure.

Tambiah, Stanley Jeyaraja. *Buddhism Betrayed: Religion, Politics and Violence in Sri Lanka*. Chicago: University of Chicago Press, 1992.

Tambiah investigates the ethnic and religious conflict in Sri Lanka that has led to a stalemate in economic development. The author identifies a number of root causes for the conflict, including the political process, strongly held religious beliefs, and the ideology of nationalism.

Tamimi, Azzam, and John L. Esposito, eds. *Islam and Secularism in the Middle East*. New York: New York University Press, 2000.

These essays examine the Islamic rejection of secularism as the harmful influence of the Western Christian tradition. The authors discuss the views of Islamists that secularism in the Muslim world has been the cause of dictatorship, human rights violations, and limitations on civil liberties.

Tessler, Mark. *A History of the Israeli-Palestinian Conflict*. Bloomington: Indiana University Press, 1994.

Tessler offers a history of the Israeli-Palestinian conflict from its origins to the late twentieth century. The author describes the rise of modern Zionism and Arab nationalism, investigates the conflict up to Israeli independence in 1948, and focuses on more recent events such as the June 1967 war, the Camp David negotiations in the 1970s, the military and political conflicts between Palestinians and Israelis in the 1980s, and the peace initiatives of the 1990s. Tessler recounts the rise of radical Islamic movements as part of the continuing Middle East conflict.

Thiemann, Ronald F. *Religion in Public Life: A Dilemma for Democracy.* Baltimore, MD: Georgetown University Press, 1996.

Thiemann, dean of the Harvard Divinity School, calls for a reassessment of the traditional separation of church and state in the United States in order to fill the vacuum left by the breakdown of the nonsectarian consensus over the last thirty years. The author proposes a liberal perspective that recognizes a place for religious views in public life, provided that the constitutional principles of freedom, equality, and toleration are respected.

Turner, Richard Brent. *Islam in the African-American Experience.* Bloomington: Indiana University Press, 1997.

Turner investigates the history and present status of African Americans who decided to associate with Islam. The author traces the development of Islam from the introduction of African American slaves into America to Elijah Muhammad and Malcolm X and more recent figures such as Louis Farrakhan. Islam has provided many African Americans with a distinctive religious, social, and political identification that has coincided with the global growth of militant Islam and has been expressed in the ascendance of Islamic leaders, businesses, mass media, and distinctive foods and clothing.

Uhalley, Stephen, and Xiaoxin Wu, eds. *China and Christianity: Burdened Past, Hopeful Future.* Armonk, NY: M. E. Sharpe, 2001.

The essays in this volume offer perspectives on Chinese-Western cultural interactions, focusing on the experience of Christianity in China. Essays are divided into two major categories: those examining the history of Christianity in China and those considering the present circumstances and prospects for the future. Authors focus on such topics as the future of the Catholic Church in Hong Kong, Christianity in contemporary Taiwan, and prospects for a dialogue about Christianity in China.

Van Der Veer, Peter. *Religious Nationalism: Hindus and Muslims in India.* Berkeley: University of California Press, 1994.

Investigating the relationship between religion and politics in India, Van Der Veer demonstrates how religious identity has been influenced by such things as migration, language development, and the print and broadcast media. The author focuses on the violent confrontation in December 1992 between Hindus and Muslims at the Babari Mosque in Ayodhya.

Van Der Veer, Peter, and Hartmut Lehmann, eds. *Nation and Religion.* Princeton, NJ: Princeton University Press, 1999.

Focusing on the varied connections between religion and nationalism, these essays challenge the conclusion that Western modernity is associated with the separation of the private domain of religion from the public sphere of politics.

Vasquez, Manuel A. *The Brazilian Popular Church and the Crisis of Modernity.* New York: Cambridge University Press, 1997.

Vasquez examines the development and fate of progressive Catholicism in Latin America from the late 1960s through the 1980s. The author focuses on a Brazilian community, investigating the influences on the movement of Vatican policy, economic vicissitudes, and humanist thought.

Vinz, Warren L., and Martin E. Marty. *Pulpit Politics: Faces of American Protestant Nationalism in the Twentieth Century.* Albany: State University of New York Press, 1997.

The authors investigate the relationship between religious expression and the formation in the United States of what they term messianic nationalism. They note that although Protestant leaders attempted to offer meaning to the American experience, they provided disparate views of nationalism, both reflecting and contributing to confused nationalistic images.

Viorst, Milton. *In the Shadow of the Prophet: The Struggle for the Soul of Islam.* New York: Anchor Doubleday, 1998.

Viorst conducted in-depth interviews with Islamic leaders and thinkers, exploring the influence of traditional Islamic theology on Middle East politics. The author investigates the conflict between the resolute desire to maintain traditional Islamic law and beliefs and the objective of achieving economic advancement and political power among the nations of the world. The discussion is placed within the larger context of the concerns of Western nations.

Waines, David. *An Introduction to Islam.* New York: Cambridge University Press, 1995.

Waines provides a comprehensive overview of Islam, from its beginnings with the Prophet Muhammad in the sixth century to the present day. The author describes the development of Muslim beliefs and practices and the rapid spread of Islam throughout the Middle East and into Southeast Asia. Over the last 200 years Muslims have contended with Western domination, and are now attempting to reestablish their own identity. A final chapter deals with contemporary issues for Islam, such as the revision of family law, the formation of the Islamic state, and relations with Western nations such as the United States and Great Britain.

Wald, Kenneth D. *Religion and Politics in the United States.* 3d ed. Washington, DC: Congressional Quarterly, 1997.

Wald investigates several topics regarding religion and public life from both a social scientific and a normative perspective. The author examines controversies over Supreme Court decisions on religious subjects, some of which have led to new legislation, such as the Religious Freedom Restoration Act, and proposals for constitutional amendments.

Walsh, David. *The Third Millennium: Reflections on Faith and Reason.* Washington, DC: Georgetown University Press, 1999.

Walsh discusses the rise of modern civilization from the Christian experience of the Middle Ages, concluding that the major beliefs of modern society ultimately are based on Christian theology. The author asserts that Christ anchors modern civilization, including all traditions of rational thought. Therefore, he argues that the Christian understanding of the new millennium has meaning for all.

Walsh, Frank. *Sin and Censorship: The Catholic Church and the Motion Picture Industry.* New Haven, CT: Yale University Press, 1996.

Walsh investigates the Roman Catholic Church's role in the censorship of Hollywood movies during the early years of the film industry. Although American Catholics had been influencing the content of movies ever since World War I, it was not until the formation of the Legion of Decency in the 1930s that Catholic pressure became a significant determinant of film content. From the 1930s to the 1960s the Legion exercised censorship, objecting to film references to such topics as pregnancy, childbirth, abortion, and divorce. Walsh derives his discussion from church archives, personal papers, and studio records.

Walsh, George. *The Role of Religion in History.* Piscataway, NJ: Transaction Publishers, 1998.

In material gathered from his lectures, Walsh offers a secularist treatment of religion from Ayn Rand's "Objectivist" perspective, which is highly critical of religious belief. The author investigates the doctrines of the major world religions and suggests how their values, sometimes conflicting but often in agreement, have influenced the formation of societies.

Watt, William Montgomery. *Islamic Political Thought.* Irvington, NY: Columbia University Press, 1998.

Watt surveys the development of Islamic political thought from the political-religious order established by Muhammad and his contemporaries to the present circumstance that pits Islamic societies against Western culture.

Wessinger, Catherine. *How the Millennium Comes Violently: From Jonestown to Heaven's Gate.* New York: Seven Bridges, 2000.

Wessinger examines several cults that have been associated with violent activities or the potential for violence toward their own members as well as the larger society. Chapters present case studies of such groups as the Branch Davidians; Aujm Shinrikyo (Supreme Truth), the violent Japanese cult; the Montana Freemen; Solar Temple, a suicide cult; and Chen Tao (True Way). The author explains why such groups become violent and offers advice to policy makers for improving their understanding of such groups and preventing the members of these organizations from committing acts of violence.

West, John G., Jr. *The Politics of Revelation and Reason: Religion and Civic Life in the New Nation.* Lawrence: University Press of Kansas, 1996.

Arguing that the founders of the Constitution intended that religion play an important role in American politics, West investigates the public activism of Christians in the period 1800 to 1835. He focuses on such issues as mail delivery on Sunday, dueling, the treatment of Indians, and other practices that professing Christians early in the republic considered immoral.

Wilkinson, Brenda. *Jesse Jackson: Still Fighting for the Dream.* Englewood Cliffs, NJ: Silver Burdett, 1990.

In this book written for juveniles, Wilkinson describes the life of Jesse Jackson, a civil rights leader and Baptist minister who ran for the Democratic presidential nomination in 1988 and 1992. The author describes Jackson's early life and experiences with racial discrimination, his educational endeavors and first involvement in politics working for North Carolina Governor Terry Sanford, his work with civil rights leader Martin Luther King Jr., the establishment of a political base in Chicago, and the ultimate move to Washington, D.C., and involvement in national politics.

Williams, Peter W. *America's Religions: Traditions and Cultures.* Champaign: University of Illinois Press, 1998.

Williams presents a religious history of the United States from the colonial period until the late twentieth century, identifying the social traditions from which it developed. The author identifies individual religious traditions and their evolution through mutual interaction and exposure to the larger U.S. culture.

Wineburg, Robert. *A Limited Partnership: The Politics of Religion, Welfare and Social Service.* New York: Columbia University Press, 2000.

Wineburg assesses the recent move by American public officials such as President George W. Bush to advocate a greater public role for private, faith-based organizations in providing welfare assistance. He argues that in order to understand welfare service delivery in the United States, greater attention must be paid to the local level. Wineburg summarizes his long experience with the welfare service system in Greensboro, North Carolina.

Winston, Diane. *Red-Hot and Righteous: The Urban Religion of the Salvation Army.* Cambridge, MA: Harvard University Press, 1999.

Winston examines the Salvation Army and its activities from the organization's introduction into the United States from England in 1880 through World War II. Today, the Salvation Army is the largest charitable fund-raiser in the United States. The Army was unique in its combination of religious proselytizing and social programs, such as soup kitchens and homeless shelters. The author portrays the organization as playing an important role in shaping social services for the urban poor and changing the role of women in modern urban society.

Wong, John, and William T. Liu. *The Mystery of China's Falun Gong: Its Rise and Its Sociological Implications.* River Edge, NJ: World Scientific, 1999.

In this brief monograph, Wong and Liu trace the rise of the Falun Gong movement in China, describe the worldwide attention it has received, and focus on the repressive reaction of the Chinese government. The authors analyze the character of the movement, delving into its religious roots in Buddhism and Daoism and charges that it constitutes a religious cult.

Woodwiss, Ashley, and Thomas Heilke, eds. *The Re-Enchament of Political Science.* Lanham, MD: Lexington Books, 2001.

The contributors to this volume discuss the nature of political science and the distinctive role that Christianity can play in the discipline. Individual essays investigate the contributions Christian thinking can make to various approaches within political theory, including liberalism, communitarianism, and critical theory. In addition, an explanation is given of how public policy studies may be conducted within a Christian framework.

Wunder, John R. *Native American Cultural and Religious Freedoms.* Levittown, PA: Garland, 2000.

Wunder recounts the struggle between Native American groups and the United States legal system over the recognition of certain religious practices. The author discusses the conflict over ownership rights to skeletal remains and artifacts illegally recovered from Native American burial sites.

Wuthnow, Robert. *Producing the Sacred: An Essay on Public Religion.* Champaign: University of Illinois Press, 1994.

Contending that cultural expressions of religion are consciously produced, Wuthnow investigates the primary organizations responsible for cultivating public religion and discusses the ways in which they form its content. The author identifies the ways in which the sacred is inadvertently and implicitly communicated in modern society.

————. *Christianity in the Twenty-First Century: Reflections on the Challenges Ahead.* New York: Oxford University Press, 1995.

In an attempt to project the future of the Christian church, Wuthnow focuses mainly on American Protestantism, and within Protestantism he targets the decline of more liberal denominations. The author admits that liberal analysts, himself included, failed to perceive the true significance of fundamentalist churches, which, he observes, arose not just as reactions to the development of the modern world, but possess a self-perpetuating, vibrant cultural force that has attracted many mainline Christians. Wuthnow urges that Christians find strength and durability in the fostering of community.

Wuthnow, Robert, ed. *The Encyclopedia of Politics and Religion.* Washington, DC: Congressional Quarterly, 1998.

This two-volume work includes 256 articles on various aspects of the relationship between politics and religion, including treatments of specific regions or countries, major religions and traditions, and religious and political leaders. An appendix includes documents dealing with the relationship between politics and religion, such as provisions in national constitutions related to religious practice.

Zelkina, Anna. *In Quest for God and Freedom: Sufi Responses to the Russian Advance in the North Caucasus.* New York: New York University Press, 2000.

Zelkina focuses on the historical background to the contemporary conflict between the Russian government and the provinces of Chechnya and Daghestan. The author describes the events of the early nineteenth century when Islam and *shari'a* (sacred law) provided a unifying force to resist Russian attempts at conquest. Zelkina notes the role still played by Sufi brotherhoods in the region.

7

Nonprint Resources

Audiotapes and Videotapes

Afghanistan: Exporting the Taliban Revolution
Type: 1/2" videocassette
Length: 23 min.
Cost: $129 (purchase); $75 (rental)
Date: Not available
Source: Films for the Humanities and Sciences
P.O. Box 2053
Princeton, NJ 08543-2053
(800) 257-5126
www.films.com

This video examines the potential conflicts between the Taliban, a militant fundamentalist Sunni group that gained control of most of Afghanistan, and the Shi'ite government of Iran. Each government is concerned about the presence of a minority population in its own country that adheres to the rival sect.

Against Great Odds
Type: 1/2" videocassette
Length: 29 min.
Cost: $14.99
Date: 1992
Source: Gateway Films / Vision Video
P.O. Box 540
Worcester, PA 19490-0540
(800) 523-0226
www.visionvideo.com

The Meserete Kristos Church suffered persecution under the

Marxist government in Ethiopia from 1982 to 1991. The govern-ment closed all congregations and imprisoned church leaders. The video emphasizes that church membership expanded greatly during the time of repression.

Altars of the World: The Eastern Religions
Type: 1/2" videocassette
Length: 53 min.
Cost: $29.95
Date: 1977
Source: Teacher's Video Company
P.O. Box WHR-4455
Scottsdale, AZ 85261
(800) 262-8837

The viewer is provided with a broad introduction to influential Eastern religions, including Hinduism, Buddhism, Jainism, Sikhism, Shintoism, and Zoroastrianism. Among the nations vis-ited are China, Japan, and India.

America Held Hostage: The Iran Crisis
Type: 1/2" videocassette
Length: 60 min.
Cost: $29.95
Date: 1990
Source: Teacher's Video Company
P.O. Box AHV-4455
Scottsdale, AZ 85261
(800) 262-8837

This video recounts the hostage crisis precipitated by Iranian mil-itants who held fifty-three Americans during the last year of President Jimmy Carter's administration. The militants were in-spired by Ayatollah Ruhollah Khomeini, the religious leader who had recently risen to power in Iran.

American Religious History
Type: 1/2" videocassette, audiocassette, and CD
Length: 720 min. (24 30-min. lectures)
Cost: $54.95 (video); $34.95 (audio); $49.95 (CD)
Date: 2001
Source: The Teaching Company
4151 Lafayette Center Drive
Chantilly, VA 20151-1232

(800) 832-2412
http://www.teach12.com

This series of twenty-four lectures presented by Patrick N. Allitt, professor of history at Emory University, covers the history of religion in the United States from the Puritans to the contemporary debate over the separation of church and state. Lectures cover such topics as the role of religion in the Revolutionary War, religious divisions over the issue of slavery, the expansion of Catholicism, the formation of Jewish communities, debates over American involvement in warfare, the civil rights movement, the counterculture movement and feminism, and the growth of Asian religious groups.

The Amish: A People of Preservation
Type: 1/2" videocassette
Length: 54 min.
Cost: $19.99
Date: 1991
Source: Gateway Films/Vision Video
         P.O. Box 540
         Worcester, PA 19490-0540
         (800) 523-0226
         www.gatewayfilms.com

In this video, producer John Ruth investigates the Amish, a religious group that has raised a number of constitutional issues in the United States. The video focuses on various aspects of the group, including its origins, dependence on farm life, the schooling of children, and the rejection of modern technology, such as reliance on horse transportation.

The Amish: Not To Be Modern
Type: 1/2" videocassette
Length: 57 min.
Cost: $29.95
Date: 1985
Source: Teacher's Video Company
         P.O. Box AHR-4455
         Scottsdale, AZ 85261
         (800) 262-8837

This video offers a depiction of the Amish, a religious sect that, through its members wish to remain separate from the rest of American society, has raised several constitutional questions within the U.S. legal structure.

Apocalypse!
Type: 1/2" videocassette
Length: 120 min.
Cost: $19.98
Date: 1999
Source: PBS Video
1320 Braddock Place
Alexandria, VA 22314-1698
(800) 344-3337

This video provides the historical background to the religious fervor generated by the new millennium. Among the topics covered are the origins of apocalyptic writing in Hebrew history, its historical development, and contemporary interpretations in the context of a scientific age.

Archbishop Desmond Tutu with Bill Moyers
Type: 1/2" videocassette
Length: 75 min.
Cost: $89.95
Date: Not available
Source: Films for the Humanities and Sciences
P.O. Box 2053
Princeton, NJ 08543-2053
(800) 257-5126
www.films.com

In this interview with journalist Bill Moyers, Archbishop Desmond Tutu of South Africa describes his work to bring an end to the discriminatory policy of apartheid. Tutu discusses the broader significance of the Truth and Reconciliation Commission, an organization opposing apartheid that he chaired.

Ashes in the River: Four Religions of India
Type: 1/2" videocassette
Length: 250 min. (four tapes)
Cost: $649 ($149 per tape)
Date: 1998
Source: Films for the Humanities and Sciences
P.O. Box 2053
Princeton, NJ 08543-2053
(800) 257-5126
www.films.com

This series on the religions of India includes four presentations:

"Spiritual India: A Guide to Jainism, Islam, Buddhism, and Hinduism," "Jainism: Ascetics and Warriors," "Islam: The Five Pillars of Faith," "Buddhism: The Great Wheel of Being," and "Hinduism: Faith, Festivals, and Rituals." The temples, festivals, and sacred rituals of these four religions are examined, along with the variety of cultural traditions.

Assassination of Martin Luther King, Jr.
Type: 1/2" videocassette
Length: 85 min.
Cost: $29.95
Date: 1993
Source: Teacher's Video Company
P.O. Box AHR-4455
Scottsdale, AZ 85261
(800) 262-8837

This video investigates the assassination in Memphis, Tennessee, of Martin Luther King Jr., Baptist minister and noted leader of the civil rights movement.

Authority and Change
Type: 1/2" videocassette
Length: 30 min.
Cost: $89.95
Date: 2000
Source: Films for the Humanities and Sciences
P.O. Box 2053
Princeton, NJ 08543-2053
(800) 257-5126
www.films.com

Sheikh Syed Tautavi, Mufti of Egypt, examines the conflict between liberal and radical Muslims in Egypt, including the challenge that the secular state and traditional scholars face from more militant Islamic groups.

Beyond the Veil: Are Iranian Women Rebelling?
Type: 1/2" videocassette
Length: 22 min.
Cost: $129 (purchase); $75 (rental)
Date: 1997
Source: Films for the Humanities and Sciences
P.O. Box 2053

Princeton, NJ 08543-2053
(800) 257-5126
www.films.com

Following the Islamic revolution in Iran in 1978, women were required to submit to more stringent social controls, such as a government-enforced dress code. In this video an undercover reporter investigates the attitudes of Iranian women toward their limited role in Iranian society.

**Bible Reading in Public Schools:
The Schempp and Murray Cases—1963**
Type: 1/2" videocassette
Length: 57 min.
Cost: $89.95
Date: 1963 (2000)
Source: Films for the Humanities and Sciences
P.O. Box 2053
Princeton, NJ 08543-2053
(800) 257-5126
www.films.com

This tape is a reproduction of the 1963 documentary on two Supreme Court cases, *School District of Abington Township v. Schempp* and *Murray v. Board of School Commissioners of Baltimore City,* in which the use of Bible reading in public schools was ruled invalid under the U.S. Constitution. Television news anchor Eric Sevareid interviews the Schempps, the Murrays, the attorneys in the cases, expert witnesses, and others having an interest in the outcome.

Birth of a God: The Dalai Lama
Type: 1/2" videocassette
Length: 90 min. (two tapes)
Cost: $149
Date: Not available
Source: Films for the Humanities and Sciences
P.O. Box 2053
Princeton, NJ 08543-2053
(800) 257-5126
www.films.com

This program is composed of two presentations. In the first, "Tibetan Buddhism: Politics, Power, and the Birth of the Dalai Lama," three historians and students of Tibetan Buddhism discuss the religious/political history of Tibet. The second presentation, "The Dalai Lama and the Rituals of Reincarnation," investigates the role of the Dalai Lama in the context of power politics and Chinese efforts at territorial expansion.

Buddhism: Spiritual Heritage
Type: 1/2" videocassette
Length: 30 min.
Cost: $29.95
Date: 1998
Source: Teacher's Video Company
              P.O. Box WHR-4455
              Scottsdale, AZ 85261
              (800) 262-8837

This brief video investigates the Buddhist heritage, including the religion's origins, beliefs, and significant traditions.

Buddhism: The Great Wheel of Being
Type: 1/2" videocassette
Length: 52 min.
Cost: $149 (purchase); $75 (rental)
Date: 2000
Source: Films for the Humanities and Sciences
              P.O. Box 2053
              Princeton, NJ 08543-2053
              (800) 257-5126
              www.films.com

This video presents the basic religious beliefs and teachings of Buddha. Included are a discussion of the "Four Noble Truths" and a presentation of religious monuments as witnesses to the long history of Buddhism.

Church of Liberation
Type: 1/2" videocassette
Length: 59 min.
Cost: $390
Date: 1985
Source: First Run / Icarus Films
              153 Waverly Place, Sixth Floor
              New York, NY 10014
              (800) 876-1710
              www.frif.com

This video presents an overview of Catholicism in Brazil and an account of the rise of liberation theology up to the mid-1980s. The tape includes subtitles.

Coping with Scientific and Social Change:
19th and 20th Centuries
Type: 1/2" videocassette
Length: 40 min.
Cost: $149 (purchase); $75 (rental)
Date: 2000
Source: Films for the Humanities and Sciences
P.O. Box 2053
Princeton, NJ 08543-2053
(800) 257-5126
www.films.com

This last tape in the "Two Thousands Years: The History of Christianity" series investigates the possibilities for the coexistence of religion and science in a post-Darwinian world. Also included on the tape is an investigation of the growing movement worldwide toward social equality.

Crescent and Cross: The Rise of Islam
and the Age of the Crusades
Type: 1/2" videocassette
Length: 59 min.
Cost: $149 (purchase); $75 (rental)
Date: 1998
Source: Films for the Humanities and Sciences
P.O. Box 2053
Princeton, NJ 08543-2053
(800) 257-5126
http://www.films.com

This video provides a background to the contemporary tensions between Christianity and Islam, discussing the Crusades as a response to the rise of Islam. Among the topics covered are the role of Christian monks in the preservation of religious and cultural traditions and the Inquisition as an attempt to counter the rise of heresy within the church as well as such practices as witchcraft and magic.

Crimes of Honor
Type: 1/2" video cassette
Length: 44 min.

Cost: $375 (purchase); $75 (rental)
Date: 1998
Source: First Run / Icarus Films
           153 Waverly Place, Sixth Floor
           New York, NY 10014
           (800) 876-1710
           www.frif.com

The troubling practice of femicide in Middle Eastern countries, the killing of women suspected of losing their virginity before marriage, is addressed. The video claims that although the practice has no basis in Islamic law, increasing numbers of incidents have been observed, setting off a debate about its religious and social origins.

Dalai Lama
Type: 1/2" videocassette
Length: 50 min.
Cost: $29.95
Date: Not available
Source: Teacher's Video Company
           P.O. Box WHM-4455
           Scottsdale, AZ 85261
           (800) 262-8837

This Arts and Entertainment channel biography presents the life of the Dalai Lama, who the people of Tibet consider the reincarnation of Buddha. Living in exile due to the Chinese invasion, the Dalai Lama has for many years worked for the independence of his people.

The Dalai Lama and the Rituals of Reincarnation
Type: 1/2" videocassette
Length: 45 min.
Cost: $149 (purchase); $75 (rental)
Date: Not available
Source: Films for the Humanities and Sciences
           P.O. Bos 2053
           Princeton, NJ 08543-2053
           (800) 257-5126
           www.films.com

Robert Thurman, professor of Indo-Tibetan Buddhist studies at Columbia University, and other scholars investigate the history of the belief in the reincarnation of the Dalai Lama in the context of Tibetan politics and Chinese aspirations for expansion.

Desmond Tutu and the Rainbow Nation
Type: 1/2" videocassette
Length: 52 min.
Cost: $149 (purchase); $75 (rental)
Date: 1996
Source: Films for the Humanities and Sciences
          P.O. Box 2053
          Princeton, NJ 08543-2053
          (800) 257-5126
          www.films.com

This video follows Nobel Laureate and Anglican Archbishop Desmond Tutu during a tour through his Cape Town, South Africa, diocese in 1996. The presentation focuses on the attempts being made to meet the challenges facing the multicultural and multiracial nation of South Africa following the abolition of apartheid.

The Evolution of Revolution: Live from Tehran
Type: 1/2" videocassette
Length: 73 min.
Cost: $79.95
Date: 1999
Source: Films for the Humanities and Sciences
          P.O. Box 2053
          Princeton, NJ 08543-2053
          (800) 257-5126
          http://www.films.com

This program investigates the reasons for the taking of fifty-three hostages at the American embassy in Teheran, Iran, during President Jimmy Carter's administration. For over a year, American diplomacy was unable to release the American prisoners held by the fundamentalist Islamic regime.

Father, Son and Holy War
Type: 1/2" videocassette
Length: 120 min.
Cost: $490 (purchase); $150 (rental)
Date: 1994
Source: First Run / Icarus Films
          153 Waverly Place, Sixth Floor
          New York, NY 10014
          (800) 876-1710
          www.frif.com

This two-part video confronts the tendency of the nation of India to divide into religious and ethnic enclaves hostile to each other. The first part ("Trial By Fire") examines the phenomenon of communal fires that have created violent religious confrontations. The second part ("Hero Pharmac") investigates the influence of male pride on the conduct of religious strife, focusing on the demands Hindus have made for revenge for Muslim acts committed centuries in the past.

444 Days: The Iran Hostage Crisis
Type: 1/2" videocassette
Length: 103 min.
Cost: $149
Date: 1999
Source: Films for the Humanities and Sciences
               P.O. Box 2053
               Princeton, NJ 08543-2053
               (800) 257-5126
               http://www.films.com

Through this detailed account of the taking of American hostages in Teheran, Iran, in 1979 is presented the rise of fundamentalist Islam in the Middle East. Included are interviews with the American hostages as well as Iranians who held them captive.

The Fundamental Question
Type: 1/2" videocassette
Length: 65 min.
Cost: $195
Date: 1994
Source: Insight Media
               2162 Broadway
               P.O. Box 621
               New York, NY 10024-0621
               (800) 233-9910

This video examines the rise of various forms of Islamic fundamentalism, including the history and characteristics of the movements from the perspective of imams, terrorists, students, government officials, and victims of fundamentalist-inspired violence.

Gandhi
Type: 1/2" videocassette
Length: 187 min.

Cost: $29.95
Date: 1982
Source: Teacher's Video Company
P.O. Box WHS-4455
Scottsdale, AZ 85261
(800) 262-8837

English actor Ben Kingsley portrays the Indian spiritual leader Mohandas Gandhi, who practiced and advocated nonviolent strategies to gain independence for his nation from Great Britain.

Gandhi Biography
Type: 1/2" videocassette
Length: 40 min.
Cost: $29.95
Date: 1990
Source: Teacher's Video Company
P.O. Box WHS-4455
Scottsdale, AZ 85261
(800) 262-8837

This video presents an overview of the life of Mohandas Gandhi, the Indian spiritual leader who led his country to independence from Great Britain. Included are Gandhi's famous march to the sea, London address, and use of the fast to bring about political victory.

Great World Religions: Beliefs, Practices and Histories
Type: audiocassette
Length: 2,250 min. (50 lectures, 45 min. each)
Cost: $299.95
Date: 2000
Source: The Teaching Company
4151 Lafayette Center Drive, Suite 100
Chantilly, VA 20151-1210
(800) 832-2412
http://www.teach12.com

These lectures on the world religions are presented by five scholars of religion (Robert Oden, Kenyon College; John Swanson, American University at Cairo; William Scott Green, University of Rochester; Robert Henricks, Dartmouth College; and Diana Eck, Harvard Divinity School). Among the topics covered are religious fundamentalism as a world phenomenon; Muslim attitudes toward the United States; the intellectual and cultural history of Judaism; the Chinese religious traditions of Daoism, Confucianism, and Buddhism; and the nonviolent tradition of Hinduism and its role in the Indian independence movement.

Hinduism: An Introduction
Type: 1/2" videocassette
Length: 29 min.
Cost: $249 (purchase); $75 (rental)
Date: Not available
Source: Films for the Humanities and Sciences
P.O. Box 2053
Princeton, NJ 08543-2053
(800) 257-5126
www.films.com

This video provides an introductory overview of Hinduism and its place within Indian culture. Among the topics covered are such spiritual ideas as karma, dharma, God as both one and many, worship practices, and Hindu scriptures.

Hinduism: Faith, Festivals, and Rituals
Type: 1/2" videocassette
Length: 51 min.
Cost: $149 (purchase); $75 (rental)
Date: 1995
Source: Films for the Humanities and Sciences
P.O. Box 2053
Princeton, NJ 08543-2053
(800) 257-5126
www.films.com

This video describes Hinduism, the majority religion of Indian, looking at Kerala, located in the southern tip of India. Topics for investigation include religious ceremonies, sacred Hindu literature such as the *Ramayana* and the *Mahabharata,* and the concept of *dharama,* or right living.

A History and Holy Sacraments of Orthodox Christianity
Type: 1/2" videocassette
Length: 90 min. (three tapes)
Cost: $59.99
Date: 1992
Source: Gateway Films / Vision Video
P.O. Box 540

Worcester, PA 19490-0540
(800) 523-0226
www.visionvideo.com

This three-part video series ("The Beginnings," "Byzantium," and "A Hidden Treasure"), produced by Greek Orthodox Telecommunications, introduces the teachings and traditions of the Orthodox Christian faith. The program presents the long history of the church, including its struggles under Eastern European communism after World War II. Church leaders offer their understanding of the Orthodox faith's significance in the contemporary world.

I Have a Dream: Martin Luther King
Type: 1/2" videocassette
Length: 25 min.
Cost: $29.95
Date: 1986
Source: Teacher's Video Company
P.O. Box AHR-4455
Scottsdale, AZ 85261
(800) 262-8837

This video focuses on the August 28, 1963, gathering at the Lincoln Memorial where Martin Luther King Jr., the Baptist preacher and civil rights leader, electrified an estimated crowd of 250,000 with his "I Have a Dream" speech.

The Image of God
Type: 1/2" videocassette
Length: 28 min.
Cost: $89.95
Date: 2000
Source: Films for the Humanities and Sciences
P.O. Box 2053
Princeton, NJ 08543-2053
(800) 257-5126
www.films.com

Bill Moyers discusses with scholars the history, sectarian divisions, basic beliefs, and political implications of Islam. The participants discuss the inaccuracies of reporting in the American media. A major topic is the notion of jihad, or holy war.

In Memory of Friends
Type: 1/2" videocassette; 16 mm film
Length: 60 min.
Cost: $390 (purchase); $125 (rental)
Date: 1990
Source: First Run / Icarus Films
            153 Waverly Place, Sixth Floor
            New York, NY 10014
            (800) 876-1710
            www.frif.com

This video describes the violent conditions in Punjab, India, which has been instigated by religious fundamentalists. Emphasis is placed on the rise of Sikh fundamentalism and the war of propaganda between the socialist state and the Khalistani separatists.

In Remembrance of Martin
Type: 1/2" videocassette
Length: 60 min.
Cost: $59.95
Date: 1986
Source: PBS Video
            1320 Braddock Place
            Alexandria, VA 22314-1698
            (800) 344-3337

This video includes comments from various individuals, including friends, advisers, and public figures, regarding the leadership that Reverend Martin Luther King Jr. provided for the civil rights movement. Also included are excerpts from King's "I Have a Dream" speech.

In the Name of God
Type: 1/2" videocassette; 16 mm film
Length: 90 min.
Cost: $490 (purchase); $150 (rental)
Date: . 1992
Source: First Run / Icarus Films
            153 Waverly Place, Sixth Floor
            New York, NY 10014
            (800) 876-1710
            www.frif.com

The presentation focuses on the danger to Indian social stability posed by Hindu fundamentalists. The militant Vishwa Hindu

Parishad (VHP) are portrayed as wanting to destroy a centuries-old mosque in Ayodhya and build a temple to Ram on the site. Subsequent religious riots resulted in the deaths of thousands of people and the destruction of the mosque following completion of the film.

The Ingathering
Type: 1/2" videocassette
Length: 52 min.
Cost: $149 (purchase); $75 (rental)
Date: 1998
Source: Films for the Humanities and Sciences
P.O. Box 2053
Princeton, NJ 08543-2053
(800) 257-5126
http://www.films.com

The video provides an account of Jewish immigration into the Middle East, efforts to create a Jewish identity in the state of Israel, and the variety of cultures that nonetheless exist in the Jewish state. Among the problems faced are the varied origins of immigrating Jews, including Poland, Russia, Hungary, Romania, Libya, Algeria, and Ethiopia.

Iran: Adrift in a Sea of Blood
Type: 1/2" videocassette
Length: 27 min.
Cost: $225 (purchase); $50 (rental)
Date: 1986
Source: First Run / Icarus Films
153 Waverly Place, Sixth Floor
New York, NY 10014
(800) 876-1710
http://www.frif.com

Although this video was produced over a decade ago, it provides a good view of the continuing fundamentalist Islamic influence in the Middle East. Various Iranians, including clergy and government officials, present their views on religion and politics.

Iran: Departure into the Unknown
Type: 1/2" videocassette
Length: 49 min.
Cost: $149 (purchase); $75 (rental)

Date: 2000
Source: Films for the Humanities and Sciences
P.O. Box 2053
Princeton, NJ 08543-2053
(800) 257-5126
http://www.films.com

This examination of life in fundamentalist-ruled Iran focuses on many aspects of Iranian social life and highlights the expectations of many Iranians for greater freedom after years of revolution, warfare, and strict social codes imposed by the Shi'ite regime.

Irish Civil War: The Madness from Within
Type: 1/2" videocassette
Length: 60 min.
Cost: $129 (purchase); $75 (rental)
Date: 1999
Source: Films for the Humanities and Sciences
P.O. Box 2053
Princeton, NJ 08543-2053
(800) 257-5126
http://www.films.com

In 1922 the people of Ireland began a civil war that lasted for decades, resulting in bloody fighting and terrorism. Those on both sides of the conflict were passionate about the political correctness of their positions, partly because of the Protestant-Catholic loyalties of the respective sides.

Islam and Christianity
Type: 1/2" videocassette
Length: 30 min.
Cost: $89.95
Date: 1993
Source: Films for the Humanities and Sciences
P.O. Box 2053
Princeton, NJ 08543-2053
(800) 257-5126
http://www.films.com

This tape investigates the historical conflict between Islam and Christianity, the continuing clash between the two religious traditions, and the possibility of increased understanding between them. Iran's ambassador to the Vatican, Mohammad Masjed

Jame'i, discusses the differences and similarities between Islam and Christianity, the Qur'an and the Bible, and the respective roles of Muhammad and Christ.

Islam and Democracy
Type: 1/2" videocassette
Length: 56 min.
Cost: $350
Date: 1994
Source: Filmmakers Library, Inc.
124 E. 40th
New York, NY 10016
(800) 555-9815

This documentary discusses the factors hindering the attainment of democracy in Islamic countries of the Middle East.

Islam and Feminism
Type: 1/2" videocassette
Length: 25 min.
Cost: $225 (purchase); $75 (rental)
Date: 1991
Source: First Run / Icarus Films
153 Waverly Place, Sixth Floor
New York, NY 10014
(800) 876-1710
http://www.frif.com

This video investigates the unequal treatment women receive under Pakistan's Islamic law. For instance, a female rape victim may be charged under Islamic law with having engaged in extramarital sex and the legal testimony of two women is valued equally to that of one man.

Islam and Pluralism
Type: 1/2" videocassette
Length: 30 min.
Cost: $89.95
Date: 2000
Source: Films for the Humanities and Sciences
P.O. Box 2053
Princeton, NJ 08543-2053
(800) 257-5126
http://www.films.com

Anwar Ibrahim, the minister of finance and deputy prime minister of Malaysia, discusses the government's multicultural policies in an Islamic society. Although Malaysia is officially Islamic, Ibrahim states that he supports tolerance. He discusses such topics as Islamic fundamentalism, non-Muslim minorities, and the effects of economic development on Islamic values.

Islam and War
Type: 1/2: videocassette
Length: 30 min.
Cost: $89.95
Date: 2000
Source: Films for the Humanities and Sciences
P.O. Box 2053
Princeton, NJ 08543-2053
(800) 257-5126
http://www.films.com

An influential political figure in the Lebanese Islamic Movement and the spiritual leader of the Hizbullah, Sasyed Fadlallah discusses the origins, rules, and place of terrorism in jihad, or holy war. In addition, the video examines the role Muslim thinkers in general grant to the use of violence in the contemporary world and their attitudes toward the idea of holy war.

Islam: The Faith and the People
Type: 1/2" videocassette
Length: 22 min.
Cost: $129
Date: 1992
Source: Insight Media
2162 Broadway
New York, NY 10024-0621
(800) 233-9910
http://www.insight.media.com

Among the topics covered in this video are the effects of colonialism, the Five Pillars of Islam and their importance to the daily life of Muslims, the mosque, and the Muslim view of Muhammad. Emphasis is placed on the influence that Islam has had on Western culture.

Islam: The Five Pillars of Faith
Type: 1/2" videocassette
Length: 52 min.

Cost: $149 (purchase); $75 (rental)
Date: 1995
Source: Films for the Humanities and Sciences
           P.O. Box 2053
           Princeton, NJ 08543-2053
           (800) 257-5126
           http://www.films.com

Focusing on the population of Kashmir to the north of India, this video examines the beliefs and religious practices of Islam. In addition to traditional Muslim festivals and holy sites, the program investigates the history of Islam in Kashmir and the religion's dissemination throughout India.

Islam: There Is No God but God
Type: 1/2" videocassette
Length: 52 min.
Cost: $129
Date: 1978
Source: Insight Media
           2162 Broadway
           P.O. Box 621
           New York, NY 10024-0621
           (800) 233-9910

This video examines the appeal that Islam has for hundreds of millions of people around the world. Various everyday scenes are presented, including an Islamic wedding ceremony at an Egyptian village, morning prayers in a small town, and everyday life in Cairo.

Islamic Fundamentalism and Democracy
Type: 1/2" videocassette
Length: 57 min.
Cost: $350
Date: 1995
Source: Filmakers Library, Inc.
           124 E. 40th
           New York, NY 10016
           (800) 555-9815

Interviews with Arab leaders highlight the difficulties faced in attempting to transform Middle Eastern countries into democracies. The program focuses on the problems of illiteracy, poverty, and Islamic fundamentalism as a barrier to the toleration of opposing political views.

Islamic Mysticism: The Sufi Way
Type: 1/2" videocassette
Length: 30 min.
Cost: $109
Date: 1971
Source: Insight Media
      2162 Broadway
      P.O. Box 621
      New York, NY 10024-0621
      (800) 233-9910

This older video still provides valuable information about Sufism, considered the mystical basis for Islam. Filmed in India and Morocco and narrated by Huston Smith, the film explores the Sufi way to God.

Islamic Resurgence and Holy War:
The Former Soviet Union and Indonesia
Type: 1/2" videocassette
Length: 52 min.
Cost: $149
Date: 2000
Source: Films for the Humanities and Sciences
      P.O. Box 2053
      Princeton, NJ 08543-2053
      (800) 257-5126
      http://www.films.com

This video investigates the increase in conflict that has occurred between Muslim and non-Muslim populations as Islam has acquired greater numbers of adherents. The first part of the video follows the lives of four divinity school students from Tatarstan who join the jihad in Chechnya, and the second part records the efforts of Indonesian President Abdurrahman Wahid to restore peace between Muslims and Christians.

Islamic Social Values
Type: 1/2" videocassette
Length: 60 min.
Cost: $89.00
Date: 1998
Source: Insight Media
      2162 Broadway
      New York, NY 10024-0621

(800) 233-9910
http://www.insight-media.com

Adding to an understanding of Islam's importance in various parts of the world, Hamza Yusuf, a Muslim educator, discusses the significance of social values from a variety of Islamic perspectives.

The Islamic State
Type: 1/2" videocassette
Length: 30 min.
Cost: $89.95
Date: 2000
Source: Films for the Humanities and Sciences
              P.O. Box 2053
              Princeton, NJ 08543-2053
              (800) 257-5126
              http://www.films.com

Hasan al-Turabi, considered the architect of the Sudanese Islamic state, discusses the structure of the Islamic state and its guiding principles. Turabi touches on such subjects as human rights, women's rights, and the status of minority groups in the Sudan.

The Islamic Wave
Type: 1/2" videocassette
Length: 48 min.
Cost: $149
Date: 2000
Source: Films for the Humanities and Sciences
              P.O. Box 2053
              Princeton, NJ 08543-2053
              (800) 257-5126
              http://www.films.com

Employing commentary by General Perevez Musharraf, Qazi Hussain Ahmad, Dr. Hasan al-Turabi, and others, this video documents the increasing popularity of Islam and investigates the use of violence by Muslim extremists. The program focuses on Pakistan, Indonesia, and Sudan, as well as the Middle East.

Israel: Birth of a Nation
Type: 1/2" videocassette
Length: 60 min.
Cost: $29.95
Date: 1997

Source: Teacher's Video Company
P.O. Box WHM-4455
Scottsdale, AZ 85261
(800) 262-8837

The video presents an overview of Israel from its formation as a Jewish state through the many armed conflicts with its Arab neighbors. Included are interviews with Israeli leaders and historical newsreel footage.

Jainism: Ascetics and Warriors
Type: 1/2" videocassette
Length: 51 min.
Cost: $149 (purchase); $75 (rental)
Date: 1995
Source: Films for the Humanities and Sciences
P.O. Box 2053
Princeton, NJ 08543-2053
(800) 257-5126
http://www.films.com

Profiled in this video are the Jains, a small religious group residing primarily in the Indian state of Rajasthan near the Pakistani border. Jainism advocates salvation through liberation from material existence by following an ascetic life of strict self-discipline. Adherents follow the doctrine of *abimsa*, refusing to injure any living thing.

Jesse Jackson: I Am Somebody
Type: 1/2" videocassette
Length: 50 min.
Cost: $29.95
Date: 1995
Source: Teacher's Video Company
P.O. Box AHR-4455
Scottsdale, AZ 85261
(800) 262-8837

Reverend Jesse Jackson was an adviser to Martin Luther King Jr. After the assassination of his mentor, Jackson went on to become an effective speaker and organizer for the civil rights cause, and twice ran for the Democratic presidential nomination.

John Brown's Holy War
Type: 1/2" videocassette

Length: 60 min.
Cost: $19.98
Date: 2000
Source: PBS Video
1320 Braddock Place
Alexandria, VA 22314-1698
(800) 344-3337

This video provides a revealing historical treatment of the crusade that John Brown conducted against slavery shortly before the American Civil War. Brown was inspired by strongly held religious beliefs to oppose the government with force and to commit murder in the name of a higher ideal.

John Paul II: The Millennial Pope
Type: 1/2" videocassette
Length: 150 min.
Cost: $19.95
Date: 1999
Source: PBS Video
1320 Braddock Place
Alexandria, VA 22314-1698
(800) 344-3337

John Paul II, the last Roman Catholic Pope of the twentieth century, has used his position of religious authority to advocate the cause of the disadvantaged, particularly those in underdeveloped countries. The video traces the influence that the Pope has had on major events of the final decades of the twentieth century.

The Journey: From Faith to Action in Brazil
Type: 1/2" videocassette
Length: 29 min.
Cost: $225 (purchase); $50 (rental)
Date: 1984
Source: First Run / Icarus Films
153 Waverly Place, Sixth Floor
New York, NY 10014
(800) 876-1710
http://www.frif.com

This case study in liberation theology explores the establishment of Christian Base Communities in a poor neighborhood outside Rio de Janeiro. Catholic and Methodist clerics are interviewed regarding attempts to improve the living conditions of poor Brazilians.

Legacy of a Dream: Martin Luther King, Jr.
Type: 1/2" videocassette
Length: 30 min.
Cost: $29.95
Date: 1990
Source: Teacher's Video Company
P.O. Box AHR-4455
Scottsdale, AZ 85261
(800) 262-8837

In this brief overview of Martin Luther King Jr., Southern Baptist preacher and civil rights leader, actor James Earl Jones narrates the key events in King's life.

The Legacy of Desmond Tutu
Type: 1/2" videocassette
Length: 40 min.
Cost: $249 (purchase); $75 (rental)
Date: 1997
Source: Films for the Humanities and Sciences
P.O. Box 2053
Princeton, NJ 08543-2053
(800) 257-5126
http://www.films.com

As South Africa attempts to come to terms with its past experiences with apartheid, Archbishop Desmond Tutu and the Truth and Reconciliation Commission that he heads encourage the process of reconciliation, healing, and forgiveness.

Living Islam: What It Means to Be
a Muslim in Today's World
Type: 1/2" videocassette
Length: 50 min.
Cost: $29.95
Date: 1993
Source: Ambrose Video Publishing, Inc.
28 W. 44th Street
New York, NY 10036
(800) 526-4663
http://ambrose.com

This video explores the Islamic faith in differing cultures, examining the "Great Tradition" of this world religion and the "Little Tradition" of regional and local cultures. The presentation is divided into six programs: "The Prophet, the Book and the Desert," "The Challenge of the Past," "Islam in the Minority," "The Muslim Family," "Islam and Modernity," and "The Last Crusade."

Mahatma Gandhi: The Great Soul Lives
Type: 1/2" videocassette
Length: 60 min.
Cost: $75.00
Date: 1998
Source: Films for the Humanities and Sciences
P.O. Box 2053
Princeton, NJ 08543-2053
(800) 257-5126
http://www.films.com

This account of Mahatma Gandhi's life and philosophy follows the Indian spiritual leader's activities from London, where he studied law, to South Africa, where he first organized a religious retreat (ashram), to India, where his leadership finally led to independence from Great Britain.

Malcolm X
Type: 1/2" videocassette
Length: 50 min.
Cost: $29.95
Date: 1995
Source: Teacher's Video Company
P.O. Box AHV-4455
Scottsdale, AZ 85261
(800) 262-8837

This Arts and Entertainment channel biography examines the life of Malcolm X, the Black Muslim leader who spoke out against racial discrimination in the United States.

Malcolm X
Type: 1/2" Videocassette
Length: 201 min.
Cost: $24.98
Date: 1992
Source: Warner Home Video
4000 Warner Boulevard
Burbank, CA 91522
(818) 954-6000

This docudrama starring Denzel Washington in the role of Malcolm X depicts the life of the controversial black activist and leader in the Black Muslim movement. The film emphasizes Malcolm X's contributions to black nationalism and racial pride.

Malcolm X: His Own Story
Type: 1/2" videocassette
Length: 92 min.
Cost: $29.95
Date: 1972
Source: Teacher's Video Company
P.O. Box AHV-4455
Scottsdale, AZ 85261
(800) 262-8837

Based on Malcolm X's autobiography, the video investigates the religious and political beliefs of this noted member of the Black Muslims and attempts to explain the popularity Malcolm X had in the African American community.

Malcolm X: Make It Plain
Type: 1/2" videocassette
Length: 150 min.
Cost: $99.95
Date: 1995
Source: PBS Video
1320 Braddock Place
Alexandria, VA 22314-1698
(800) 344-3337

This extensive filmed biography traces Malcolm X's life, including a prison term in his younger years, and his becoming a major spokesperson for the Nation of Islam. The video includes lesson outlines to be used for instruction.

Martin Luther King, Jr.
Type: 1/2" videocassette
Length: 50 min.
Cost: $29.95
Date: 1997
Source: Teacher's Video Company
P.O. Box AHR-4455
Scottsdale, AZ 85261
(800) 262-8837

This Arts and Entertainment channel biography presents an overview of the life of Martin Luther King, the southern black preacher who became a noted civil rights leader. The video analyzes King's speeches and sermons and offers commentary on the civil rights leader's influence on American politics.

Martin Luther King Jr.: The Legacy
Type: 1/2" videocassette
Length: 80 min.
Cost: $149 (purchase); $75 (rental)
Date: 1988
Source: Films for the Humanities and Sciences
P.O. Box 2053
Princeton, NJ 08543-2053
(800) 257-5126
http://www.films.com

This treatment of the life of religious and civil rights leader Martin Luther King Jr. examines his personality and presents his campaign for equal rights through his speeches and the recollections of colleagues such as Andrew Young and Ralph Abernathy.

The Martyr's Cry
Type: 1/2" videocassette
Length: 26 min.
Cost: $19.99
Date: 2000
Source: Gateway Films / Vision Video
P.O. Box 540
Worcester, PA 19490-0540
(800) 523-0226
http://www.visionvideo.com

David Goodnow narrates this account of the persecution of Christians in Sudan, Southeast Asia, and Indonesia. Individual Christians in interviews on location provide accounts of their willingness to risk suffering for their religious faith.

The Martyr's Smile
Type: 1/2" videocassette
Length: 52 min.
Cost: $129 (purchase); $75 (rental)
Date: Not available
Source: Films for the Humanities and Sciences

P.O. Box 2053
Princeton, NJ 08543-2053
(800) 257-5126
http://www.films.com

This documentary recounts the actions—including the bombing of the U.S. Marine barracks in the early 1980s—that Lebanon's Hizbullah and Islamic Jihad organizations have taken in the attempt to free southern Lebanon from Israeli occupation. Interviews are conducted with Sheikh Hassan Nasralla, Hizbullah suicide soldiers, and those caught in Israeli air attacks.

Middle East: Cradle of Conflict
Type: 1/2" videocassette
Length: 60 min.
Cost: $29.95
Date: 1991
Source: Teacher's Video Company
P.O. Box WHM-4455
Scottsdale, AZ 85261
(800) 262-8837

This video describes the conflicts between Arabs and Jews that extend back to biblical times. Religious differences play a role in the inability of Israel and Arab nations to agree on a lasting peace.

Money: Man-Made or a Divine Gift from Allah?
Type: 1/2" videocassette
Length: 52 min.
Cost: $149 (purchase); $75 (rental)
Date: 2000
Source: Films for the Humanities and Sciences
P.O. Box 2053
Princeton, NJ 08543-2053
(800) 257-5126
http://www.films.com

After examining the third pillar of faith—*zakat,* or alms-giving—this video investigates the Islamic financial system, which forbids usury and speculation and mandates profit-sharing. The implications of *zakat* are highlighted, including the effects of no-interest banking on the Albaraka Group, a Saudi Arabian multinational associaton.

Muhammad: The Voice of God
Type: 1/2″ videocassette
Length: 43 min.
Cost: $149 (purchase); $75 (rental)
Date: 2001
Source: Films for the Humanities and Sciences
          P.O. Box 2053
          Princeton, NJ 08543-2053
          (800) 257-5126
          http://www.films.com

Presenting a biography of Muhammad, the merchant from Mecca who claimed to have received a call from Allah to become a prophet, this video explores the wide appeal of Islam and the fear of its spread throughout the world. Included are illustrations of Muslim holy sites and contemporary life in the desert of Saudi Arabia.

Muslims in America: The Misunderstood Millions
Type: 1/2″ videocassette
Length: 22 min.
Cost: $29.95
Date: 1995
Source: Teacher's Video Company
          P.O. Box WHS-4455
          Scottsdale, AZ 85261
          (800) 262-8837

This video explains the basic beliefs of Islam and portrays the life of Muslims in the United States in an attempt to dismantle popular stereotypes.

Nation of Islam: Its Mission and Beliefs
Type: 1/2″ videocassette
Length: 50 min.
Cost: $129 (purchase); $75 (rental)
Date: 1999
Source: Films for the Humanities and Sciences
          P.O. Box 2053
          Princeton, NJ 08543-2053
          (800) 257-5126
          http://www.films.com

This video traces the history of the Nation of Islam from its roots in the rise of black separatism and its promotion by Marcus Garvey to the present leadership of Louis Farrakhan. The topics covered include the differences between the Nation of Islam and Islam, the life and work of Malcolm X, and the objectives of the organization. Excerpts of interviews with organization members, including Elijah Muhammad and Muhammad Ali, are presented.

The Night of San Lazaro
Type: 1/2" videocassette
Length: 35 min.
Cost: $235 (purchase); $50 (rental)
Date: 1997
Source: First Run / Icarus Films
          153 Waverly Place, Sixth Floor
          New York, NY 10014
          (800) 876-1710
          http://www.frif.com

Focusing on the revival of religious belief in Cuba, this video depicts a religious event in which people take part in frenzied devotion to San Lazaro, considered by some a saint of healing and to others an African divinity.

On Buddhism
Type: 1/2" videocassette
Length: 220 min. (3 tapes)
Cost: $29.95
Date: 1999
Source: Teacher's Video Company
          P.O. Box WHR-4455
          Scottsdale, AZ 85261
          (800) 262-8837
          http://www.teachersvideocompany.com

This video provides detailed information about the origins, traditions, and contemporary practices of Buddhism.

**One Nation Under God? School Prayer
and the First Amendment**
Type: 1/2" videocassette
Length: 30 min.
Cost: $59.95
Date: 1995
Source: Close Up Publishing, Dept. B2
          44 Canal Center Plaza

Alexandria, VA 22314-1592
(800) 765-3131
http://www.closeup.org

The major participants in the 1985 *Wallace v. Jaffree* Supreme
Court case discuss the legal controversy over the establishment
clause of the First Amendment and the Court's decision that an
Alabama law providing for silent prayer was unconstitutional.
The large number of separate opinions that justices issued
demonstrates the complex nature of the question.

119 Bullets + Three

Type: 1/2" videocassette
Length: 60 min.
Cost: $390 (sale); $75 (rental)
Date: 1995
Source: First Run / Icarus Films
153 Waverly Place, Sixth Floor
New York, NY 10014
(800) 876-1710
http://www.frif.com

The title of this video refers to the 119 bullets that religious extremist Baruch Goldstein fired in 1994 to kill thirty-nine praying
Muslims in Hebron, and to the three bullets that law student
Yigal Amir fired to kill Israeli Prime Minister Yitzhak Rabin. The
video highlights the conflict between religious and secular Jews
in Israel over the direction to be taken by Zionism.

Onward Christian Soldiers

Type: 1/2" videocassette
Length: 52 min.
Cost: $390 (purchase); $75 (rental)
Date: 1989
Source: First Run / Icarus Films
153 Waverly Place, Sixth Floor
New York, NY 10014
(800) 876-1710
http://www.frif.com

This video documents the concern among Latin Americans about
the spread of Protestant evangelical movements in the broadcast
media. The fear is expressed that fundamentalist sects manipu-
late the religious heritage of the native population.

Pillars of Faith: Religions around the World
Type: 1/2" videocassette
Length: 48 min.
Cost: $29.95
Date: 1998
Source: Teacher's Video Company
              P.O. Box WHR-4455
              Scottsdale, AZ 85261
              (800) 262-8837

This video presents a good overview of the world's major religions, including Christianity, Judaism, Islam, and Buddhism, emphasizing the similarities as well as the differences among these faiths.

Poverty, Politics, and Religion: The Plight of India's Poor
Type: 1/2" videocassette
Length: 31 min.
Cost: $129 (purchase); $75 (rental)
Date: Not available
Source: Films for the Humanities and Sciences
              P.O. Box 2053
              Princeton, NJ 08543-2053
              (800) 257-5126
              http://www.films.com

This video examines the campaign of militant Hindu revivalists against Christian missionaries, charging them with unlawfully seeking converts and desecrating Hindu shrines. Acts of violence against the Christian minority in India are described and political reasons for the violence are offered.

The Qur'an and the American Dream
Type: 1/2" videocassette
Length: 52 min.
Cost: $149 (purchase); $75 (rental)
Date: 2000
Source: Films for the Humanities and Sciences
              P.O. Box 2053
              Princeton, NJ 08543-2053
              (800) 257-5126
              http://www.films.com

This video focuses on the expansion of Islam in New York City and that religion's role in providing services to Muslim citizens, recent immigrants, and converts largely from the less affluent segments of society. The Council on American-Islamic Relations, an organization opposing prejudice and stereotyping, is also profiled.

The Real Malcolm X
Type: 1/2" videocassette
Length: 60 min.
Cost: $29.95
Date: 1992
Source: Teacher's Video Company
P.O. Box AHR-4455
Scottsdale, AZ 85261
(800) 262-8837

This video provides an account of the life of Malcolm X, a member of the Black Muslims and a controversial leader in the civil rights movement of the 1950s and 1960s.

Reflections on the Islamic Revolution
Type: 1/2" videocassette
Length: 40 min.
Cost: $99
Date: 1993
Source: Insight Media
2162 Broadway
New York, NY 10024-0621
(800) 233-9910
http://www.insight.media.com

With commentary by Guity Nashat and Said A. Arjomand, this video explains how the Iranian revolution came about and why it led to the taking of American hostages in 1979.

Religion
Type: 1/2" videocassette
Length: 30 min.
Cost: $139
Date: 1991
Source: Insight Media
2162 Broadway
New York, NY 10024-0621
(800) 233-9910
http://www.insight.media.com

As a background to the political implications of religion, this video examines several major religions, focusing on their relationship to societal values. Religion is viewed as a social structure that alters according to shifting needs within society. Recent religious trends are noted.

Religion and Race in America: Martin Luther King's Lament
Type: 1/2" videocassette
Length: 60 min.
Cost: $149 (purchase); $75 (rental)
Date: 1994
Source: Films for the Humanities and Sciences
P.O. Box 2053
Princeton, NJ 08543-2053
(800) 257-5126
http://www.films.com

Employing Martin Luther King's theme that churches should engage in the development of morality and the elimination of prejudice, this video focuses on four situations: a church that holds separate services for whites and blacks; a predominantly white church that a black couple attends; a black church attended by a white woman; and an interracial church.

Religion, Rap, and the Crisis of
Black Leadership: Cornel West
Type: 1/2" videocassette
Length: 50 min.
Cost: $89.95
Date: Not available
Source: Films for the Humanities and Sciences
P.O. Box 2053
Princeton, NJ 08543-2053
(800) 257-5126
http://www.films.com

Bill Moyers interviews philosopher and lay preacher Cornel West, who has spoken to community groups and high school students about religious faith. West discusses such topics as liberation theology, black politicians, and the crisis of black leadership.

Religions of the World
Type: 1/2" videocassette
Length: 300 min. (6 tapes)
Cost: $99.99

Date: 1999
Source: Gateway Films / Vision Video
P.O. Box 540
Worcester, PA 19490-0540
(800) 523-0226
http://www.gatewayfilms.com

Ben Kingsley narrates this overview of the major religions of the world, including Protestantism, Catholicism, Judaism, Islam, Hinduism, and Buddhism. The video emphasizes the ways in which religions have influenced cultures and contributed to either peace or to conflict.

Romero
Type: 1/2" videocassette
Length: 105 min.
Cost: $29.95
Date: 1989
Source: Teacher's Video Company
P.O. Box WHM-4455
Scottsdale, AZ 85261
(800) 262-8837

This docudrama portrays the life of Archbishop Oscar Romero of El Salvador (played by Raul Julia) who was transformed from an apolitical priest into an activist who resisted political persecution and social injustice.

The Roots of Hate: The New Testament and Anti-Semitism
Type: 1/2" videocassette
Length: 25 min.
Cost: $129 (purchase); $75 (rental)
Date: 1997
Source: Films for the Humanities and Sciences
P.O. Box 2053
Princeton, NJ 08543-2053
(800) 257-5126
http://www.films.com

Bishop John Spong participates in this dialogue among Christian and Jewish religious leaders who challenge the idea of Jewish responsibility for Jesus' death. Participants investigate the hostility over the centuries toward Jews that supposedly arose from New Testament accounts. They hope to encourage communication and understanding between adherents of the two religions.

Sacred Memory: Buddhism, Islam, Hinduism, and Christianity

Type: 1/2" videocassette
Length: 20 min.
Cost: $89.95
Date: 1998
Source: Films for the Humanities and Sciences
P.O. Box 2053
Princeton, NJ 08543-2053
(800) 257-5126
http://www.films.com

This video focuses on the subject of sacred memory in Buddhism, Islam, Hinduism, and Christianity. Adherents maintain the collective memory of their faith through such holy days as Ramadan in the Muslim religion and Christmas and Easter in Christianity. Martin E. Marty explains the importance of the Christian liturgical calendar, and Sayyid M. Syeed discusses the Islamic calendar as a means of commemorating important events in the Prophet Muhammad's life.

The School Prayer Case: Engel vs. Vitale—1963

Type: 1/2" videocassette
Length: 55 min.
Cost: $89.95
Date: 1963 (2000)
Source: Films for the Humanities and Sciences
P.O. Box 2053
Princeton, NJ 08543-2053
(800) 257-5126
http://www.films.com

Shortly after the famous Supreme Court case, *Engel v.* Vitale, in which a twenty-two-word prayer introduced into the New York public school system was declared unconstitutional, the litigants, legal counsel, political and religious leaders, and academics shared their views on the issue of prayer in the public schools.

Searching for God in America

Type: 1/2" videocassette
Length: 240 min.
Cost: $250
Date: 1996
Source: PBS Video

1320 Braddock Place
Alexandria, VA 22314-1698
(800) 739-5269

Hugh Hewitt speaks with some of the most noted contemporary religious leaders, including Charles Colson, Rabbi Harold Kushner, Father Thomas Keating, Seyyed Nasr, and the Dalai Lama, about the challenges that secular society pose for their religious faith.

A Separate Peace: Hinduism, Buddhism, Taoism, and Shintoism
Type: 1/2" videocassette
Length: 54 min.
Cost: $149 (purchase); $75 (rental)
Date: Not available
Source: Films for the Humanities and Sciences
P.O. Box 2053
Princeton, NJ 08543-2053
(800) 257-5126
http://www.films.com

This video examines the main doctrines of four eastern religions, including the Hindu belief in the spiritual master, the Buddhist belief in reincarnation and nonviolence, the Chinese Daoist emphasis on the equilibrium of forces, and the Japanese Shintoist notion of animism, which involves the belief that nature contains many deities.

Shrine under Siege
Type: 1/2" videocassette
Length: 42 min.
Cost: $350 (purchase); $60 (rental)
Date: 1985
Source: First Run / Icaraus Films
153 Waverly Place, Sixth Floor
New York, NY 10014
(800) 876-1710
http://www.frif.com

This documentary investigates the theological basis of the coalition between fundamentalist Christians in the United States and militant Israeli Jews who want to destroy the Dome of the Rock, a holy shrine of Islam, in order to build a Jewish temple.

Sikhism: The Golden Temple
Type: 1/2" videocassette
Length: 15 min.
Cost: $59.95
Date: Not available
Source: Films for the Humanities and Sciences
          P.O. Box 2053
          Princeton, NJ 08543-2053
          (800) 257-5126
          http://www.films.com

The Sikh religion, which has been the focus of recent violence in India, is briefly investigated. The origins of Sikhism as well as its adherents' major beliefs, including belief in one God, the equality of all, and the importance of performing good deeds, are presented.

Solidaridad: Faith, Hope, and Haven
Type: 1/2" videocassette
Length: 57 min.
Cost: $390
Date: 1989
Source: First Run / Icarus Films
          153 Waverly Place, Sixth Floor
          New York, NY 10014
          (800) 876-1710
          http://www.frif.com

The video provides an account of a Catholic organization in Chile, Vicaria de la Solidaridad, which offers assistance to victims of human rights abuses.

SOS In Iran
Type: 1/2" videocassette
Length: 52 min.
Cost: $390 (purchase); $75 (rental)
Date: 2001
Source: First Run/Icarus Films
          153 Waverly Place, Sixth Floor
          New York, NY 10014
          (800) 876-1710
          www.frif.com

Sou Abadi filmed this presentation in Iran, revealing aspects of the day-to-day lives of Iranians at the beginning of the twenty-first century. Among the sights revealed to the camera are the Committee of the Imam, a charity for the poor created by the Ayatollah Khomeini; the Health Ministry's mandatory premarital sex education courses; psychotherapy sessions for the elite of Tehran; and the Marriage Foundation, an Islamic matrimonial agency.

Speeches of Martin Luther King, Jr.
Type: 1/2" videocassette
Length: 60 min.
Cost: $29.95
Date: 1990
Source: Teacher's Video Company
P.O. Box AHR-4455
Scottsdale, AZ 85261
(800) 262-8837

This video includes some of Martin Luther King's most memorable speeches and quotes. It emphasizes King's skill as an orator during the days of the civil rights movement.

Spiritual India: A Guide to Jainism, Islam, Buddhism, and Hinduism
Type: 1/2" videocassette
Length: 50 min.
Cost: $149 (purchase); $75 (rental)
Date: 1995
Source: Films for the Humanities and Sciences
P.O. Box 2053
Princeton, NJ 08543-2053
(800) 257-5126
http://www.films.com

This video treats the great variety of religious traditions in India, including Jainism, Islam, Buddhism and Hinduism. The discussion of religions refers to Indian history, the country's diverse geography, and the plurality of cultures and languages.

The Story of Islam: A History of the World's Most Misunderstood Faith
Type: 1/2" videocassette
Length: 120 min.
Cost: $29.95
Date: 1989

Source: Teacher's Video Company
P.O. Box WHM-4455
Scottsdale, AZ 85261
(800) 262-8837

This video charts the history of Islam from its beginnings to the late twentieth century, explores the religion's major articles of faith, and recounts recent events significant to the Islamic religion. Also included is a comparison and contrast of Islam to the beliefs of Judaism and Christianity.

Televangelism in Brazil
Type: 1/2" videocassette
Length: 41 min.
Cost: $149 (purchase); $75 (rental)
Date: 1999
Source: Films for the Humanities and Sciences
P.O. Box 2053
Princeton, NJ 08543-2053
(800) 257-5126
http://www.films.com

The dominance of the Catholic Church in Brazil has recently been challenged by Pentecostal Protestants who began a television campaign that resulted in shifts in religious affiliation. The program relates the efforts of charismatic Catholics to compete with Protestants through their own television programming. The competition between Protestant and Catholic denominations may have significant consequences for the role of religion in Brazilian society and the effectiveness of liberation theology.

Three Pillars: Confucius, Jesus, and Mohammed
Type: 1/2" videocassette
Length: 53 min.
Cost: $75
Date: 1998
Source: Films for the Humanities and Sciences
P.O. Box 2053
Princeton, NJ 08543-2053
(800) 257-5126
http://www.films.com

This video examines the influence of three religious traditions on social values. The influence of Confucianism on the Chinese social and political structure is discussed. Other subjects include the contrasting views of Jesus among Muslims and Christians and Mohammed and the codification of the Qur'an.

Tibet
Type: 1/2" videocassette
Length: 58 min.
Cost: $29.95
Date: 1989
Source: Teacher's Video Company
P.O. Box WHJ-4455
Scottsdale, AZ 85261
(800) 262-8837

This video provides an overview of Tibetan life, focusing on the ways in which mystical religious beliefs are integrated into the daily lives of Tibetans.

Tibet: On the Edge of Change
Type: 1/2" videocassette
Length: 58 min.
Cost: $29.95
Date: Not available
Source: Teacher's Video Company
P.O. Box WHJ-4455
Scottsdale, AZ 85261
(800) 262-8837

This video provides an overview of Tibetan society and the long traditions that continue to influence religious beliefs and social interactions. The continuing struggles with Chinese dominance are highlighted.

Tibet: The Survival of the Spirit
Type: 1/2" videocassette
Length: 92 min.
Cost: $29.95
Date: 1991
Source: Mystic Fire Video
524 Broadway, Suite 604
New York, NY 10012
(800) 292-9001
http://www.mysticfire.com

This video documents Chinese attempts to destroy Tibetan opposition to their rule and the efforts of Tibetans to maintain their culture. Included is an account of the Chinese attack on the Johkang Temple that led to the arrest of monks.

**Tibetan Buddhism: Politics, Power,
and the Birth of the Dalai Lama**
Type: 1/2" videocassette
Length: 45 min.
Cost: $149 (purchase); $75 (rental)
Date: Not available
Source: Films for the Humanities and Sciences
P.O. Box 2053
Princeton, NJ 08543-2053
(800) 257-5126
http://www.films.com

Robert Thurman, Michael Harris Goodman, and Shagdaryn Bira investigate the historical development of Tibetan Buddhism, including early efforts to resist Chinese intervention and the institution of the Dalai Lama.

Tibet's Stolen Child
Type: 1/2" videocassette
Length: 57 min.
Cost: $29.95
Date: 2000
Source: Amazon.com
P.O. Box 81226
Seattle, WA 98108-1226
http://amazon.com

This video presents an account of the 1995 kidnapping of the six-year-old Tibetan child, Gedhun Choekyi Nyima, by the Chinese government. The child had been determined to be the eleventh incarnation of the Panchen Lama, the second ranking Tibetan Buddhist spiritual leader. Political motives for the kidnapping are offered.

Tu Wei-ming: A Confucian Life in America
Type: 1/2" videocassette
Length: 30 min.
Cost: $89.95
Date: 1990
Source: Films for the Humanities and Sciences
P.O. Box 2053

Princeton, NJ 08543-2053
(800) 257-5126
http://www.films.com

Tu Wei-ming argues that the humanism of Confucius contributes to the resolution of contemporary ethical problems, and suggests that Eastern humanistic philosophy, when combined with Western technology and democratic values, may determine the future characteristics of industrialized East Asia.

Under One Sky: Arab Women
in North America Talk about the Hijab
Type: 1/2" videocassette
Length: 44 min.
Cost: $129
Date: 1999
Source: Films for the Humanities and Sciences
P.O. Box 2053
Princeton, NJ 08543-2053
(800) 257-5126
http://www.films.com

Arab women living in North America discuss the symbolism behind the *hijab*, or veil, which is worn by fundamentalist Islamic women. The program offers information about the history of Arab women from the early colonial time period to the post–Gulf War era.

A Veiled Revolution
Type: 1/2" videocassette
Length: 26 min.
Cost: $280 (purchase); $55 (rental)
Date: 1982
Source: First Run / Icarus Films
153 Waverly Place, Sixth Floor
New York, NY 10014
(800) 876-1710
http://www.frif.com

Although Egyptian women took part in political demonstrations as early as 1919, renounced the wearing of veils in 1923, and gained free secular education in 1924, by the 1980s many of them had decided to return to Muslim tradition in a return of Islamic fundamentalism and a rejection of Western influences. This video explores the reasons for Egyptian women reverting to old social and religious customs.

Walking with Buddha
Type: 1/2" videocassette
Length: 29 min.
Cost: $99
Date: Not available
Source: Films for the Humanities and Sciences
P.O. Box 2053
Princeton, NJ 08543-2053
(800) 257-5126
http://www.films.com

Filmed in Thailand, this video examines the life of Buddha and investigates the development of Buddhism in various countries. Focusing on the Buddhist notion of compassion, the lives of Buddhist priests as they counsel, teach, and meditate, are portrayed.

Wars in Peace: Iran/Iraq, Afghanistan
Type: 1/2" videocassette
Length: 80 min.
Cost: $29.95
Date: 1995
Source: Teacher's Video Company
P.O. Box WHM-4455
Scottsdale, AZ 85261
(800) 262-8837

This is an exploration of the eight-year conflict between the Middle Eastern nations of Iran and Iraq as well as the civil conflict in Afghanistan. Emphasis is placed on the role of religion in intensifying these conflicts.

Which Way Next for Iran?
Type: 1/2" videocassette
Length: 52 min.
Cost: $149 (purchase); $75 (rental)
Date: 2000
Source: Films for the Humanities and Sciences
P.O. Box 2053
Princeton, NJ 08543-2053
(800) 257-5126
http://www.films.com

Iranian President Mohammad Khatami, Vice President Masoumeh Ebtekar, and others discuss the questions that separate Iran from the United States, Egypt, Israel, and other countries.

The video investigates students at the Faizieh Divinity School, who demonstrate the strong local support for Islam.

Whose State? Whose Religion?
Type: 1/2" videocassette
Length: 53 min.
Cost: $149 (purchase); $75 (rental)
Date: 1998
Source: Films for the Humanities and Sciences
P.O. Box 2053
Princeton, NJ 08543-2053
(800) 257-5126
http://www.films.com

Although the original founders of Israel viewed the nation as the homeland of the Jewish people of the Bible, many Israelis today tend to de-emphasize religion and focus on Israel as a nation. The video describes how the religious versus secular divisions over the definition of Israel affect the nation's politics and public policy.

Women and Islam
Type: 1/2" videocassette
Length: 30 min.
Cost: $89.95
Date: 2000
Source: Films for the Humanities and Sciences
P.O. Box 2053
Princeton, NJ 08543-2053
(800) 257-5126
http://www.films.com

Leila Ahmed, professor of women's studies at Amherst University, explains the origin of the veil in the Islamic world and discusses the issues of marriage and women's rights within marriage.

Women in Islam
Type: 1/2" videocassette
Length: 42 min.
Cost: $99
Date: 1998
Source: Insight Media
2162 Broadway
New York, NY 10024-0621
(800) 233-9910
www.insight-media.com

Offering a unique perspective on their culture, Guity Nashat and Sule Ozler discuss their experiences as women who were raised in the Islamic tradition.

Women in Islam
Type: 1/2" videocassette
Length: 60 min.
Cost: $89
Date: 1997
Source: Insight Media
           2162 Broadway
           New York, NY 10024-0621
           (800) 233-9910
           http://www.insight-media.com

Azizah Al-Hibri, a law professor, discusses the role of women in Islam. The video touches on Islamic values and law and the various difficulties with which modernization has confronted Islamic culture.

World Sikhism Today
Type: 1/2" videocassette
Length: 49 min.
Cost: $149 (purchase); $75 (rental)
Date: Not available
Source: Films for the Humanities and Sciences
           P.O. Box 2053
           Princeton, NJ 08543-2053
           (800) 257-5126
           http://www.films.com

This video details Sikh beliefs and investigates the present status of the religion in India, Europe, and North America. Facing discrimination and at times violence from the Hindu majority in India, this group has responded with violence and has called for an independent state.

Internet Resources

The Bible and Public Policy: Biblical Axioms on Public Issues
http://users.churchserve.com/nz/bibpp/biblepp.htm

This site presents positions on public policy issues based on interpretations of the Bible. Among the issues treated are the basic purpose of government, justice, inflation, taxation and government spending, international trade, immigration, public health, education, welfare, and the environment.

Bibliography of Hinduism
http://www.carthage.edu/~lochtefe/bibhin.htm

This site contains a long list of references on Hinduism, including such topics as art and literature, ascetics, modern religious life, philosophy, and religion and politics.

Briefing Notes on Islam, Society, and Politics
http://www.csis.org/html/isp1298.html

This site, begun in 1998 and maintained by the Center for Strategic and International Studies, records the claimed increase in the influence of extremist religious groups in politics. Examples discussed include the Taliban in Afghanistan and the continuing conflict between Hindus and Muslims in India.

Buddhism
http://internets.com.buddha.htm

This site offers links to other sites related to Buddhism, including "Fundamental Buddhism Explained," "Government of Tibet in Exile," "Journal of Buddhist Ethics," and "Center for Buddhist Ethics."

Buddhism in Vietnam
http://mcel.pacificu.edu/as/students/vb

This site provides a comprehensive history of the Buddhist religion in Vietnam. An important aspect of the site is an emphasis on the importance of Buddhism to an understanding of the Vietnam War. Information is also presented about Buddhism after the United States withdrawal from Vietnam.

Christian Politics and World-View
http://www.aliensonearth.com/catalog/pub/christian/politics

This site contains reading materials on Christianity and politics that may be ordered online. Included among the titles are *The Culture of Disbelief, Handbook of Today's Religions,* and *The New Age Cult.*

Christianity and Libertarianism
http://libertarian.faithweb.com/libertarianism

This site contains several sources on libertarianism and its possible connection to Christianity. Among the issues discussed are abortion, charity and welfare, economics, foreign policy, gun control, and taxation.

Church and State, Religion and Politics
http://www.frontiernet.net/~kenc/relandpo.htm

Beginning with the position that people of faith can appropriately express their religious beliefs and moral and social preferences through political activity, Kenneth Cauthen provides various observations about political involvement for Christians and how religious beliefs may conflict with secular law.

Counter-Cultural Christianity, Changing Times, and Changing Minds
http://chalcedon.edu/report/97jan/507/htm

Brian Abshire presents his observations about conservative theology, conservative politics, and Christian reconstructionists who claim that Christians tend to take humanistic positions on political issues because they are ignorant of biblical teaching and because the present society is out of touch with the Bible. Abshire contends that conservative politicians fail to present an adequate political agenda because they too are unfamiliar with scripture.

Cross Currents
http://crosscurrents.org

This online periodical is supported by various religious faiths that are "committed to connecting the wisdom of the heart and the life of the mind." Subjects include the interaction of religion and the use of violence and the increasing involvement of religious groups in political activity.

DharmaNet's Buddhist Info Web
http://www.dharmanet.org/infoweb.html

The Buddhist Info Web contains a directory of lay and monastic Dharma centers and organizations and links to other sites. The main purpose of this site is to support Buddhist teaching and practice.

Fitting Christianity into Politics
http://str.org/free/commentaries/social_issues/fitting.htm

Gregory Koukl argues that Christians logically will take certain positions on political issues. For instance, he argues that anyone who accepts the permissibility of abortion is taking an un-Christian position because it is inconsistent with biblical teaching.

Fundamental Buddhism Explained
http://www.fundamentalbuddhism.com/english.htm

The Buddhist Instruction Ministry provides a basic introduction to Buddhist belief and practices as well as links to other sites. The religion is founded on the teaching of Siddhartha Gautama (circa 557 B.C. to 477 B.C.), known as "The Buddha," which means "Supremely Enlightened One." The site notes that Buddhism does not adhere to specific creeds or rites but rather is a "Path to Enlightenment."

The Gifts of Islamic Civilization
http://astrolabepictures.com

This site provides information about Islam, including such topics as Muslim history and Islamic law (*shari'a*). Various literature is on sale, including books on Islamic science, military history, culture, and politics.

Hamas
http://palestine-info.net/hamas/about/index.htm

The site provides information about Hamas, the Islamic Resistance Movement. Among the topics covered are the development of the organization, the conflict with Zionism, the role of military action, and positions of various issues specific to the Middle East conflict.

Hezbollah
http://www.hezbollah.org

Although not affiliated with the militant Islamic organization Hezbollah, this site presents a highly positive view of the group, describing it as "an Islamic struggle movement" composed of "individuals concerned about bringing the truth to the public." The goals of the organization are discussed.

Hindu Power Politics
http://www.en.monde-diplomatique.fr/1999/09/11india

This site contains an essay by Romain Maitra dealing with the rise of Hindu nationalism in India. India has witnessed a long history of conflict between Hindus and Muslims, which has continued in recent years with the rise of the Indian People's Party, or Bharatiya Janata Party (BJP) and its emphasis on "one nation, one people, one culture." This alternative to the long-ruling Congress Party has been associated with renewed opposition to the Christian community and perceived attempts to convert Hindus to Christianity.

Hindu Unity
http://www.hinduunity.com

This site offers goals for Hindu nationalism, which is considered to be the object of dangerous attacks, including the threat of religious conversion of Hindus by other religious faiths, such as Christianity and Islam. This site advocates banning such conversion efforts in India.

Hinduism
http://members.attcanada.ca/~raj/hinduism.html

This site provides basic information on Hinduism, briefly describing the three basic divisions—Shivites, Vaishnavas, and Shaktas—and four objectives—duty (dharma), material prosperity (artha), enjoyment (kama), and salvation (moksha). Significant Hindu locations are listed.

How Should People of Faith Become Involved in Politics?
http://www.discovery.org/lewis/chapter5.html

Fred Barnes of *The Weekly Standard*, Don Bonker, a former U.S. congressman, and Dale Foreman, a former majority leader in the Washington State House of Representatives, provide advice to Christians about political involvement, focusing on the dangers and temptations that religious people confront when becoming politically active.

Information on ISLAM in the Internet
http://www.iso.gmu.edu/~mbeg/n.html

This site offers various information on Islam, including news reports from Islamic sources, information on the Qur'an, explanations of the relationship between Judaism, Christianity, and Islam, and pamphlets on such topics as human rights and Islam, Islam as the true religion, and Muslim contributions to science.

Introduction to Sikhism
http://www.sikhs.org/summary.htm

This site presents some of the basic beliefs of the Sikh religion, which considers itself a faith in contrast to both Hinduism and Islam. Guru Nanak is mentioned as the founder of the Sikh religion in 1469. The most significant historical religious center is Harmiandir Sahib (The Golden Temple) at Amritsar in the Indian state of Punjab.

Islam and Politics
http://atheism.miningco.com/religion/atheism/cs/islamandpolitics

This site approaches Islam from an atheistic perspective, offering critiques of Islamic history and society, including positions on such topics as democracy, tolerance, and secularization. Specific items available include an interview with Salman Rushdie, the British writer condemned to death by Ayatollah Ruhollah Khomeini for publishing *The Satanic Verses*, which was declared blasphemous; an analysis of Islam and liberal democracy; and a treatment of Muhammad.

Islam and Politics in the Middle East
http://jinx.sistm.unsw.edu.au/~greenlft/1993/105/105p12.htm

This interview about Islamic fundamentalism with Ahmad Shboul, associate professor of Arabic and Islamic studies at Sydney University, concentrates on Islamic activism in Algeria and Palestine and the distinction between religious and secular factions in the respective areas.

Islamic Art, Religion and Politics
http://www.ocnsignal.com/aword1.shtml

This site contains resources on the Qur'an as well as links to English language sites providing news about the Middle East. The site has had reports on the alleged Princess Di and Dodi al-Fayed murder conspiracy and other more popular news stories involving Muslims.

Islamic Unification Movement
http://www.oneummah.net

This Web site is maintained by the Islamic Unification Movement, which does not claim to be an organization, but a movement. The site calls for unity among Islamic organizations and encourages dialogue among groups and education to create strong religious faith.

IslamiCity
http://www.islamicity.org

The site contains information about Islamic communities around the world. News items are available regarding events in Islamic countries and announcements of Islamic conferences. Other topics covered include travel, religious observances, education, and business and finance.

IslamOnline.net
http://www.muslims.net/English

This site contains recent news accounts of events in various countries that are of relevance to Muslims, such as updates on Bosnian Muslims and peace talks in the Middle East. An archive of past political reporting is also available.

Journal of Buddhist Ethics
http://jbe.la.psu.edu

The exclusively electronic publication contains scholarly articles that present a Buddhist perspective on such topics as medical ethics, jurisprudence, human rights, ecology and the environment, and social and political philosophy.

Muslim Brotherhood Movement Page
http://ummah.org.uk/ikhwan

Although not officially associated with the organization, this site provides basic information about the Muslim Brotherhood from a sympathetic perspective. Included are writings from Hasan al-Banna, founder of the Brotherhood.

Panchen Lama Web Site
http://tibet.ca/panchenlama

This site provides information about, and a call of support for, the eleventh reincarnation of the Panchen Lama, Gedhun Choekyi Nyima, a young Tibetan boy determined to be second to the Dalai Lama as a Tibetan Buddhist leader. The boy and his parents were kidnapped by the Chinese government in 1995 in an apparent attempt to establish another child as a Tibetan spiritual leader more to the liking of Chinese officials.

Politics and Organizations Topics
http://www.cust.idl.com.au/fold/Politics_topics.html

This site contains summaries of articles dealing with "secular politics, church politics, and principles of leadership in the kingdom of heaven." Among the topics of articles are Christians and the law, Christian politicians, civil disobedience, and tolerance and pluralism. Individual articles may be purchased through the site.

Politics and Religion Academic Network
http://psa.ac.uk/spgrp/paran/politics_and_religion.htm

A subgroup in the Political Studies Association, a British organization, the Politics and Religion Academic Network was established "to facilitate the academic scrutiny of issues relating to the relationship between politics and religion." The site is intended to encourage debate, discussion, and research in the area of religion and politics. Bibliographies of published materials are available.

Politics by Other Means: Attacks against Christians in India
http://www2.viaweb.com/hrwpubs/india1099.html

This site provides a brief description of the publication *India: Politics by Other Means*, published in 1999. The report claims that the Hindu nationalist Bharatiya Janata Party, the ruling party in India, has condoned violence against Christians. Allegedly, Christian schools and churches have been destroyed and priests have been killed.

Popular Buddhism, Politics and the Ethnic Problem
http://www.c-r.org/acc_sri/buddhism.htm

Priyath Liyanage reports on the ethnic violence in Sri Lanka, which is aggravated by religious tensions between Buddhists and Hindus.

Religion and Politics
http://fx.nu/quest/relpol.html

This site, maintained by Al Khilafah Publications in London, discusses the rise of secularism in Western society in contrast to the Islamic stance on the relationship between religion and society. The presentation provides a discussion of the meanings of religion and politics from an Islamic perspective.

Religion and Politics in India
http://findarticles.com/m1321/5_182/59474877/pl/article.jhtml

This article, written by Lancy Lobo, reports on the Hindu nationalists' categorization of Christianity as an "outsider religion," claiming that India persecutes Christians that have "made bold attempts to empower the poor of India."

Religion of Islam
http://www.templemount.org/islam.html

This Web site provides an overview of Islam, including an explanation of the Qur'an. The site recommends speaking of the Judeo-Christian-Islamic tradition because Islam shares in "the sacred history of the other Abrahamic religions."

Religion, Politics, and the State: Cross-Cultural Observations
http://www.crosscurrents.org/Demerath.htm

This article from the online publication *Cross Currents* (1996) presents an overview of the various contemporary religious movements, including liberation theology, Islamic fundamentalism, Solidarity in Poland, and the religious right in the United States, which have become involved in national politics.

Retrospect: Christianity in India
http://hindubooks.org/Retrospect_of_Christianity

This site claims that the strained relations between Hindus and Christians in India can be traced to Christian attempts to convert Hindus through threats, deception, persecution, and financial temptations. The author, Shripaty Sastry, argues that such conversion attempts are considered aggression on Hindu society and should not be condoned.

The Shadow of the Dalai Lama
http://www.trimondi.de/en/front.html

This site is devoted to the book *The Shadow of the Dalai Lama: Sexuality, Magic, and Politics*, a critical treatment of Buddhism written by German authors Victor and Victoria Trimondi. The site contains the introduction and postscript to the book as well as reviews and reader comments.

Talk Islam
http://www.talkislam.com

This site is a guide to various subjects relevant to Islam, including studies of Muslim countries, organizations (including political, student, and finance groups), bookstores, and Islamic history. News reports relevant to Islam are also available.

Why Christians Need to Be Involved in Politics
http://worthynews.com/co . . . tary/christians-politically-in-volved.html

The author, B. K. Eakman, offers many of the standard arguments for conservative Christians to become actively involved in politics. Although the United States is claimed to have been based on Christian principles, the author insists that while other groups' interests are protected, those of Christians are not.

World Religions Index
http://wri.leaderu.com

This site contains a wide variety of material on religions around the world, including comparative studies of religions, data on various religions and sects, personal accounts by people of differing faiths, and links to other sites dealing with religions, cults, and philosophies.

Glossary

ayatollah Derived from the Arabic *Ayat Allah,* meaning "sign of God," this is a term of respect which came into vogue in the twentieth century in Iran. In Twelver Shi'ism it refers to an Islamic jurisprudent, or a leading *mujtahid* who interprets *shari'a,* a body of sacred law.

bodhisattva In Tibetan Buddhism, this is a spiritual adept who desires rebirth in this world in order to assist suffering humanity. This belief, which dates from the thirteenth century, undergirds the idea that each succeeding lama is the reincarnation of the previous one.

caliph Meaning "successor to the Prophet," the term refers to Islamic rulers who followed Muhammad.

charismatic movement Characterized by emotional, ecstatic forms of worship in which speaking in tongues and faith healing are encouraged, this is a twentieth-century phenomenon. Protestants and Catholics in the United States, especially since the 1960s, have been influenced by this movement.

charitable choice This term refers to the practice of allowing faith-based organizations in the United States to bid on federal contracts for various social services, such as housing, job training, and drug and prison rehabilitation. The welfare reform legislation passed by the U.S. Congress in 1996 permits this, and many religious and social conservatives applaud it, convinced religious institutions do a better job than secular ones at providing certain services for the needy. A concern of many critics is that charitable choice, aside from the fundamental issue of church-state separation, neither proscribes faith-based organizations from proselytizing nor ensures compliance with federal laws regarding such things as gender, sexual, and racial discrimination.

Christian reconstructionism   Drawing primarily upon Genesis 1:26–28 and Matthew 28:16–20, this movement, which apparently evolved from teachings at J. Gresham Machen's Westminster Theological Seminary, attempts to reconstruct society in accordance with God's law. Guided by the example of the seventeenth-century American Puritans, who had sought to build the Massachusetts Commonwealth on biblical principles, Christian reconstructionists want to subordinate all aspects of life to God's authority. Accordingly, they encourage Christian schooling, certain that public education has been corrupted by secular humanism; condemn the modern state, convinced it has usurped the authority of God; and embrace an optimistic eschatology, persuaded of the possibility of constructive change. In pursuit of their objectives, however, Christian reconstructionists do not advocate civil disobedience.

civil religion   Broadly, the term refers to the usage of transcendent religious symbols to explain and justify national purpose and destiny. On one hand, civil religion in America provides a unifying set of values for people of all persuasions, values that inspire the pursuit of justice and equality of treatment for everyone; on the other hand, when suffused with an intense nationalism where God and country become one, civil religion easily gives support to American aggression abroad and intolerance at home.

compassionate conservatism   Derived in large part from Marvin Olasky's *The Tragedy of American Compassion* (1992), this phrase was bandied about quite a lot in the 2000 presidential race in the United States. In contrast to the allegedly false compassion of the existing welfare state, which purportedly doles out material aid without imposing discipline on the poor or providing spiritual guidance, compassionate conservatism nourishes both the soul and the body. Based on the assumption that religion and government have in America's past worked closely together, compassionate conservatism today looks to faith-based institutions to administer various programs to help the needy. And for doing this, faith-based institutions would receive tax support.

dar al-harb   Referring to those areas of the world not under Muslim rule, this term means the abode of war and is considered the zone of unbelievers. Islamists intend ultimately to integrate all of *dar al-harb* into the Islamic community, or *dar al-Islam*.

dar al-Islam Meaning the domain of Islam, this term refers to those lands in which Muslim rulers prevail and Islamic law, *shari'a*, is observed.

dharma In Hinduism, refers to the way life *should* be lived in *all* its aspects. And since dharma makes no distinction between the religious and secular, the sacred and profane, politics involves *moral* obligations. Thus, politics and religion are essentially one.

dominion (kingdom) theology Used by politically involved evangelicals, this term lends biblical sanction to efforts to Christianize America's political, economic, legal, educational, military, and communications institutions. Dominion theology undergirds much of Christian reconstructionism.

election (predestination) The belief that certain people and groups have been foreordained to fulfill God's divine purposes. This view undergirds Israel's position as God's chosen people, as well as the New Testament doctrine of humanity's undeserved grace. Given the influence of such conservative Presbyterians as Charles Hodge, Benjamin Warfield, J. Gresham Machen, and Carl McIntire, this sentiment runs deep among many American fundamentalists.

eschatology Derived from two Greek words, eschatology means "end" or "final." Central to eschatology, therefore, are beliefs about death, resurrection, the return of Jesus, judgment, and the Kingdom of God. In both the Old and New Testaments eschatological writers were concerned with the ultimate triumph of God over evil.

ethic of life See seamless garment of life.

fatwa This reference to Islamic law refers to legal pronouncements or decrees of religious leaders. The most well-known case of *fatwa* is Ayatollah Ruhollah Khomeini's edict condemning Salman Rushdie to death for writing the novel *The Satanic Verses (1988)*, thus causing Rushdie to go into hiding in order to protect his life.

fitna This Arab term refers to a division, rupture, separation, or splitting of the community, which, according to Islam, is a serious political transgression and is to be avoided. Any separation into social, economic, or political groups is considered a cause of *fitna*.

fundamentalism In the United States the terms "fundamentalist," "evangelical," and "conservative Christian" were more or less synonymous by the 1920s, each referring broadly to those Christians who subscribed to the five or six basic fundamentals set forth at the Niagara Bible Conference of 1895 and in *The Fundamentals: A Testimony to the Truth* (1910–1915). But the term "fundamentalism," coined in 1920, increasingly became identified with an aggressively strident and exclusionist variety of conservative Christianity, and critics increasingly applied the term pejoratively and indiscriminately to all conservative Christians. As a result, conservative Christians such as those who founded the National Association of Evangelicals in 1942 preferred the term evangelical to fundamentalist. The difference today between a Christian fundamentalist and an evangelical is more a matter of temperament than theology. Within other religious traditions, such as Islam or Judaism, for instance, the term is often used to describe efforts to make society conform to religious precepts.

Hadith The sayings and deeds of the Prophet Muhammad, as recorded by his close friends and family members. Hadith does not appear in the Qur'an, but, along with the Qur'an, provides the basis for Islamic law.

halakha The Jewish legal system, which is built on the Talmudic compendium of 613 divine commandments.

heterodoxy (heresy) Departure from established beliefs and traditions. To American fundamentalists, for instance, the denial of such things as the virgin birth and resurrection of Jesus would be heterodoxy.

hijrah The term originally referred to the Prophet Muhammad's flight from Mecca to Medina in 622, but in modern times it has been used by Islamic fundamentalists to mean a temporary escape from societies considered to have departed from Islam.

Identity Christianity Based upon the belief that white Anglo-Saxons are God's chosen people and that Jews and all other so-called nonwhites are a subspecies of humanity. Identity Christianity unites such white supremacist groups in the United States as the Ku Klux Klan and Aryan Nations.

imam To Sunni Muslims, the term refers to a prayer leader; to Shi'ites, one of the historical leaders of the Shi'ite community (for example, one of the twelve in Twelver Shi'ism). Modern Shi'ites use the term as one of respect for outstanding religious leaders, such as Ayatollah Khomeini.

imminency The belief within Christianity that the second coming of Jesus could occur at any moment. This idea fuels much of the millennial speculation regarding the end of time.

intifada In Arabic, meaning literally "to shake off," the term has been used since the late 1980s to refer to the Arab uprising against the Israeli occupation of the West Bank and Gaza Strip.

jihad In popular parlance, the term refers to a holy war waged by Muslims against infidels. In this context, there is considerable debate within Islam regarding the circumstances justifying such a war. A more spiritual meaning of the term refers to an individual's struggle against bad habits and irreligious conduct.

kafir In Islam, this term refers to an unbeliever or infidel. The leader of a Muslim government can be declared in a state of infidelity and war can justly be waged against such a leader.

madrasha The traditional educational institution of Islamic countries, the madrasha stresses religion, especially Islamic law, as well as history, literature, and Arabic grammar. Some madrasha in recent years have added modern, Western learning to the curriculum.

mahdi According to Islamic eschatology, God will send a messiah, the mahdi, to defeat the enemies of Islam and establish global peace, a prelude to the final judgment. Such a belief has given rise to false mahdis from time to time in Islamic history.

millennialism This refers to a thousand-year period in which the kingdom of God will prevail. Christians are usually divided over whether the second coming of Jesus will occur before (premillennialists) or after (postmillennialists) the thousand-year reign. Millennial expectations are fueled by the apocalyptic portion of the Bible, especially the Book of Revelation, and groups such as the Seventh Day Adventists and Jehovah's Witnesses reflect the influence of millennial ideas.

modernism Although many conservative Christians in the United States by the 1920s used modernism loosely to cover a multitude of alleged sins, scholars usually use the term more precisely to mean the adjustment of religious ideas to contemporary culture, the immanence of God in human development, and the belief that history is evolving toward the Kingdom of God. As this suggests, modernism is an optimistic view, one at sharp odds with the conservative Christian emphasis upon original sin and human depravity.

mujahidin   In Islam, this term refers to those who fight in a holy war, or jihad. For instance, those combatants in Afghanistan who fought against Soviet occupation were called the *mujahidin.*

mullah   A title of respect for one learned in the sacred law of Islam.

New Age Movement   Drawing upon both Eastern and Western religious traditions, this phenomenon gained momentum in the United States in the 1980s. Its adherents subscribe to an eclectic assortment of beliefs and practices, such as reincarnation, astral projection, astrology, extraterrestrial life, immortality of the soul, miracles, angels, and yoga.

orthodoxy   Derived from the Greek words *orthos*, "correct," and *doxa*, "opinion," orthodoxy refers to "correct" or "right" beliefs.

postmillennialism   The belief that steadily improving world conditions will culminate in the second coming of Jesus. By this interpretation, Jesus will return *after* a millennium of human progress. This optimistic viewpoint not only reinforced the reform efforts of liberal social gospel ministers in the late nineteenth and early twentieth centuries but also undergirds the labors of contemporary Christian reconstructionists.

premillennialism   The belief that steadily deteriorating world conditions (wars and rumors of wars) will precede the second coming, at which time Jesus will establish a thousand-year reign. Thus, Jesus will return *before* the millennium. This viewpoint is generally more harmonious with a conservative, pessimistic assessment of contemporary world conditions.

pro-choice   A term commonly used in the United States by those who support a woman's right to choose whether or not to have an abortion.

pro-life (right to life) movement   Originating among Roman Catholics, this movement today embraces Catholics, Protestants, and others opposed to abortion. The U.S. Supreme Court's decision in *Roe v. Wade* (1973), which legalized abortion during the first two trimesters of pregnancy, gave impetus to the movement.

prophecy   Derived from a Greek word meaning one who speaks for another, prophecy supposedly is an expression of divine will.

Unlike apocalyptic literature, however, which forecasts the end of time, prophetic literature is present-minded, predicting dire consequences in this life if "God's people" persist in their wicked ways. Examples of the prophetic tradition among the ancient Hebrews are Amos, Joel, Isaiah, Jeremiah, Ezekiel, and Elijah.

Ramadan   The holy month of Ramadan, lasting twenty-eight days, commemorates the revelation of the Qur'an to the Prophet Muhammad about 1,400 years ago. It is a time not only of fasting when devout Muslims abstain from eating, drinking, smoking, and sexual intercourse from sunrise to sunset to renew themselves spiritually, but also of generosity as wealthy Muslims feed the poor.

salafism   Derived from the Arabic word *salaf*, meaning ancestor, this is a purist, militant, and stridently anti-Western form of Islam. Its essence is that Muslims should avoid the corrupt ways of the modern world and return to the simple ways of the Prophet Muhammad.

sangha   Refers collectively to the followers who have embraced and seek to spread the teachings of Buddha. Symbolizing their disinterest in bodily adornment and material possessions, the sangha shave their heads and wear simple robes.

satyagraha   Coined by Gandhi, the term means "truth-force," and practitioners of *satyagraha* practice civil disobedience to accomplish justice and reconciliation without resorting to violence and hatred.

schism   Refers to a factious division, or split, of a religious body. Although sometimes used synonymously, schism and heresy are not the same. Heresy always involves doctrinal matters, whereas schism results primarily from disputes over authority and organizational structure.

seamless garment of life   A phrase increasingly used by many American Catholics and Protestants to denote opposition to not only abortion, but also capital punishment, euthanasia, and nuclear warfare. The phrase also indicates support of programs to assist children, pregnant women, and the impoverished in general. This broadens the debate over abortion to include life in virtually all its aspects.

secular humanism   The belief that humans, relying upon reason and acting independently of God, are sufficient unto themselves. Some intellectual leaders of the religious right in the United States, such as Francis Schaeffer, trace this human-centered view from the Greeks through the Renaissance to the Enlightenment. An alleged consequence of this outlook is the replacement of God-centered absolutes with moral relativism. Much like "modernism" in the 1920s, secular humanism today has become for the religious right in the United States a popular catchall for practically all social ills. By contrast, other religious traditions, such as Buddhism, have a more positive view of humanism, emphasizing that contentment results from human efforts to overcome worldly pleasures.

secularization   Refers to a decline of religious influence in public life.

shahada   An Arab term meaning martyrdom, this involves undergoing extreme suffering or death in the struggle against the enemies of God. Suffering martyrdom can have as much significance as victory over the enemy, for the holy war, or jihad, is primarily concerned with the relationship between God and the believer.

Shari'a   Derived primarily from the Qur'an and secondarily from the Sunna, the oral traditions of the Prophet Muhammad, this is the sacred law of Islam. It prescribes a divinely ordained way of life and regulates every aspect of behavior. Among Sunnis, there are four schools of Shari'a; among Shi'ites, one.

Shastras   Literally meaning "sacred book" in Sanskrit, this is a general term for the four categories of Hindu scriptures: *purana, shruti, smrti,* and *tantra.*

social gospel   A movement in the United States that emerged among more liberal Protestants in the late nineteenth century and reached its peak in the optimistic years preceding World War I. Convinced the gospel message was social as well as personal, ministers such as Washington Gladden and Walter Rauschenbusch sought to focus the attention of the churches on social ills spawned by industrialization and urbanization. Many conservative Christians objected to the social gospel, believing its social emphasis detracted from the primary responsibility of individuals.

Sufism   Refers to a mystical tradition in Islam in which adherents seek union with Allah through renunciation and love. This practice has come to be associated primarily with Shi'ism.

Sunna Taken from the Qur'an and the *hadith*, refers to the customs and practices of the Prophet Muhammad. All Muslims, ideally, are expected to live by the Sunna, which serves as a model of behavior for all aspects of life.

Sutra A literary formulation of the ancient Hindu Vedas and later works of Mahayana Buddhism, these verses, or aphorisms, provide the rules for such things as grammar, ritual, and philosophy.

talibs Seekers of Islamic truths

theonomy Coined by Cornelius Van Til of Westminster Theological Seminary, theonomy, derived from two Greek words, *theos* (God) and *nomos* (law), is submission to God's law. As such, it is an argument for Christian reconstructionism, one steeped in Calvinistic influences. To Van Til, God's elect could grasp divine laws and live accordingly, while those who relied on human judgment, or autonomy, lived in darkness. Broadly, theonomy holds that Old Testament law differentiates between right and wrong and, therefore, should be the basis for modern society.

Tripitaka Meaning "Three Baskets of the Law," this is the holy scripture of Buddhism, the earliest and most authoritative of Buddha's teachings.

ulama In Islam, refers collectively to jurists or religious scholars.

umma This term refers to the ideal of Islamic society, the unified egalitarian community of believers, and can be contrasted with *fitna*, or division within the community. The community of Muslims is considered to transcend social classes, ethnic identity, tribal divisions, and national boundaries. Muslims throughout the world are regarded as members of a single community of the faithful.

Vedas Sacred knowledge of Hinduism, consisting of the Rig-Veda (some 1,000 hymns), Sama-Veda (a rearrangement of the aforementioned hymns), Yajur-Veda (prose formulas), and Atharva-Veda (charms, incantations, and spells).

Zionism Emerging in the late nineteenth century, Zionism represents a fusion of Jewish nationalism and the desire for nationhood for Europe's persecuted Jewish population. The movement was inspired in large part by Theodor Herzl, author of *The Jewish State* (1896) and founder of the Zionist Congress (1897).

Index

323

About the Authors

John W. Storey, educated at Lamar University, Baylor University, and the University of Kentucky, is a specialist in southern religious history. His writings have appeared in numerous scholarly publications, and two of his previous studies, *Texas Baptist Leadership and Social Christianity, 1900–1980* (1986) and *Southern Baptists of Southeast Texas, 1888–1988* (1988), won the Texas Baptist Historical Society's Church History Award. He is currently professor and chair of the History Department at Lamar University.

Glenn H. Utter, professor and chair of the Political Science Department at Lamar University, was educated at Binghamton University, the University of Buffalo, and the University of London. Utter specializes in modern political theory and American political thought. He coedited *American Political Scientists: A Dictionary* (1993), cowrote *Campaign and Election Reform* (1997), and most recently published *Encyclopedia of Gun Control and Gun Rights* (2000). He has written a number of articles for political science journals and other scholarly publications.